GUIDE TO RESOURCES
FOR COMMONWEALTH STUDIES

GUIDE TO RESOURCES
FOR COMMONWEALTH STUDIES
IN LONDON OXFORD
AND CAMBRIDGE

WITH BIBLIOGRAPHICAL AND OTHER INFORMATION

by

A. R. HEWITT

Secretary and Librarian
The Institute of Commonwealth Studies

UNIVERSITY OF LONDON
PUBLISHED FOR THE
INSTITUTE OF COMMONWEALTH STUDIES
THE ATHLONE PRESS
1957

Published by
THE ATHLONE PRESS
UNIVERSITY OF LONDON
at 2 Gower Street, London, w.c.1
Distributed by Constable & Co. Ltd.
12 Orange Street, London, w.c.2

Canada
University of Toronto Press
Toronto 5, Ontario

U.S.A.
Essential Books Inc
Fair Lawn, New Jersey

Printed in Great Britain by
WESTERN PRINTING SERVICES LTD
BRISTOL

FOREWORD

The purpose of this *Guide* is to assist advanced research workers, particularly those who have come to Great Britain from overseas, to locate material for the study of the British Commonwealth. The materials listed fall mainly, but not exclusively, within the fields of history and the social sciences and are limited to libraries and other institutions in London, Oxford and Cambridge. It is realized, of course, that much valuable material is available elsewhere in this country and it is hoped that the geographical range of the *Guide* may be extended if and when a future edition is called for. Meanwhile the compiler would welcome criticisms of the present work and suggestions for its improvement.

Users of the *Guide* will realize that many of the libraries and institutions enumerated contain much other material besides that which possesses a particular value for students of the Commonwealth.

The selection of bibliographical works for mention has been difficult but it is hoped that the most important have been included. There exists at the moment no comprehensive Commonwealth bibliography of bibliographies and the *Guide* may also, to some extent, serve the same purpose.

The arrangement and scope are the results of suggestions received from members of staff of this and other universities and from others to whom a draft was submitted before completion of the work. It was not possible to adopt all the suggestions that were made but they were most helpful and greatly appreciated. Errors of omission and commission are, however, the sole responsibility of the compiler. He would like to acknowledge the great debt he owes to his colleagues in the University of London, particularly in the Institute of Commonwealth Studies, and to many others in London, Oxford, Cambridge and, indeed, throughout the Commonwealth, whose names are too numerous to mention individually.

A.R.H.

27 Russell Square,
London, w.c.1.
March, 1957

TABLE OF CONTENTS

Part I

GENERAL SURVEY OF RESOURCES

Part I

GENERAL SURVEY OF RESOURCES

I. INTRODUCTION

The National Archives

The Public Record Office is the repository of the national archives to which government departments transfer their records from time to time. Papers which have been transferred include those of the Colonial Office to the year 1938 and the Commonwealth Relations Office to the year 1935, except those of the former India Office which are retained in the Indian Records Section of the Commonwealth Relations Office. Official records less than fifty years old are not available for consultation.

The National Libraries

The great national repositories in England are the British Museum (p. 98), the Bodleian Library, Oxford (p. 160), and the University Library, Cambridge (p. 173). These three libraries contain vast collections of printed and manuscript material on all subjects having enjoyed for many years rights under the Copyright Acts of receiving copies of all books published in the United Kingdom—in the case of the Bodleian and the University Library, Cambridge, on demand only. A description of the Bodleian in the *Handbook* of the University of Oxford might well apply to the other two great libraries; it states that 'in a great and ancient depository like this there is hardly any field of human knowledge which is not represented by some greater or smaller body of raw material for research'.

For the purposes of research specifically in Commonwealth affairs three other libraries might well be described as 'national' Commonwealth libraries, namely, those of the Colonial Office (p. 104) and Royal Empire Society (p. 139) in London and of Rhodes House, Oxford, which is, of course, part of the Bodleian (p. 166).

Although there are many 'special' libraries to which the research worker may tend to go first the great general libraries frequently contain more material on particular subjects than the smaller specialized libraries. Some frequently claim to possess special collections which are not in fact as comprehensive as the appropriate sections in the general libraries where it is neither necessary nor practicable to describe particular classes of material as 'special collections'. Because of their size, machinery in the great libraries for obtaining books from closed shelves and stacks involves unavoidable delay in bringing material to the reader. This is certainly true of the British Museum which should, perhaps, be reserved for use when other sources fail. It must be realized, however, that the collections in the Museum are, generally speaking, of a quality and comprehensiveness which is beyond the scope of most libraries. The State Paper room, for example, contains a magnificent collection of parliamentary papers on the open shelves—they are available (to persons holding readers' tickets) for consultation without application. Many readers, however, prefer the more intimate reading room of the smaller library, particularly where the majority of works required are on open shelves.

The General Libraries of London

Of the great concentration of libraries in London some may well be described as being 'general' libraries, namely, the University of London library (including the Goldsmiths' collection) (p. 153), the library of University College (p. 152) and, notwithstanding its special interest in the field of the social sciences, the British Library of Political and Economic Science in the London School of Economics (p. 125). Of public libraries two call for special mention, those of the City of London (p. 109) and the City of Westminster (p. 158).

METROPOLITAN PUBLIC LIBRARIES

Each of the twenty-eight Metropolitan boroughs maintains a public library service and their combined stock numbers approximately 5,000,000 volumes. Limitations of space prevent any attempt at description of them, with the exception of the Guildhall Library, City of London, and the City of Westminster Central Reference Library. Information concerning them all, however, is to be found in the following works:

Rye: *Students Guide to the Libraries of London*, 1927.
Harrod: *Libraries of Greater London*, 1951.
Irwin, ed.: *The Libraries of London* (chapter xvi, the London borough libraries, by J. D. Stewart), 1949.

Resources of the Metropolitan public libraries are made available on personal application to the Central Public Library in each borough and a reader's ticket issued in one borough can now, with one exception, be used elsewhere in the Metropolitan area.

To avoid duplication and incomplete coverage and to meet the needs of the advanced student and research worker in special fields a scheme is in operation in the Metropolitan boroughs whereby the whole field of knowledge has been divided into convenient branches and allocated to individual boroughs. Each then specializes in that branch and undertakes to provide a collection of material thereon so as to ensure the availability of a wide selection of books. Particulars of the branches allocated to individual borough libraries can be obtained from any Central Public Library.

The 'Specialist' and other Libraries of London

Many other libraries in London, belonging to colleges, institutions, societies and government departments, are available to research workers. Those which contain material on the Commonwealth are mentioned in the appropriate sections which follow and are listed, with particulars as to their scope and contents, in Part II.

Guides to the Libraries of London

Some libraries have issued catalogues of, or guides to, their collections; they have been mentioned individually in the appropriate entries in Part II. Guides to library resources generally include the following works:

Aslib Directory—*a guide to sources of specialised information in Great Britain and Ireland*, ed. G. F. Barwick. Association of Special Libraries and Information Bureaux (Aslib). London, 1928. [Out of print but most of the larger libraries have copies for reference. A new and revised edition is in the press.]

Besterman (T.). *British sources of reference and information—a guide to societies, works of reference and libraries.* 1947. [Also issued by Aslib; a considerably smaller work than the *Aslib Directory*.]

Government information and the research worker, ed. R. Staveley. London, 1952. [A collection of lectures published by the Library Association. Deals, *inter alia*, with the problem of elimination of records of public departments, the Commonwealth Agricultural Bureaux, the Central Office of Information, the Central Statistical Office, the Board of Trade, the D.S.I.R. and last, but not least, the Colonial Office and the Commonwealth Relations Office; the latter section contains appendices listing official publications of Commonwealth interest, including a complete list of the Colonial numbered series.]

Guide to Government department and other libraries and information bureaux. 9th edition, London, 1956. [Issued by the Joint Intelligence Bureau, Ministry of Defence. Although intended mainly to facilitate interdepartmental lending of, and reference to, books and official publications, it is an invaluable guide to resources about which there is insufficient knowledge.]

Harrod (L. M.). *The libraries of London.* London, 1951. [Gives brief information of educational, institutional and public libraries of the metropolis. May be used in conjunction with Rye's *Guide*.]

Libraries of London, ed. R. Irwin. London, 1949. [A collection of lectures published by the Library Association. It deals with twelve individual libraries and the Public Record Office, with general chapters on government libraries, law

libraries, medical libraries and borough libraries. It supplements Rye's *Guide*
which is brought up to date to the year 1949 in some respects.]

Philip (A. J.). *An index to the special collections in libraries, museums and art galleries
(public, private and official) in Great Britain and Ireland*, 1949 (F. G. Brown,
Hammersmith, London). [Useful but of limited value to the advanced
research worker.]

Rye (R.). *Students Guide to the Libraries of London*. 3rd edn, London, 1927.
[Although somewhat out of date it is still the standard guide. It also contains
'an account of the most important archives and other aids to study'.]

The Libraries of Oxford

Commonwealth studies are well provided for in Oxford by two of the
Bodleian's dependent libraries, Rhodes House and the Indian Institute,
as well as by other libraries. To Rhodes House has been transferred the
Bodleian's collection of material on the Commonwealth, other than
that relating to India and Pakistan and excepting works published before
1760. All new British publications in the field are also deposited there as
they are received with the result that Rhodes House is one of the fore-
most Commonwealth libraries in the country. The library of the Indian
Institute houses the Bodleian's works on India and Pakistan, except
manuscripts and the older printed books.

Other libraries of particular value to the student of Commonwealth
affairs are those of the Agricultural Economics Research Institute, the
Department of Agriculture, the Imperial Forestry Institute, Nuffield
College, the Oxford Institute of Commonwealth Studies and the
School of Geography.

The Libraries of Cambridge

Cambridge is perhaps not so well served as London and Oxford in the
matter of Commonwealth studies. The University Library, of course,
contains a wealth of material. In addition, there are the Marshall Library,
the Seeley Memorial Library, the Squire Law Library and the library of
the School of Agriculture. None of them, however, lays particular stress
on Commonwealth material.

The National Lending Library Service

A national lending library service is provided by the National Central
Library, Malet Place, London, W.C.1, which is the headquarters of
library co-operation in Great Britain. Its service ensures that practically
all the scarcer, more specialized or more expensive books and periodicals, whether British, Commonwealth or foreign, in the country are
made available to a research worker through the library at which he is

registered. Under certain circumstances foreign books of which no loanable copies are available in this country may be obtained from libraries abroad. Loans are arranged only through the borrower's university, local or other library and applications from individuals are not entertained. The Library either lends books from its own stock of about 150,000 volumes, or arranges the loan through one of the Regional Systems of which there are ten throughout the British Isles, or from university or specialized libraries. Apart from this service, it maintains two great Union Catalogues of Books (other than fiction) in most of the libraries of Great Britain. These contain well over 1,750,000 entries. In addition, it houses the London Union Catalogue, maintained by the London public libraries inter-lending system.

Further information may be obtained from the Librarian. See also *The Libraries of London* (ed. Irwin), 1949 (ch. xvii, The National Central Library, by S. P. L. Filon).

II. PUBLIC ARCHIVES

The national historical records and archives of government are deposited in the Public Record Office,[1] London, to which government departments have transferred the bulk of their records for preservation.

In addition to Colonial Office papers and Commonwealth Relations Office papers other departmental records of Commonwealth interest include those of the Admiralty (deposited to the year 1920), the Board of Trade and its predecessors (to the year 1885), the Foreign Office (to the year 1920), the Treasury (to the year 1914) and the War Office (to the year 1913).

Colonial Office

Transfers of Colonial Office papers have been made to the year 1938; deposits are usually made annually, about fifteen years in arrears. Official publications of oversea territories (i.e. Gazettes, Minutes and Journals of legislative bodies, Sessional papers and similar material) are open without restriction but office papers are available for consultation only before the year 1903, except in most exceptional cases by permis-

[1] For information concerning facilities at the Public Record Office, hours of opening, etc., see p. 136.

sion of the Secretary of State. These papers consist of files of minutes and correspondence with oversea governments, with government departments in this country, with chartered companies and with other bodies and individuals.

A detailed description of the Colonial Office records is outside the scope of this work but, briefly, they have been arranged 'as far as possible topographically under Colonies, separate classes being formed under their respective colonies of (1) the original correspondence, reports, etc. (in-letters); (2) entry books of out-letters, commissions, warrants, etc.; (3) Colonial Acts; (4) Sessional papers consisting of minutes and journals of Colonial Councils and Assemblies; (5) Government Gazettes; and (6) Miscellaneous, comprising Colonial newspapers, blue-books of statistics, shipping and other returns, and accounts and memoranda of various sorts. An exception from this arrangement has to be made in the case of the general series of papers relating to the American and West Indian Colonies between the years 1574 and 1688, with addenda extending to 1697, which had already been arranged chronologically and bound into volumes in accordance with their existing calendar references' (Giuseppi). Each class, which may consist of a few volumes or several hundreds, is identified by a reference C.O. followed by a number; for example, 'Original Correspondence' of New South Wales, 1784 to 1894, consisting of 618 volumes, is referred to as C.O.201. In addition to material classified by territory other miscellaneous classes of records include original correspondence on Colonies generally, Entry books, Board of Trade registers and indexes of letters received and sent, Correspondence on Emigration, Minutes of the Board of Trade and Accounts. Manuscript contemporary registers of the Board of Trade correspondence and Minutes of the correspondence in the Colonial Secretary's office serve as indexes to the originals; in addition, many Entry books are indexed and tables or indexes of contents are to be found in volumes of original correspondence.

Commonwealth Relations Office

Papers have been transferred to the Public Record Office to the year 1935, except the records of the former India Office which are preserved in the Indian Records Section of the Commonwealth Relations Office.

Foreign Office

The Foreign Office was responsible for a period of years (c. 1885 to 1905) for administering most of the African territories, and its papers, therefore, are of particular interest. (Much valuable material on British interests in Africa before 1885 is also to be found in the Slave Trade Series of papers (F.O. 84).) Transfers have been made to the year 1920.

Calendars

Many of the public records have been officially calendared and printed; a list is to be found in *Government Publications, Sectional List No. 24*, referred to below. Those already published include:

> *Calendars of State Papers, Colonial*, covering the period 1513 to 1736, in 42 volumes, London, 1860–1954.
>
> *Journals of the Board of Trade and Plantations*, 1704 to 1782, in 14 volumes, London, 1920–38.

Lists, Indexes and Guides

Public Record Office Lists and Indexes available include the following:

> No. 18. List of Admiralty Records, vol. i (1904).
> 28. List of War Office Records, vol. i (1908).
> 36. List of Colonial Office Records (1911).
> 43. List of State Papers, Domestic, 1547–1792, and Home Office Records, 1782–1837 (1914).
> 46. List of Records of the Treasury, etc., to 1837 (1922).
> 52. List of Foreign Office Records to 1878 (1929).
> 53. Alphabetical guide to War Office Records, etc. (1931).

The printed List of Colonial Office Records (No. 36) and List of Foreign Office Records (No. 52) are virtually superseded by typed lists of documents available in the search rooms at the Public Record Office. There is also a 'Summary of Records' in which all classes of documents transferred from government departments are noted, whether available or not yet available to research workers. The Colonial Office and the Institute of Historical Research possess up-to-date duplicated copies of the 'Summary'.

Many Public Record Office publications, unfortunately, are out of print; those still available are noted in *Government Publications, Sectional List No. 24, Record Publications* (revised from time to time and issued by H.M. Stationery Office).

Other guides, etc., to the public archives include the following:

> Andrews (C. M.). *Guide to the materials for American history to 1783 in the Public Record Office of Great Britain*. 2 vols., Washington, 1911–14. [Includes West Indian material.]
>
> Galbraith (V. H.). *Introduction to the use of the public records*. 2nd edn, London, 1952. [Contains a bibliography.]
>
> Galbraith (V. H.). *Studies in the public records*. London, 1956.
>
> Giuseppi (M. S.). *Guide to the manuscripts preserved in the Public Record Office*. 2 vols., London, 1923–4. [Vol. i relates to legal records and is based on Scar-

gill-Bird, referred to below; vol. ii relates to State Papers and records of
public departments.]

Guide to the public records. London, 1949, in progress. [A new work to be issued
in parts of which only one, Introduction, has so far been published.]

Higham (C. S. S.). *The Colonial Entry Books: a brief guide to the Colonial records in
the Public Record Office before 1696.* ('Helps to Students of History'.) London
(S.P.C.K.), 1921.

Irwin (R.), ed. *The Libraries of London.* London, 1949. [Ch. v, The Public
Record Office, by Sir Hilary Jenkinson.]

Malcolm (H.). *List of documents relating to the Bahamas islands in the British
Museum and the Public Record Office, London.* Nassau, 1910.

Report of the Committee on Departmental Records. London, 1954. [Cmd. 9163.]

Scargill-Bird (S. R.). *Guide to the various classes of documents preserved in the
Public Record Office.* 3rd edn, London, 1908.

Staveley (R.), ed. *Government Information and the research worker.* London, 1952.
[Ch. 3, The problem of elimination in the Records of Public Departments,
by Sir Hilary Jenkinson.]

See also other works by Sir Hilary Jenkinson.

In addition to the various printed sources of information the Public
Record Office provides detailed inventories, lists, etc., as well as the two
previously mentioned, all of which are available for consultation. There
are also indexes made by various government departments to their
own records. Galbraith describes them as 'a huge array of volumes
which are in the nature of indexes and abstracts, made by the various
departments, and therefore at once themselves archives and a means of
access to archives. Nothing gives one so just a conception of the vast
concentration of records at Chancery Lane as these 14,000 volumes,
which fill three great rooms, adjacent to the Literary Search Room.
They are numbered straight through and form by themselves a great
class of Indexes.' This Index class is correlated with other means of
reference provided in the Literary Search Room by means of a *Catalogue of Lists and Indexes* in eight volumes, copies of which are deposited
in the British Museum, the Institute of Historical Research and the
Bodleian Library. The *Catalogue* directs the searcher to all the known
means of reference to every section of the Public Records. This catalogue
is somewhat superseded by a card-index kept in the Literary Search
Room; in addition, another card-index records many unofficial publications of public records.

Records of Parliament

The Records of Parliament have been preserved continuously in the
House of Lords since 1497 in the charge of the Clerk of the Parliaments.
The House of Commons has never had custody of the official records
since the formal actions of Parliament as a whole are performed in the

Lords' Chamber, itself more correctly entitled the 'Parliament Chamber'. From the later sixteenth century onwards the Commons acquired a fairly extensive series of records but, with the exception of the Journals, they were entirely lost in the fire of 1834. The Commons' record series, formed since then, are mainly kept with the Lords' records and are in the immediate care of the Lords' Record Office. This Record Office was established in 1946 as a separate department within the Parliament Office to provide suitable storage for documents and facilities for consultation. The Record Office is open throughout the year (certain public holidays excepted), Mondays to Fridays from 10 a.m. to 5 p.m. and documents may be consulted free of charge, unless the search is for legal or business purposes, in which case a small fee is charged. It is advisable to give twenty-four hours' notice of a search, by letter or telephone, to the Clerk of the Records, House of Lords, S.W.1. Access to the Office is by the Chancellor's Gate, Old Palace Yard.

The main classes of records include Acts of Parliament, Private Bills, Public Bills, Committee Proceedings, House of Commons Records, Journals of the House of Lords, Judicial Records, Main Papers, Parliament Office Papers, and Peerage Claims and Petitions. The Main Papers series include documents laid on the Table, Petitions to the House, draft Bills, Judicial appeals and Reports on any subject ordered by the House or the Government (including, today, 'Command Papers' and 'Statutory Instruments').

Since 1950 a series of House of Lords *Record Office Memoranda* have been issued (in duplicated form) and include the following guides:

No. 1: *List of main classes of records* (rev. Feb. 1957).
No. 3: *The House of Lords Calendars of Manuscripts.*
No. 13: *The Journals, Minutes and Committee books of the House of Lords.*
No. 16: *Private Bill Records of the House of Lords.*

Annual reports by the Clerk of the Records, also issued as *Memoranda*, include each year's accessions.

Calendars of manuscripts have been printed, first as Appendices to the Reports of the Historical Manuscripts Commission and later as separate publications; the House took over the responsibility of compilation and publication in 1894, since when nine volumes have been published (H.M.S.O.). A tenth volume is in course of preparation together with a supplementary volume to include papers discovered since the original calendars were made. The volumes are listed in *Memorandum No. 3*, referred to above.

A complete guide to the Record Office is in course of preparation.

III. PRIVATE PAPERS

Royal Commission on Historical Manuscripts

The Royal Commission on Historical Manuscripts was appointed in 1869 to enquire into the existence of unpublished manuscripts in the possession of private persons and institutions. Its administration is housed in the Public Record Office. Since its establishment the Commission has reported on the manuscripts of over 600 individuals and institutions. Published reports on collections now number more than 200—they are listed in *Government Publications, Sectional List No. 17.* Guides to the publications of the Commission have been issued or are in preparation as follows: Part I, *Topographical Guide to Reports issued 1870–1911* (Cd. 7594), 1914, now out of print; a new edition is in preparation and will include Reports issued 1911–47. Part II, *Index to Persons in Reports issued 1870–1911,* section i, A–L, 1935, and section ii, L–Z, 1938, now out of print. Part III, *Index to Persons in Reports issued 1911–1947,* in preparation. Part IV, *Analytical Survey of subject matter in Reports issued 1870–1947,* in preparation.

National Register of Archives

According to *Sectional List No. 17,* the Commission originally 'aimed at giving brief summaries of the contents and principal features of the collections submitted to it for inspection, but the extent of the material submitted was so great that it could only deal even in a summary fashion with a comparatively small proportion of the unpublished archives of corporate bodies and private owners. Its reports, though increasing in volume, were unable to deal comprehensively with all the collections they covered: and in recent years it has tended to concentrate on dealing more fully with a small number of collections.' The Commission, therefore, set up the National Register of Archives charged with the task of making comprehensive and less detailed surveys of material in the hands of individuals, local authorities, institutions, societies, etc. The Register fosters and encourages the establishment of County Archive Offices throughout the country and organizes groups of voluntary helpers, usually on a county basis, to send in information for co-ordination and recording in the registry. It regularly acquires reports on collections of papers not only from the County offices and voluntary helpers but from its own teams of investigators and inspectors. These reports are frequently detailed and, on occasions, are in the nature of Calendars of the papers to which they relate. Lists and indexes maintained by the Register include those of owners (or custodians), documents relating to individuals, documents dealing with specific localities, documents deposited in specific places and, finally, a comprehensive subject index. The work of listing and indexing continues.

The activities of the Register are recorded in its *Bulletin* published once a year, approximately, since 1948. The *Bulletin* contains summaries of selected reports on material located during the period covered. Issue No. 7 (Winter, 1955) also contains a review of the Register's first ten years, 1945 to 1955. The Registrar and staff are available to answer queries and to supply information, and enquiries from research workers as to the existence and location of manuscripts are encouraged: *they strongly recommend that permission to consult privately owned papers be requested through the Register and not directly from owners or custodians.*

The Register is situated in the Public Record Office, Chancery Lane, London.

Sources of Information on Location of Papers

NATIONAL REGISTER OF ARCHIVES

The task of ascertaining the existence of papers in private hands has been simplified by the work of the National Register to which reference is made above.

THE NATIONAL COLLECTIONS

Details of the collections of manuscripts in the national libraries—the British Museum, the Bodleian and the University Library, Cambridge —can be obtained from published catalogues and lists or on application to the Librarian in each case. The British Museum, which possesses over 100,000 manuscripts (nearly 50,000 relating to India, Pakistan, Ceylon and Burma), has issued several catalogues particulars of which are to be found in Esdaile's *The British Museum Library* (1946), and in the printed pamphlets referred to at p. 100. Both the Bodleian Library, Oxford, and the University Library, Cambridge, maintain catalogues of manuscripts. Additions to the Bodleian collection are recorded in the *Bodleian Library Record*, the Bodleian's *Annual Reports* and the *Bulletin* of the Institute of Historical Research; the latter also records additions to the Cambridge collection.

Information concerning the collections of private papers in the Public Record Office is to be found in the catalogues and indexes maintained there; some are noted in Giuseppi's *Guide*, vol. i (1923), pp. 348–51.

BRITISH RECORDS ASSOCIATION

General information and guidance may be obtained from the British Records Association, 1 Lancaster Place, Strand, W.C.2, and its Records Preservation Section, The Charterhouse, E.C.1. A *List of Record Depositories in Great Britain* was published by the Association in 1956.

BUSINESS ARCHIVES COUNCIL
See p. 17.

INSTITUTE OF HISTORICAL RESEARCH

The Institute's collection of catalogues of manuscripts is particularly good. Since 1927 its *Bulletin* has noted accessions of manuscripts into national and local collections, as well as those changing hands in the sale room. In 1955 the National Register of Archives took over the recording of accessions to local collections but the Institute's *Bulletin* continues to record those going into the great national collections.

SCHOOL OF ORIENTAL AND AFRICAN STUDIES

The School assembles information on the location of manuscripts in other libraries and private collections relating to India and other Asian countries and to Africa.

Collections

(Chartered and other Company papers are listed separately)

Information concerning collections in some of the libraries included in Part II, to which reference should be made under individual institutions, may be briefly summarized as follows:

AFRICA

British Museum. Dilke papers; Khartoum journal and other papers of General Gordon.

Cambridge University Library. Badger papers, Zanzibar.

Christ Church, Oxford. Letters from Johnston to Salisbury.

Church Missionary Society. Archdeacon Walker letters, Uganda; Alex. MacKay's journal, East Africa.

London School of Economics library. Morel papers, Congo and West Africa generally. Courtney letters, and a manifesto and speech about the Boer war. Sidney Webb, East Africa papers (1929–31).

New College, Oxford. Milner papers.

Miss Margery Perham, Nuffield College, Oxford. Lugard's diaries and personal papers (they will be transferred to the Bodleian (Rhodes House Library) on the completion of Miss Perham's biography of Lugard, perhaps in 1958 or 1959).

Rhodes House Library, Oxford. A large and varied collection, particularly the Rhodes papers, see p. 167.

Royal Geographical Society. Letters from Johnston to H. W. Bates.
School of Oriental and African Studies. Mackinnon papers on the Imperial British
East Africa Company.

ASIA

Bodleian Library, Oxford. Some papers of Indian interest, see p. 161.
British Museum. Some 50,000 manuscripts are available in oriental languages on
India, Pakistan, Ceylon and Burma as well as some in English, including the
Warren Hastings papers, the Wellesley correspondence and papers, the
Broughton correspondence and papers and some of the East India Company.
Cambridge University Library. Hardinge of Penshurst papers and Cowell papers,
India.
Church Missionary Society. Bishop Tucker and Dr Pennell correspondence,
India.
India Office Library. Records of the East India Company and many other papers
relating to India (see p. 114) as well as some 20,000 manuscripts in oriental
languages.
Public Record Office. Cornwallis papers, East Indies, 1741–1819; papers of Lord
Ellenborough (governor-general of India, 1841–4).
Royal Asiatic Society. Some material in Sanskrit, Malay, Burmese and Singhalese.
Royal Empire Society. Burney papers, 1820–30, on Burma and Siam.

AUSTRALIA AND NEW ZEALAND

London School of Economics library. Beatrice Webb's diaries, containing sections
on the Webbs' tour of Australia and New Zealand in 1898 and letters written
during the tour. The library also possesses letters written by men of mark in
New Zealand to the Hon. W. P. Reeves (agent-general for New Zealand),
ms. and typescript, c. 1895–1908, in 1 vol. Some *Notes* on the trade of New
South Wales, c. 1835–40 are also available.
Rhodes House, Oxford. Sturt's journals, letters and maps, and a few other miscellaneous papers.

CANADA

British Museum. General Haldimand correspondence, including records of his
commands in Canada.
Rhodes House, Oxford. A few miscellaneous papers.

MALAYA

Cambridge University Library. Raffles papers.
India Office Library. Raffles letters and papers.

PACIFIC AREA AND FAR EAST

Cambridge University Library. Jardine Matheson & Company's papers; Raffles
papers.
India Office Library. Mackenzie papers, Java and the Dutch East Indies; Raffles
papers, Java and Malaya.
School of Oriental and African Studies. Oriental manuscripts.

WEST INDIES, BAHAMAS, BERMUDAS

London School of Economics library. Account book of a Trinidad sugar planter, 1793–1819.
Public Record Office. Manchester papers, the Bermudas, James I and Charles I; Rodney and Shaftesbury papers. Jamaica, Barbados and the Bahamas.
Rhodes House, Oxford. Correspondence and papers relating to estates, Young (1768–1835) and Greg (1765–1834).
Royal Empire Society. Sir George Arthur's papers, British Honduras, 1814–22.

COMMONWEALTH AFFAIRS GENERALLY

London School of Economics library. Beatrice Webb's diaries, containing section on Sidney Webb's Colonial Office period in 1929–31, and letters. Giffen collection, including section on Imperial organization; statement and letters, mostly by or on behalf of Sir Frederick Pollock, 1904–5.
Royal Empire Society. Childers papers and correspondence.
University of London (Goldsmiths' Library). Some miscellaneous papers.
War Office Library. Military Intelligence reports on Colonial territories.

MISSIONS

Church Missionary Society.
International Missionary Council.
London Missionary Society.
Methodist Missionary Society.
Society for Promoting Christian Knowledge.
Society for the Propagation of the Gospel.
Universities Mission.
Rhodes House, Oxford. Codrington diaries, letters, etc., Melanesia, 1867–87.
(The Scottish Missionary societies also possess archives of considerable value.)

NAVAL AND MARITIME HISTORY

Admiralty Library. Early voyages of discovery and exploration sponsored by the Royal Navy.
National Maritime Museum. An immense collection of manuscripts.

SLAVERY

Rhodes House, Oxford. Anti-Slavery Society's archives and copies of some American documents on suppression.
University College, London. Lord Brougham's papers.

MISCELLANEOUS

City of London, Guildhall. History of London.
London School of Economics library. Political and economic history and history of local government in England.
Public Record Office. In addition to official records, collections of private papers are available; see further, p. 136.
University College, London. Social reform and political history.

IV. PAPERS OF CHARTERED AND OTHER COMPANIES

Papers of companies having special interests in the Commonwealth and which are still operating are normally to be found in the companies' archives. Those of companies no longer functioning are to be found in the head offices of successor companies (where appropriate), in the Public Record Office, in libraries or in private hands.

Many such papers are available for consultation by research workers. Collections which have been located during the compilation of this *Guide* are listed in the following paragraphs, but the list is by no means exhaustive.

Registrar of Companies

Much useful information relating to public companies may be obtained from the office of the Registrar of Companies, Bush House (S.W. Wing), Strand, W.C.2. Registration under the Companies Acts involves deposit with the Registrar of certain documents, including Memoranda and Articles of Association, lists of directors, lists of shareholders, registration of mortgages, charges, etc., copies of agreements and particulars of capital formation. (Chartered companies, not being registered under the Companies Acts, are not obliged to lodge information with the Registrar, although their allied or subsidiary companies may be so registered.) From time to time the Registrar disposes of selected lists of shareholders of companies which have been dissolved for more than twenty-one years but all other material deposited with him is retained either in his office or by the Public Record Office. Material may be consulted in the Registrar's office on payment of a small charge; the fee, however, may be reduced in the case of historical research workers. Documents relating to companies which were dissolved up to 1933 have been transferred to the Public Record Office.

Colonial Office and Foreign Office correspondence with Chartered Companies has also been deposited in the Public Record Office.

Business Archives Council

The location of business archives and records of companies can be established with the help of the Business Archives Council which exists primarily to assist in the preservation of sources of economic history by the prevention of destruction of material. It endeavours to remind business houses of the importance of their records to historians. The

C

Council will assist research workers in locating documents required for research. It does not maintain a central repository of documents but an index of available material is in course of preparation. The Council also assembles information about the old Chartered Companies and defunct trading companies in addition to firms still functioning. Its offices are at Devereux Buildings, Devereux Court, Strand, W.C.2. A small library of about 200 volumes, mainly printed histories of business houses, is available to non-members, on prior application by letter to the Honorary Secretary. The ninth Report of the Council (1954) contains a list of such works.

Individual Collections

AUSTRALIA AND NEW ZEALAND BANK

The Bank's historical records are private and are not accessible to research workers. The Bank, however, is willing to give information on specific points. Applications should be addressed to the Head Office, 71 Cornhill, London, E.C.3.

BANK OF BRITISH WEST AFRICA

The records of the Bank are not available for consultation but applications for specific information from accredited research workers will be considered; they should be addressed to 37 Gracechurch Street, London, E.C.3.

BARCLAY'S BANK (DOMINION, COLONIAL AND OVERSEAS)

The archives and records of the Bank are not generally available for consultation. The Bank is, however, willing to answer questions submitted by research workers. The Head Offices are at 11 Lombard Street, London, E.C.3.

A history, *A Banking Centenary* (1836–1936), was published in 1938 for private circulation.

BRITISH NORTH BORNEO COMPANY

The bulk of the Company's papers are now part of the official archives of the Secretariat, Jesselton; they happily escaped destruction during the Japanese occupation. These records cover almost the entire period of the Chartered Company's rule, i.e. from 1882 to 1941, and consist of bound volumes of despatches between the Governor and the President of the Court of Directors, and a variety of correspondence and miscellaneous records, including copies of agreements, official publications, annual and other reports.

Other papers are housed in the Colonial Office library, many of which are due for transfer to the Public Record Office. The latter consist of correspondence of the Colonial Office (1881–1910), Admiralty (1881–1909), War Office (1881–1910), Crown Agents (1890–1910) and other departments; Company's correspondence with H.M. Government (1882 to 1911), and other letters; Letter books; Ledgers, 1882 to 1908, and other financial papers; the B.N.B. Provisional Association letter books; and British Borneo Exploration Company's correspondence books. Material to be retained in the Colonial Office consists of a variety of papers including private correspondence, diaries and printed official publications. A list of these papers and documents is in the Institute of Commonwealth Studies as well as in the Colonial Office library.

Rhodes House, Oxford, also possesses some miscellaneous material relating to W. C. Cowie, founder of the Company, and a set of Reports, 1st to 33rd, 1882–94.

BRITISH SOUTH AFRICA COMPANY

Most of the Company's records relating to the administration of Rhodesia were passed to the Southern Rhodesia Government when its administrative responsibilities ended in 1923. They now form part of the Official Archives in Salisbury. Unfortunately many other records were lost during air-raids on London in the Second World War. The Company still possesses, however, copies of Directors' reports and accounts from 1889 which are available for reference by accredited research workers on application to the Secretary of the Company, 11 Old Jewry, London, E.C.2. Minutes of Directors' Meetings, which are confidential, are not available, even for inspection.

Rhodes House, Oxford, possesses the Rhodes papers (see p. 167) and holds on deposit the Cawston papers consisting of Company reports and miscellaneous papers and correspondence from 1888 to 1911.

CANADA COMPANY

The Guildhall Library, City of London, possesses a few of the Company's papers.

CHARTERED BANK OF INDIA, AUSTRALIA AND CHINA

The Bank's historical records are not available for consultation but it is willing to give assistance by answering specific questions. Applications for information should be addressed to the Head Office, 38 Bishopsgate, London, E.C.2.

In 1953 the Bank celebrated the centenary of its incorporation; a centenary history, by Compton Mackenzie, *Realms of Silver: one hundred years of banking in the East*, was published in 1954. It contains much historical information.

EAST INDIA COMPANY

The extant papers of the Company are to be found in the Indian Records Section of the Commonwealth Relations Office, the successor to the India Office.

In the Bank of England Record Office are deposited the East India Stock Records; the papers available include transfer books and registers, 1676–1874; ledgers, 1706–1874; miscellaneous journals of the seventeenth and early eighteenth centuries; registers of letters, lists of stockholders, etc., 1698–1794; unpaid warrants; redemptions; powers of attorney; etc. The Bank is willing to permit accredited research workers to consult the papers.

A few other papers relating to the Company are scattered and items are to be found in the British Museum, the Bodleian Library, Oxford, the Goldsmiths' Library, University of London, and in the Guildhall Muniment Room, City of London.

Some of the Company's papers have been published, including:

Calendars of the Court Minutes of the East India Company (E. B. Sainsbury), 1635 to 1679. 11 vols., Oxford, 1907–38.
Letters received by the East India Company from its servants in the East, 1602 to 1617. 6 vols., London, 1896–1903. The narrative is continued in *The English Factories in India*, 1618 onwards. Oxford, 1906 in progress.

ELDER DEMPSTER LINES LIMITED, LIVERPOOL

The records of the Company and of its predecessors were unhappily destroyed during the Second World War and it now possesses very little of value to the research worker.

ENGLISH, SCOTTISH AND AUSTRALIAN BANK

The London offices of the Bank, 5 Gracechurch Street, E.C.3, possess only an 'outline of early records' which, together with balance sheets from the Bank's inception, are available for consultation.

ALFRED HOLT AND COMPANY OF LIVERPOOL
(OCEAN STEAM SHIP COMPANY)

The bulk of the historical records of the Company was destroyed during the war when its offices were burnt out. A quantity of material, however, is still in the Company's possession and in other hands, a list of which is to be found in appendix iv of Prof. F. E. Hyde's *Blue Funnel: a history of Alfred Holt and Company of Liverpool from 1865 to 1914*, Liverpool, 1956.

JOHN HOLT AND COMPANY (LIVERPOOL) LIMITED

The Company possesses a large collection of its archives which have recently been arranged and catalogued by Mr. John Flint. They contain an almost complete record of the Company's activities, both in commerce and politics, from 1865 to 1916. In addition to normal commercial material—minute books, ledgers, invoice books and business correspondence—they include personal correspondence of John Holt and his family, collections of letters of Mary Kingsley and E. D. Morel, some correspondence with George and Alexander Miller (of Alexander Miller Bros. & Co. Ltd.) and some papers of the African Association Ltd., and the Royal Niger Company, including some correspondence with Sir George Goldie.

The papers have been arranged broadly into three categories:

Series I: Correspondence on the internal commercial development of the Company, 1868–1915.

Series II: Correspondence with other trading and shipping firms in West Africa, general correspondence and correspondence on political affairs.

Series III: Miscellaneous correspondence with Coast Agents, which gives some idea of life on the Coast in the years 1860–80.

These series are arranged under subjects. There is also a collection of correspondence arranged under persons. Other material includes diaries, pamphlets, news cuttings and West African photographs.

Further information about these records is available to accredited research workers only, from Mr. C. R. Holt, 250 India Buildings, Liverpool 2.

HUDSON'S BAY COMPANY

The Company's archives are housed in its Record Room at Beaver House and are under the care of an Archivist. They consist of minutes, correspondence, account books, records of stockholders, journals and reports of daily events at the fur trade posts, journals of exploration, maps, ships' logs, servants' contracts, wills, etc. Except under special circumstances only archives up to the year 1870, the date of the Deed of Surrender of Rupert's Land to the Crown, are available for inspection. Documents after that date are produced only on such conditions as the Governor and Committee may determine. Use of the documents is subject to rather stringent conditions and a set of Rules and Regulations to be observed has been drawn up. Applications from accredited research workers for permission to consult them must be addressed to the Secretary of the Company, Beaver House, Great Trinity Lane, London, E.C.4, and must indicate the precise subject of the proposed research. All applications must be accompanied by two references or letters of recommendation.

The records of the Company are being published by the Hudson's Bay Record Society. Since 1938 nineteen volumes have been issued; they include early minutes of the Company, letters and journals.

(The Company's archives have been copied on microfilms, a set of which is available for consultation at the Public Archives of Canada, Ottawa, under similar terms and conditions to those which apply to the use of the originals in London.)

The Goldsmiths' Library, University of London, also possesses some miscellaneous papers relating to the Company.

IMPERIAL BRITISH EAST AFRICA COMPANY

The School of Oriental and African Studies possesses the papers of Sir William Mackinnon, the Company's first President.

Rhodes House Library, Oxford, possesses E. J. H. Russell's diaries, 1895 to 1900, and the letters, papers and diaries of F. G. Hall, District Officer, 1880–1901.

A history of the Company, compiled from its records by P. L. McDermott, *British East Africa or Ibea*, was published in 1893 (London).

JARDINE MATHESON AND COMPANY OF CHINA

The nineteenth-century records of the Company are housed in the University Library, Cambridge, particulars of which are noted at p. 174. They may be consulted only by permission of the Company.

NEW ENGLAND COMPANY

The Guildhall, City of London, possesses a complete collection of the Company's archives from 1650 to 1941.

NEW ZEALAND COMPANY

The Company's records are now in the Public Record Office; they consist of original correspondence, minutes, accounts and miscellanea covering the period 1839 to 1858.

NORTH WEST COMPANY OF CANADA

The Royal Empire Society possesses a small collection of papers of the eighteenth and early nineteenth centuries.

ROYAL AFRICA COMPANY

The Goldsmiths' library, University of London, possesses a few of the Company's papers.

ROYAL NIGER COMPANY

Rhodes House, Oxford, possesses the Scarbrough papers relating to the Company covering the period 1884 to 1930 as well as some Lugard correspondence, 1901 to 1919. Other papers are in the possession of the United Africa Company to which reference is made below.

SOUTH SEAS COMPANY

Stock records of the South Sea Company are deposited in the Bank of England Record Office; the papers available include early lists of subscribers and schedules of Tallies, but the majority relate to the Company annuities, including ledgers, 1751–1854; indices to certificates, 1723–54; sundry journals; registers of death, 1752–1851; transfer books, 1791–1854; and certificates, 1808–54. Accredited research workers will be granted facilities to consult these papers. (The Company ledgers were deposited with Bosanquet & Co., but are believed to be no longer in existence.)

A few miscellaneous papers relating to the Company are in the Guildhall Muniment Room, City of London.

STANDARD BANK OF SOUTH AFRICA

The Bank's archives are not available for consultation. Consideration will, however, be given to requests for specific information from research workers. The Bank's Head Office is at 10 Clement's Lane, London, E.C.4.

A *History* of the Bank (1862–1913), by G. T. Amphlett, was published in 1914 (Glasgow). A short account, by J. A. Henry, appeared in 1953 (Salisbury, S.R.): *Sixty years north of the Limpopo: the story of the coming of the Standard Bank to Rhodesia and Nyasaland, with some account of its early days there.*

UGANDA COMPANY

The Company's archives, which include annual reports, minute books and correspondence, are deposited in the library of Makerere College, Kampala. C. Erlich's *The Uganda Company—the first fifty years* was published in 1953 (Kampala).

UNION CASTLE MAIL STEAMSHIP COMPANY

The Company's papers are not available for consultation. It will, however, endeavour to answer specific enquiries, within reason, from research workers; requests should be addressed to the Head Office, 3 Fenchurch Street, London, E.C.3. A fairly detailed history of the Company was published in 1953 to commemorate its centenary: *Union-Castle Chronicle, 1853–1953*, by Marischal Murray (London).

UNITED AFRICA COMPANY

The Company's papers are not generally available for consultation. It will, however, give consideration to requests from accredited research workers to consult specific documents or classes of documents.

The Company also possesses some of the papers of the Royal Niger Company, its predecessor, which are in course of being sorted and examined by the Secretarial Department, U.A.C., Unilever House, Blackfriars, E.C.4, to which applications for information should be addressed.

Charles Wilson's *The History of Unilever: a study in economic growth and social change* (2 vols., London, 1954) contains some information on the Company as well as on other African enterprises of Unilever.

MISCELLANEOUS

The Guildhall, City of London, possesses records of some business and trading companies not mentioned above, as well as the papers of Thomas Bowrey (1650–1713), a sea captain and merchant dealing, *inter alia*, with trading in the East Indies and the south seas. A few firms and insurance offices in the City have also deposited their early business papers in the Muniment Room.

The Goldsmiths' library, University of London, possesses a few miscellaneous papers of various companies in addition to those of the East India, the Hudson's Bay and the Royal Africa Companies mentioned above.

The records of other banking houses contain much valuable information relating to development and projects they have helped to finance and to companies trading overseas which were their clients. The house of Glyn, Mills & Co., as an example, played an important part in the development of Canada during the period 1835 to 1893 and its archives contain many documents covering the period. Application for permission to consult Bank records should be addressed to the Head Offices in each case.

V. PARLIAMENTARY PAPERS AND OFFICIAL PUBLICATIONS

A: BRITISH

Parliamentary Papers

A number of sets of Parliamentary papers (bills, reports, accounts and papers of both Houses) are available in London, Oxford and Cambridge, some complete from their commencement, some with imperfections and gaps. Part sets are more plentiful.

The British Museum State Paper room (where a staff of specialists is available and at the disposal of readers) has a fine and comprehensive collection of all Parliamentary papers as well as a set of the scarce 'Abbot Collection' in 110 volumes, covering the period 1731 to 1800,[1] much of which is not included in the First Series of Reports, 1701 to 1801 (the fifteen-volume folio reprint issued in 1803). Its set of House of Lords papers, however, is not complete but a good proportion of the missing nineteenth-century items are being obtained.

The Bodleian and Cambridge collections are almost complete except that the Lords papers in each case have imperfections.

Her Majesty's Stationery Office possesses the only complete set of House of Lords papers of the nineteenth century; photostat copies are obtainable.

The Board of Trade possesses a nearly complete collection. The University of London library's set is good but not complete (see p. 154); its Lords papers date only from 1940, although individual papers of earlier date are in the library, especially in the Goldsmiths' collection. University College library, London, possesses a valuable run of the scarce

---

[1] Four sets were put together by Speaker Abbot; of the other three one is in the House of Lords, one in the House of Commons and one (1738 to 1800 only) in University College library, London.

papers in the Abbot collection, mentioned above, namely from 1738 to 1800. It also has a run of papers from 1801 to 1850 but practically nothing since. The London School of Economics library also has an almost complete set from 1801 as well as the fifteen-volume folio re-print, except for the exclusion of those Lords papers which are dupli-cated in the Commons collection. The Institute of Historical Research has few House of Lords papers and an imperfect set of House of Com-mons papers but most of those concerning the Commonwealth are in-cluded up to the year 1900. The Guildhall library, City of London, has a complete collection from 1837. The City of Westminster's collection is almost complete from 1920 but it also has a considerable quantity of earlier material.

British Parliamentary Papers on the Commonwealth

Several libraries possess good collections of Parliamentary papers of Commonwealth interest—the Colonial Office, the Royal Empire Society and Rhodes House, Oxford, the best of which is probably that in the Colonial Office. The Royal Empire Society's collection includes valuable sets of papers from 1867 arranged and bound together by territory. The Institute of Commonwealth Studies has a good selection from about 1901, with much material of the nineteenth century, mainly relating to South Africa. As mentioned above, the Institute of Historical Research also has most of those of Commonwealth interest up to 1900.

Papers relating to India are to be found in the India Office library, the most comprehensive collection, in India House and in the Indian Institute, Oxford.

Non-Parliamentary Papers

Except in the case of the British Museum non-Parliamentary papers are impossible to locate as 'collections'. The British Museum aims at com-plete coverage; it arranges material by department of issue. The 'Commonwealth libraries'—Colonial Office, Royal Empire Society, Rhodes House, the Institute of Commonwealth Studies and, to a lesser extent, the Oxford Institute of Commonwealth Studies—acquire those of Commonwealth interest, whilst other specialist libraries acquire those within their own fields. The general libraries, of course, select papers covering a wide range of subjects.

Parliamentary Debates

Sets of *Hansard*, together with earlier historical material containing debates, are available in several libraries, including the British Museum, the University of London library, the London School of Economics library (almost complete), the Bodleian and the University library, Cambridge. In the Institute of Historical Research the set is almost complete. University College, London, and King's College, London, also possess sets, the latter having some gaps after 1909.

Journals

Several complete sets of the *Journals* of both Houses of Parliament are available in the British Museum, the University of London library, the London School of Economics library, University College, London, King's College, London, the Guildhall, City of London, the Bodleian and the University library, Cambridge. A set in the Institute of Historical Research is complete to the year 1936.

London Gazette

Sets of the *London Gazette* are to be found in the British Museum and the Guildhall library, City of London. The Bodleian has a fine set but some of the earliest volumes are imperfect. The University library, Cambridge, has a collection from 1665 to 1724, 1742 to 1746 and 1755 to date. The Institute of Historical Research contains some *Gazettes* of the seventeenth century, but the eighteenth and nineteenth centuries are complete; the set ends in 1899. The Goldsmiths' library, University of London, has the *Gazette* from 1801 to 1829 complete, 1868 to 1930 imperfect, and from 1931 to date, and London School of Economics library for 1693–4 (with gaps) and from 1927 to date. Other libraries possess sets in varying degrees of completeness.

Calendars of State Papers

Complete sets are in many libraries, including the British Museum, the London School of Economics library, the University of London library, the Institute of Historical Research, the Bodleian and the University library, Cambridge.

Consular and Diplomatic Reports

Reports from 1855 are to be found in the British Museum, the London School of Economics library, the Bodleian, the University library, Cambridge, and, with some gaps, in the University of London library.

British and Foreign State Papers

The *State Papers* are to be found in the British Museum, the University of London library, the Institute of Historical Research, the London

School of Economics library, the Bodleian and the University library, Cambridge.

'International' Papers

League of Nations and United Nations publications (including the *Treaty Series*) are in the British Museum, the London School of Economics library, the Bodleian and the University library, Cambridge, all of which are depository libraries. The Royal Institute of International Affairs also possesses a set. The City of Westminster Central Reference Library has a large collection and good selections are to be found in several other libraries, notably those of the University of London and Nuffield College, Oxford.

For *Treaty Series* of Australia, Canada, Ceylon, New Zealand and Pakistan, see p. 35.

The United Nations Information Centre, London, also maintains a reference library of United Nations publications and documents.

International Labour Office publications are in the British Museum, the London School of Economics library and the City of Westminster Central Reference Library. The University library, Cambridge, also possesses a nearly complete set. They are well represented in the University of London library and in the library of Nuffield College.

Publications of other international organizations are also available; for information as to the location of these and other series see Barbara Kyle's *Resources on International Affairs in London Libraries*, in *International Affairs*, 32, pp. 190–8, April 1956.

Indexes, Lists and Guides

Over the years many indexes (sessional, general and special) of Parliamentary papers have been printed by H.M. Stationery Office (or the earlier Government printers), London, and published by Authority. Unfortunately some are out of print but copies are available for reference in several libraries. Many of the indexes were issued in the numbered series of House of Commons Papers and given a sessional number and date. Libraries possessing sets of papers will, therefore, contain the indexes in their sets.

Catalogue of Parliamentary Reports and Breviate of their contents, arranged under heads according to subjects, 1696–1834. (H.C. 626, 1834, o.p.); Ford's reprint, Oxford, 1953.

Catalogue of Papers printed by order of the House of Commons, 1731–1800 (1807, o.p.); reprint, 1954. [The index to the 'Abbot Collection'.]

General Index to the Reports from Committees of the House of Commons (the series of fifteen volumes). 1803. [Being the index to the 'First Series' of Reports, 1715–1801.]

the thoughts off, but they would not leave. The period with Christina seemed so far away and yet so near, so much like an experience in a different, delicate world and yet so full of pain and anguish. One can never explain such things. And still they mean so much to a writer — not at the time, God knows, when only the happiness and pain are present, but later, in retrospect. Flashes of memory — scenes and incidents — passed through his mind with the very swiftness of the train that was taking him to Boston.

Christina was a fragile and exquisite, almost otherworldly, person, and Marquand had fallen deeply in love with her. They became engaged in Rome — a classic spot for such an event — in 1922. At the time, he was travelling abroad to look with fascinated eyes at the cathedrals and paintings he had had no time to observe during the war, and she was travelling with her parents. The Sedgwicks moved about Europe with quiet, unhurried, *fin-de-siècle* elegance. Wherever they went, they ran into other Sedgwicks, or collateral Sedgwicks, or, at the very least, people from Boston. Journeying with the Sedgwicks through Italy, looking with wonderment at the glorious relics, at the Tintorettos and the Raphaels, and joining up at the end of each day in some hotel lobby or restaurant with a group of understand-

the staid *Atlantic Monthly.* The Sedgwick family, although it came from Stockbridge, Massachusetts, where the frogs in the spring were all said to sing, "Sedgwick, Sedgwick, Sedgwick," was one of the intellectual prides of intellectual Boston — scholars, writers, teachers, ministers. They were among the select group who were final arbiters of taste. They were steeped in the traditions of the city, where American culture had been founded and had flourished, and they were nourished by their family traditions. They were a tightly knit group, proud, even arrogant, and to young Marquand from Newburyport and the *Saturday Evening Post* they had an indefinable, awesome quality. Marquand nervously crossed his legs in the parlor car. He tried to shake off his thoughts, but they persisted against his will. He rose and walked to the vestibule of the car, and stood for a moment looking out at the countryside of Rhode Island, but still the thoughts were with him. One can never dismiss some thoughts that lie most deeply within one; no effort of the will can do it. Christina, the mother of his first two children, was dead now. She had died not long ago — many years after she and Marquand were divorced. The marriage lasted nearly thirteen years, a tenderly happy and tenderly unhappy period for him. He tried to shake

Classification of Parliamentary Reports and Breviate of their Contents, 1801–1826. (H.C. 81, 1830.)

List of Reports of the House of Commons, including those of the year 1832, with indexes thereto. (H.C. 626.I to 626.XI, 1834.) [Includes reports on Colonies and slavery, 1804–34, and on emigration, 1826–7.]

Indexes to Reports of the House of Commons, 1801–1834, 1835–1837. (H.C. 498 and 498.I to 498.VIII, 1837.) [Includes East India affairs, 1805–32.]

Indexes to the Reports of Commissioners. (H.C. 710.I to 710.XVII, 1847; all o.p.) [Include Colonial land and emigration, 1828–47; W. Indies and Mauritius (Labour), 1828–47; Colonies, 1812–40; East India, 1837–47.]

Index to Reports from Select Committees, 1800–45. (H.C. 396, 1845, o.p.)

Annual Lists and General Index of the Parliamentary Papers relating to the East Indies published during the years 1801–1907 inclusive. (H.C. 89, 1909, o.p.)

General Index to the Reports of Select Committees, printed by order of the House of Commons, 1801–52. (H.C. 9, 1854, o.p.)

General Index to the Accounts and Papers, Reports of Commissioners, Estimates, &c., printed by order of the House of Commons, or presented by Command, 1801–52. (1854, o.p.): reprint, 1938.

General Index to the Bills, Reports, Estimates, Accounts and Papers and to the Papers presented by Command, 1852–99. (1909, o.p.) [Unfortunately sessional and Command numbers are omitted.]

It is understood that a new fifty-year Index is in preparation; it will cover the period 1900–49.

Other indexes have been published (1829 to 1951) covering varying periods from 1801 to 1948/49, sixteen in all, supplemented by annual sessional indexes to date.

HOUSE OF LORDS

General index to the Sessional Papers of the House of Lords or presented by special Command, 1801–1859. (1859, o.p.; reprint, 1938). *1859–1870* (1872, o.p.). *1871–1884/5* 1890, o.p.).

Subsequent to the publication of the Index for the period 1871–1884/5 annual indexes only were issued up to and including the year 1920, most of which are out of print.

Since 1920 annual 'lists of titles' only are available. A numerical list is included in the Annual (consolidated) lists of Government Publications (H.M.S.O.).

NON-PARLIAMENTARY PAPERS

There are no general indexes or consolidated lists of non-Parliamentary papers. Such papers are recorded in the Annual (consolidated) lists issued by H.M. Stationery office—they have been issued under various titles since about the middle of the nineteenth century and only since 1936 have five-year indexes to the annual lists been published. The lists before 1900 are scarce and not easily located. Current non-Parliamentary papers are also included in the *Sectional Lists*, referred to below.

CURRENT LISTS

H.M. Stationery Office issues Daily Lists, Monthly Catalogues and Annual Catalogues to which five-year indexes are published at intervals.

The Stationery Office also issues a series of *Sectional Lists* (revised from time to time) comprising a catalogue of all current non-parliamentary publications with a selection of important Parliamentary publications. So far sixty lists have been prepared and issued including the following:

No. 3. D.S.I.R.
    7. Treaty Series.
   17. Historical Manuscripts.
   24. Record Publications. [Contains *all* the Department's publications.]
   34. Colonial Office. [Contains a list of papers by subject (issued in and since 1925), complete lists of publications in the Colonial Numbered series, the Colonial Research studies, the Colonial Research publications, the Colonial Advisory Council of Agriculture, Animal Health and Forestry publications, the Falkland Islands Dependencies Survey (Scientific Reports) and Fishery publications.]
   50. Miscellaneous. [Includes publications of the British Commonwealth Scientific Conference, the Commonwealth Agricultural Bureaux, the Commonwealth Economic Committee, the Commonwealth Relations Office, the Commonwealth Shipping Committee and the former India Office.]
   51. Board of Trade.
   53. Colonial Office. Special. [Books, maps, etc., on the Colonies.]
   58. Foreign Office.
   59. Royal Commissions, 1936–54.

BRITISH PARLIAMENTARY PAPERS ON THE COMMONWEALTH

In about the year 1902 the Colonial Office issued, for limited circulation, a *List of Parliamentary Papers relating to South Africa, 1860 to 1901.* [A copy is in the library of the Royal Empire Society and photographic reproductions are in the Colonial Office and Institute of Commonwealth Studies libraries.]

The Office of the Agent-General for Western Australia in London possesses a bibliography of British Parliamentary Papers on Western Australian affairs from 1829 to 1890.

Lists of Parliamentary and non-Parliamentary papers relating to Colonial affairs appear in the *Colonial Office Lists*; at one time the list covered the period from 1864 to 1877, later from 1877 to 1886, from 1886 to 1940, and from 1925 to 1950; subsequently the lists are annual. The former *India Office Lists* included annual lists of papers relating to India.

The Colonial Office *Monthly Lists of Official Colonial Publications*, 1948 onwards, include H.M.S.O. publications on the Colonies.

The Colonial Office *Reading List on Development and Welfare* (revised January 1951) includes United Kingdom official publications.

The Colonial Office (Information Department) issues from time to time, in duplicated form, a list of *British Government Publications of Colonial Interest* (latest issue, revised to September 1953, with Supp. September 1953–September 1955).

MISCELLANEOUS LISTS

Indexes to *Consular and Diplomatic Reports* were regularly issued covering the period 1886 to 1914, namely 1886–96, 1896 and 1897, 1898–9, 1900 annually until 1914, the last issued. Several are now out of print.

Guide to Current Official Statistics, annually from 1922 to 1938, 17 issues, most of which are now out of print. The series has not been resumed since the Second World War.

House of Commons, Library. *A bibliography of Parliamentary Debates of Great Britain* (H. of C. Library Doc. No. 2), 1956.

House of Lords. *The journals, Minutes and Committee books of the House.* (H. of L. Rec. Office Memo. No. 13), 1956.

WORKS ON INDEXES, LISTS, ETC., OF PARLIAMENTARY PAPERS

British Parliamentary Papers: Catalogues and Indexes. Institute of Historical Research *Bulletin*, xi, 1933/4, pp. 24–30.

Ford (P. and G.). *Guide to Parliamentary Papers—what they are, how to find them, how to use them.* New edn, London, 1956.

Government Publications: Official Indexes, Lists, Guides, Catalogues. H.M.S.O., London, 1956.

Horrocks (Sidney). *The State as Publisher.* London, 1952.

UNOFFICIAL INDEXES, LISTS, ETC., OF PARLIAMENTARY PAPERS

Adams (M. I.), Ewing (J.) and Munro (J.). *Guide to the principal Parliamentary papers relating to the Dominions, 1812–1911.* Edinburgh, 1913.

Association of Research Libraries, Philadelphia. *Catalogue of Great Britain entries represented by Library of Congress.* Issued to July 31, 1942. Ann Arbor, Mic., 2 vols., 1943–4.

Brown (E. S.). *Manual of Government Publications—United States and Foreign.* New York, 1950.

Cambridge History of the British Empire, Cambridge, 1929 in progress (eight vols. have so far been published). [Bibliographies, including British Parliamentary papers, etc., are to be found in vols. ii (New Empire), iv (British India), v (Indian Empire), vi (Canada), vii, pt. i (Australia), vii, pt. ii (New Zealand), and viii (South Africa).

Childs (J. B.). *Government document bibliography in the United States and elsewhere*, 3rd edn. Library of Congress, Washington, 1942.

Ford (P. and G.). *A breviate of Parliamentary Papers, 1917–1939.* Oxford, 1951.

Ford (P. and G.). *Select List of British Parliamentary Papers, 1833–1899.* Oxford,

1953. [Unfortunately neither this work nor the previous one contain much relating to the Commonwealth.]

Gabine (B. L.). *Finding list of British Royal Commission Reports, 1860–1935*. Cambridge, Mass., 1935.

Government Information and the Research Worker, ed. R. Staveley. London, 1952. [Ch. xxiv, Colonial Office and Commonwealth Relations Office, by A. B. Mitchell. Contains lists of Command Papers presented by the Secretary of State for the Colonies, 1946 to 1951, Colonial Numbered series, complete to 1951, Colonial Research publications, Colonial Research studies, Colonial Advisory Council of Agriculture, Animal Health and Forestry publications, Fishery publications, Unnumbered publications, 1947 to 1951, Command Papers presented by the Secretary of State for Commonwealth Affairs, 1946 to 1951, Dominions Numbered series and Command Papers of Commonwealth Interest presented by other Ministers, a selection from 1946 to 1951.]

Gregory (W.). *List of Serial Publications of Foreign Governments, 1815 to 1931*. New York, 1932; o.p.

Jones (H. L.), comp. *Catalogue of Parliamentary Papers, 1801–1900*, with Supplements 1901–10 and 1911–20. 4 vols. London, 1904–22. [Sometimes known as P. S. King's Lists. Unfortunately all numbering of papers is omitted.]

King (P. S. & Son). *Catalogue of parliamentary reports, papers, etc., relating to Africa, 1800 to 1899*. London, 1899.

Ragatz (L. J.), comp. *A check-list of House of Commons sessional papers relating to the British West Indies and to the West Indian slave trade and slavery, 1763–1834*. London, 1923.

Ragatz (L. J.), comp. *A check-list of House of Lords sessional papers relating to the British West Indies and to the West Indian slave trade and slavery, 1763–1834*. 2nd edn, London, 1932.

Scholefield (G. H.). *Union list of New Zealand official papers and British official papers relating to New Zealand*. Wellington, 1938. [A microfilm copy is in the library of the Institute of Commonwealth Studies.]

Simpson (D. H.), comp. *A checklist of British official publications relating to Malta, 1801–1950*. In *Melita Historica*, vol. i, 1954.

Temperley (H.) and Penson (L. M.). *A century of diplomatic Blue-books, 1814–1914*. Cambridge, 1938.

B: COMMONWEALTH

Commonwealth Generally

The most comprehensive collection of official publications of the Commonwealth is that in the Colonial Office which possesses reports, papers, journals, debates, gazettes, legislation, etc., from the earliest times to date. Transfers of this material are made to the Public Record Office about fifteen years in arrears of the current date where it is available for consultation, perhaps, though, not so readily as elsewhere.

The Commonwealth Relations Office possesses material similar to that in the Colonial Office, in respect of the self-governing countries of the Commonwealth from about 1925.

The library of the Royal Empire Society is almost comparable with that of the Colonial Office and is an outstanding collection; some of its holdings are listed on pp. 139–41.

Rhodes House library, Oxford, except in regard to the Asian countries of the Commonwealth, ranks with those of the Colonial Office and Royal Empire Society although it is not quite so complete in some respects; material is still being acquired to fill gaps (see pp. 168–70).

Under a Colonial Office directive, copies of all Colonial official publications are sent to the British Museum. Publications of the other countries of the Commonwealth are sent under international exchange arrangements. As a result, the State Paper room has a good and comprehensive collection of official publications from all parts of the Commonwealth.

Material in the London School of Economics library is fairly comprehensive; particulars of some of its holdings are to be found on pp. 127–9.

The University library, Cambridge, has a representative collection. It is incomplete in certain sections although, with the exception of India and Pakistan, all Commonwealth countries now send copies of their more important official publications. Material is also being regularly received from most Colonial governments. In April 1948 it issued, in duplicated form, a list of *Dominion Government Publications* in the library.

The Institute of Commonwealth Studies has a selective collection regularly acquired since 1950, except for India and Pakistan, but much earlier material is available, particularly that of Australia, Canada and South Africa.

Legislation is to be found in the Institute of Advanced Legal Studies, the Squire law library, Cambridge, the School of Oriental and African Studies, some of the Inns of Court and the Bar library, Royal Courts of Justice, in addition to the libraries of the Colonial Office, the Commonwealth Relations Office, the Royal Empire Society and Rhodes House. Of the Inns of Court the libraries of the Middle Temple, Lincoln's Inn and the Inner Temple, particularly the two former, are the most comprehensive—they possess the very early legislation, annual and sessional volumes as well as many of the previous revised editions of the laws. Admission to the Inns of Court and Bar libraries is restricted but applications from research workers are considered individually.

Australasia

Official publications of Australia are also to be found in the reference library of Australia House, p. 94, and State publications in the offices

D

of Agents-General in London—New South Wales, p. 133; Queensland,
p. 137; South Australia, p. 150; Tasmania, p. 150; Victoria, p. 156;
Western Australia, p. 158.

New Zealand official publications, from earliest times, are in the
library of New Zealand House, Office of the High Commissioner in
London (p. 134).

See also Commonwealth, above.

Canada

Canadian material is in Canada House library (p. 101), whilst provincial
publications are available in the Offices of the Agents-General for
Alberta, p. 93; British Columbia (a particularly good set), p. 97;
Ontario, p. 135; and Saskatchewan. Material of the provinces not
represented in London is to be found in Canada House. See also
Commonwealth, above.

Ceylon

The Office of the High Commissioner in London has some material
from about 1947, but the best collections are in the Colonial Office and
the Royal Empire Society.

India

Indian publications are to be found in the India Office Library and the
Indian Records Section of the Commonwealth Relations Office which
possess virtually complete collections from earliest times. India House
has a fine set from 1920 to date. It also has the Minutes and Debates of
the Legislative Council of India and its successors, which commence in
the year 1854 and continue to the present time. The University of
London Library has some papers covering the period 1850 to 1936—
debates and proceedings of various legislative councils and reports on
the administration of particular provinces. The Indian Institute, Oxford, also possesses a selection of papers from 1921 onwards.

Pakistan

The Office of the High Commissioner in London has some publications
but the most comprehensive set is perhaps in the India Office Library
which is still in the process of acquiring Pakistani material.

South Africa

Official publications of the Union of South Africa are to be found in
South Africa House. See also Commonwealth, above.

Overseas Territories

East African official publications are well represented in East Africa House, in the Office of the High Commissioner for Rhodesia and Nyasaland and in Northern Rhodesia House. Other current publications are in the London Offices of the Governments of Cyprus, Malta and Nigeria. See also Commonwealth, above.

Miscellaneous

Complete sets of the *Treaty Series* of Australia, Canada, Ceylon, New Zealand and Pakistan are to be found in the British Museum, the Commonwealth Relations Office library and the Royal Institute of International Affairs.

Official publications in specialized fields are available at the offices of other organizations in London, for example, the Commonwealth Economic Committee (p. 106), the International Wool Secretariat (p. 123), etc., and in the two libraries at the Imperial Institute (p. 111).

Indexes, Lists and Guides

Indexes, lists, guides, etc., relating to official publications and legislative journals of the Commonwealth are available. Most of them are noted in the following paragraphs but the lists are not exhaustive; additional information may be found in some of the bibliographies referred to at pp. 73–85.

COMMONWEALTH

Cole (A. H.). *Finding-list of Royal Commission reports in the British Dominions.* With an introductory essay by H. McD. Clokie. Cambridge, Mass., 1939.

AUSTRALIA

Parliament. *General Papers Indexes,* approximately every ten years, from 1901; *Indexes to Papers* are also issued sessionally. Both series are included in appropriate sessional volumes of papers. A *First consolidated index to the papers presented to Parliament, 1901–1949,* was published in 1955 (Canberra).

South Australia. *Index to parliamentary papers of the Legislature,* 1857–81; 1881–5; 1886–94 (Adelaide). *Index to the votes and proceedings of the House of Assembly* (to which is added a catalogue of all printed parliamentary papers other than those laid before the House), 1857–67; 1867–73; 1874–1900 (together with a schedule of bills introduced in the House . . . 1857 to 1900, which did not pass into law, and a schedule of papers presented to both Houses and of printed petitions from 1881 to 1900); 1901–15 (Adelaide). *Index to the papers laid before Parliament* (and petitions), 1901–15; 1916–37 (Adelaide). *Index to the Minutes of the Proceedings of the Legislative Council,* 1857–74; 1875–84; 1885–1904; 1905–15 (Adelaide).

Tasmania. *Index to parliamentary papers . . . 1856 to 1921*. Hobart, 1922.

Victoria. *Index to the parliamentary papers, reports of select committees, and returns to orders, bills, etc. 1851 to 1909*. Melbourne [1910?].

Western Australia. *General index to the printed papers presented to the Legislative Council, 1870–1889, and to Parliament, 1890–1908*. Perth, 1908. *General index to the printed papers presented to Parliament, 1908–1923*. Perth, 1925.

Current Lists

Commonwealth National Library. *Annual Catalogue of Australian publications*, from 1936 (Canberra), (containing a separate section devoted to official publications of the Commonwealth and the several States).

Commonwealth National Library. *Monthly lists of Australian Government publications*, from 1952 (Canberra).

CANADA

Todd (Alfred). *General index to the journals of the Legislative Assembly of Canada*, 1841–51 (Montreal, 1855); 1852–66 (Ottawa, 1867).

General Index to the journals of the House of Commons of the Dominion . . . and of the sessional papers of Parliament, 1867–76, 1877–90, 1891–1903, 1904–15, 1916–30 (Ottawa).

Canada Year Book, 1940 (Ottawa). [Contains in ch. xxix lists of publications of Dominion Departments and of Provincial Governments, together with a list of Reports of Dominion and Provincial Royal Commissions, with a selection of Reports of British Royal Commissions having a bearing on Canada. The list of Reports of Dominion and Provincial Royal Commissions has been continued in the Year Books for 1942, 1943–4, 1945, 1946, 1947, 1948–9 and 1951.]

Canada, Mines and Survey Dept. *Catalogue of, and guide to, the publications of the Geological Survey, Canada*, 1845–1917, with suppl., 1917–52. Ottawa, 1920, 1952.

Current Lists

Queen's Printer, Ottawa. *Annual Catalogues*. [The latest *consolidated* issue is that for 1953, with annual volumes since. Daily and monthly lists are also issued.]

Queen's Printer, Ottawa. *Sectional lists*.

National Library, Ottawa. *Canadiana*, monthly and yearly issues, 1951 onwards. [Includes publications of the Government of Canada and of the Provincial Governments.]

Queen's Printers in the several Provinces regularly issue lists of government publications.

Ontario, Legislative Assembly. *General index to the journals and sessional papers*, 1867/8 to 1927. 6 vols., Toronto, 1888–1927.

Ontario, House of Assembly. *General index to the journals*, 1825 to 1839/40. Montreal, 1848.

Quebec, Legislative Assembly. *General index to the journals*, 1867 to 1887. Quebec, 1891.

Ellis (Margaret). *Calendar of official correspondence and legislative papers, Nova Scotia, 1802–1815*. Halifax, N.S., 1936.

Higgins (M. V.). *Canadian Government publications.* Chicago, 1935. [Includes lists of Government Departments and their publications; publications of the Provinces are not included.]

Holmes (M. C.). *Royal Commissions and Commissions of Inquiry, British Columbia, a checklist.* Victoria, B.C., 1945.

Holmes (M. C.). *Publications of the government of British Columbia, 1871–1947.* Victoria, B.C. [1950].

MacDonald (C.). *Publications of the Governments of the North-West territories, 1876–1905, and of the Province of Saskatchewan, 1905–1952.* Regina, 1952.

Weston (S. M.). *Publications of the government of British Columbia, 1871–1937. A checklist.* Victoria, B.C., 1939. [But see Holmes, 1871–1947, above.]

CEYLON

Index to papers and sessional papers laid before the Legislative Council, 1855 to 1931, and before the State Council, 1931 to 1933. S. Gunawardana, comp. Colombo, 1934, reprinted 1950. Supplements, 1934–51, 1951–2 in progress.

Ceylon Civil List, 1948. [Contains an index to Sessional papers, 1934–47.]

Record Office. *Catalogues of government publications.* Colombo, 1926; 1930; 1934.

Ceylon Government Gazette. Supplements containing quarterly *Statements of Books printed in Ceylon.*

Crown Agents. *Lists of Publications,* monthly. [These lists continue to include publications of Ceylon.]

INDIA

Campbell (Francis), comp. *Index-catalogue of Indian official publications in the library, British Museum.* London [1900].

India, Government of. *Quarterly Catalogues;* publications registered in the various Provinces of British India since 1867. [Include official publications; from 1947 the Catalogues have been issued only for certain states and territories.]

India Office, Record Branch. *Classified list, in alphabetical order, of reports and other publications, December, 1892.* London, 1894.

India Office, Record Branch. *Publications received.* Annually, 1880 to 1936.

There are many other lists of official publications, non-confidential publications, publications of various departments of government and publications of the former provincial governments; particulars are to be found in Besterman's *World Bibliography of Bibliographies,* 3rd edn, 1955, vol. ii, and Childs' *Government document bibliography,* 3rd edn, 1942 (Library of Congress, Washington).

Current Lists

India, Government of. *Catalogue of Civil Publications,* 1948, with annual supplements and monthly lists.

Office of the High Commissioner, London, Library. Monthly lists.

NEW ZEALAND

Legislative Council and House of Representatives. *Index to the appendices to the journals of the Legislative Council and House of Representatives, 1854–1913, 1914–1922.* 2 vols., Wellington, 1915–24.

House of Representatives. *General index to the journals of the House . . .*, 1893–1902, 1903–17, 1918–23, 1923–38. 4 vols., Wellington, 1903–52.

General Assembly. Library. *Catalogue*. 2 vols., Wellington, 1897; Suppl., Wellington, 1899. [Includes official publications.]

General Assembly. Library. Monthly and annual Copyright Lists, 1934 onwards.

Government Printing and Stationery Department. Catalogues and price lists issued from time to time.

New Zealand Official Year-book, 1940 (Wellington). [Contains lists, not comprehensive, of annual Parliamentary papers, of recent special reports of statistical interest presented to Parliament and of regularly issued reports, etc., containing original statistical data. The lists do not seem to have been kept up-to-date.]

Scholefield (G. H.). *A union list of New Zealand official papers and British official papers relating to New Zealand*. Wellington, 1938.

PAKISTAN

Pakistan, Government. *Catalogue of the Government of Pakistan publications*. Karachi, 1952.

Pakistan Government Gazettes. [Contain lists of official publications.]

SOUTH AFRICA

Cape of Good Hope. House of Assembly. *Index to the annexures and printed papers . . . and also to the principal resolutions adopted, and to the bills and printed select committee and commission reports*, 1854–97; 1898–1903; 1904–10. 3 vols., Cape Town, 1899–1910.

Parliament. House of Assembly. *Index to the manuscript annexures and printed papers . . . including select committee reports and bills and also to principal motions and resolutions and commission reports*, 1910–30; 1930/1–40; 1940/1–50. 3 vols., Cape Town, 1931–51 (to be issued decennially).

Official Year-book of the Union, No. 12, 1929–30. Pretoria, 1931. [Contains a classified list of the principal reports and similar publications issued by Government departments from 1910 to 1929; subsequent issues contain information as to publications in later years.]

Isaacson (I.). *Official publications of the Union . . . and of the provinces of the Union*, 1949. Reprints from *South African Libraries*, vol. v, 1939, and vol. xi, 1943. [The latter contains lists of Provincial official publications. A list of indexes and guides to Union and pre-Union publications appears in the same journal, vol. i, 1934.]

Current Lists

State Library, Pretoria. *Publications acquired in terms of . . . the Copyright Act*, 1933 onwards.

Government Printing and Stationery Department, Pretoria. *Lists of Official publications*. Pretoria, 1938; 1939–43. Pretoria, 1944. Lists are also issued at frequent intervals.

South African Library. *Quarterly Bulletin*, 1946 onwards. [Includes lists of official publications.]

See also Boston University: *Bibliography of periodical publications*, referred to below, which includes the Union of South Africa.

SOUTHERN RHODESIA

Printing and Stationery Department. *Government publications. Catalogue and price list to Dec. 1951.* Salisbury, 1951. [Revised from time to time.]

COLONIES AND OTHER TERRITORIES

The most comprehensive information on Colonial official publications is to be found in two monthly lists—Colonial Office: *Monthly lists of Official Colonial Publications,* 1948 onwards; Crown Agents: *Lists of publications,* 1950 onwards. They are complementary to each other as both contain information not in the other; the Crown Agents lists also include publications of Ceylon.

A *Bibliography of Periodical Government publications of selected African countries and territories,* issued by Boston University, 1955, contains comprehensive lists of serial publications (departmental annual reports and other publications issued at regular intervals) of territories in British Africa, South West Africa and the Union. It lists only titles of publications issued by the Governments included and omits all bibliographical detail.

A specimen range of official publications of a territory is to be found in *Government Information and the Research Worker* (ed. R. Staveley), London, 1952, ch. xxiv, which lists all those of Northern Rhodesia.

Caribbean

Current Caribbean Bibliography. Caribbean Commission, Port of Spain, Trinidad, 1951 onwards. [Contains lists of official publications of all Caribbean countries; the issue for December 1953 (1955) is a consolidated list, 1950–3.]

Fiji

Publications Bulletin, annually.

Kenya

Annual Reports of the Printing and Stationery Departments. [Include lists of official publications printed in the current year.]

Malta

Annual reports on Archives. [Contain lists of official publications.]

Mauritius

Annual reports of the Archives Department. [Contain lists of publications issued during the year under review.]
Toussaint (A.). *Bibliography of Mauritius, 1502–1954.* Port Louis, 1956. [Contains a list of government and semi-official publications, 1810 to 1954.]

Nigeria

University College, Ibadan. *Nigerian Publications,* 1950 onwards. [Contain lists of works received under the Publications Ordinance, including official publications.]

Other territories issue modest catalogues and lists of Government publications, including Ghana, the Federation of Malaya, Northern Rhodesia, Singapore and Tanganyika. This list of territories is not comprehensive.

VI. PERIODICALS AND NEWSPAPERS

A: PERIODICALS

The field of periodical literature is very large and it is not possible here to do more than give some general indications on availability. The publication of union lists is, fortunately, making the task of location somewhat easier today; many of them, together with lists issued by individual libraries, are mentioned in the following paragraphs.

The national libraries and the larger general libraries have large holdings in all subjects and each 'specialist' library takes those within its own and allied fields. Reference should be made to the appropriate entries in Part II for some further indication as to the number and range of periodicals held in individual libraries. In the case of British periodicals the British Museum has the most comprehensive range. The Bodleian and the University library, Cambridge, both possess very large collections; they have each published lists of their holdings.

In London the best collections, British, Commonwealth and foreign, apart from that in the British Museum, are in the London School of Economics library (over 6,000 titles, apart from government publications), the University library (over 3,000), the library of University College (over 3,000, with a bias towards the scientific), the Board of Trade (2,300, mainly in the field of social science with an emphasis on trade and economics). The public libraries of the Cities of London and Westminster each have a wide range of serials; the former, however, retains them only for limited periods up to three years; the latter binds and keeps for permanent reference about 500 titles, mainly historical and economic. Principal historical periodicals are in the Institute of Historical Research, together with some in allied fields—efforts are made by the library to provide at least one periodical representative of every country or area. Some other large collections are those of the Patent Office (12,000, scientific and technical, of which 4,000 are current and include many of the Commonwealth); the Science Museum library (8,000 current titles, which are by no means confined to the field of science); the Ministry of Agriculture (2,000), and the libraries in the Imperial Institute (1,200).

Of 'Commonwealth' collections the Royal Empire Society has over 2,000 current and non-current serials which are retained permanently; the London School of Economics library and Rhodes House Library, Oxford, take all those of importance. The Colonial Office library (together with the Commonwealth Relations Office library) and the Institute of Commonwealth Studies have reasonable selective collections. The Oxford Institute of Commonwealth Studies has a small select range, including some of the French Union and Belgian colonies. Periodicals of the Asian countries of the Commonwealth are to be found in the India Office library and the School of Oriental and African Studies. The Indian Institute, Oxford, takes about eighty current titles. All English language periodicals published officially are in the library of India House. The International African Institute has some 140 current series. Periodicals are also available in the libraries of the various offices of the High Commissioners in London—Australia House, particularly, possesses a good collection.

Holdings in 'specialist' libraries are, in some cases, considerable; e.g.:

Empire Forestry Association—640 titles.
Institution of Bankers.
Institution of Mining and Metallurgy—300.
International Wool Secretariat—220.
Iron and Steel Institute and Institute of Metals—850.
Oxford, University. Department of Agriculture—200.
Oxford, University. Imperial Forestry Institute—280.
Royal Anthropological Institute—320. [A unique collection from the mid-nineteenth century, from all parts of the world.]
Royal Geographical Society—700.
Royal Institute of International Affairs—700.
Royal Statistical Society—400.

Information in detail concerning catalogues, lists, etc., of periodicals is to be found in *Catalogues and Bibliographies of Periodicals*: a survey of the more important works published in the British Commonwealth and the United States of America since 1945, by H. M. Gummer, *Journal of Documentation* 12 (March 1956), pp. 24–38.

Lists

Libraries which have issued lists in duplicated form of their own holdings include:

Aslib.
Australia House Reference library.
Cambridge, University. Haddon library.
Imperial Institute libraries.
India Office Library. Current periodicals, Dec. 1956. [Serial publications in European languages currently acquired. A detailed catalogue of both current and those which have ceased publication is being compiled for publication.]
London, University:
  Institute of Education.
  Institute of Education Department of Education in Tropical Areas.
  School of Oriental and African Studies.
Oxford, University:
  Department of Agriculture.
  Nuffield College.
  Rhodes House library.
Royal Geographical Society.
Royal Institute of International Affairs.

Others have printed and published their lists, including the following:

Bristol, University. *Catalogue of the periodical publications in the libraries of the University*, J. Shum Cox, comp. Bristol, 1940.
Cambridge, University Library. *Current periodicals in the University library and other libraries connected with the University.* Cambridge, 1955.
Liverpool, University. *List of periodicals and other serial publications currently received by the University library* [and other libraries in Liverpool]. 2nd edn, Liverpool, 1950, with suppl., 1953.
London School of Economics, British Library of Political and Economic Science. *A London Bibliography of the Social Sciences.* 1932, vol. 4, and supplements.
London, University Library. *List of periodicals.* London, 1956.
Oxford, Bodleian Library. *Current foreign and Commonwealth periodicals in the Bodleian and in other Oxford libraries.* Oxford, 1953; suppl. No. 1 (1951-5), Oxford, 1956.
Oxford, University. *List of periodicals and serials in the library of the Department of Forestry.* Oxford, 1949.
Rothamsted Experimental Station, Harpenden. *Catalogue of serial publications in the Library, 1953.* D. H. Boalch, ed. Harpenden, 1954.
Science Museum. *Hand-list of short titles of current periodicals in the Science Library.* 6th edn, London, 1949.
Westminster Public Libraries. *Periodicals.* London, 1949.

Information generally on periodicals may also be obtained from the following lists:

Ayer (N. W.) and Sons' *Directory.* Newspapers and periodicals. 89th edn, Philadelphia, 1957. [U.S.A. and its possessions, Canada, Bermuda.]

Gregory (W.). *Union list of serials in libraries of the United States and Canada.* 2nd edn, New York, 1943, with suppls., 1945–53.

Library of Congress. *New serial titles: a union list of serials commencing publication after Dec. 31, 1949.* Monthly, with annual and five-year cumulations. Washington, 1950 in progress.

Newspaper Press Directory. London, 1956.

Ulrich (C. F.). *Periodicals directory.* 8th edn, New York, 1956.

Unesco. *Bibliographies in the social sciences: a selected inventory of periodical publications.* Paris, 1951.

Unesco. *World list of social science periodicals.* 2nd edn, Paris, 1957.

Willing's Press Guide. London, 1956.

Union Lists

British Union Catalogue of Periodicals—a record of periodicals of the world from the 17th century to the present day in British Libraries. London, 1955 in progress. [A most valuable 'aid'. The work is to be completed in four volumes, the first, A–C, appeared in 1955, the second, D–K, in 1956, and the third, L–R, in 1957. It supersedes Roupell's *Union Catalogue.*]

Mallaber (K. A.) and de Paris (P. M.), eds. *London union list of periodicals.* London, 1951. [Records holdings of the municipal and county libraries of Greater London.]

Roupell (M. G.), comp. *Union Catalogue of the periodical publications in the University libraries of the British Isles.* London, 1937. [Now out of print; it will be superseded by the *British Union Catalogue* referred to above.]

World List of Scientific Periodicals, 1900–1950. 3rd edn, London, 1952. [This work 'lists not only those periodicals which are actually held by one or more British libraries, but also those of which, so far as is known, there is no copy in this country. It is thus a bibliography as well as a union list'.]

Other union lists available include:

Aslib, Economic Group. *Union list of periodicals—a tentative list.* London, 1953.

British Iron and Steel Federation. *Union list of periodicals on metallurgy.* n.p.

Cambridge, University. School of Agriculture. *Agricultural periodicals of the British Isles, 1681–1900, and their location.* F. A. Buttress, comp. Cambridge, 1950.

Harris (C. D.) and Fellmann (J. D.). *Union list of geographical serials.* 2nd edn, Chicago, 1950.

Institutes of Education. *Union list of periodicals held.* Birmingham, 1955.

Library Association, N.W. Branch. *Periodicals currently received in the libraries of the North West.* Manchester, 1952.

Library Association, Reference and Special Libraries Section. *Union list of scientific and technical periodicals in Northern libraries.* Newcastle-upon-Tyne (Public Library), 1955.

London, University. *List of current medical periodicals taken by the London Medical Schools.* London, 1954.

London, University. *List of botanical periodicals in London libraries.* London, 1954.

London, University. Institute of Advanced Legal Studies. *Survey of legal periodicals . . . in British libraries.* 2nd edn, London, 1957. [Includes Commonwealth material.]

Royal Anthropological Institute. *Anthropological journals in the United Kingdom.* n.p. [Lists holdings in many libraries.]

Commonwealth Lists

Lists and union lists of periodicals issued in other parts of the Commonwealth include the following:

AFRICA

Advertising and Press Annual of Africa (formerly the *African Press and Advertising Annual*). Cape Town, annually.

Freer (P.). *Catalogue of Union periodicals*, with suppls., 4 vols., Johannesburg, 1943–53.

Ibadan, University College. *Nigerian periodicals and newspapers, 1950–55*. Ibadan, 1955.

Johannesburg Public Library. *List of serial publications available*, ed. J. B. Brown. Johannesburg, 1947.

Library of Congress. *Research and information on Africa: continuing sources*. Washington, 1954. [Includes periodicals and newspapers.]

Plowman (J. I.). *South African periodical publications, 1875–1910: a bibliography*. (University of Cape Town School of Librarianship.) Cape Town, 1952.

Saul (C. D.). *South African periodical publications, 1800–1875: a bibliography*. (University of Cape Town School of Librarianship.) Cape Town, 1949.

South African Library. *Handlist of South African periodicals*, comp. C. D. Saul. (Grey Bibliographies, No. 5.) Cape Town, 1951.

State Library, Pretoria. *List of periodicals currently received in terms of . . . the Copyright Act*. Pretoria, 1956.

ASIA

Ghani (A. R.). *Guide to current scientific journals received in various libraries of West Pakistan*. Lahore, 1950.

Ghani (A. R.). *Periodical publications of Pakistan*. 2nd edn, Lahore, 1953.

Indian book-trade and library directory, 1950–51, containing . . . periodicals in India, Pakistan, Burma and Ceylon. New Delhi.

Indian Press Year-book, 1951–52. Madras.

Kaula (P. N.) and Saxena. *Periodicals currently published in India*. In *Public Library Provision*, etc., Indian Library Association, 1951.

Moid (A.) and Siddiqui (A. H.). *A Guide to periodical publications of Pakistan*. Karachi, n.d.[?1954].

National Information Service. *Guide to Indian periodicals*. Poona, 1955.

Ranganathan (S. R.) and others. *Union catalogue of learned periodical publications in South Asia*. Vol. 1, *Physical and biological sciences*. Delhi and London, 1953. [Includes Ceylon, India, Malaya and Singapore.]

Unesco. *List of scientific and technical journals published in South East Asia*. Manila, 1951. [Includes Malaya and Hong Kong.]

AUSTRALIA

Australian advertising rates and data service (GAARDS). Sydney, 1953. [Includes periodicals.]

Commonwealth National Library. *Annual catalogue of Australian publications* containing a 'select list of . . . periodicals, annuals and serials'. Canberra, 1936 in progress. [Periodicals published officially are listed under 'Official publications'.]

Commonwealth National Library. *Union list of serials in the humanities and social sciences* [in the libraries of Australia]. Issued in card form; compilation completed to letter Q. Canberra, in progress.

Foxcroft (A. B.). *The Australian catalogue. A reference index to the books and periodicals published and still current in the Commonwealth of Australia.* Melbourne, 1911.

Ferguson (J. A.). *Bibliography of Australia from 1784* [to 1850]. 4 vols., Sydney, 1941–55.

Greenap's *History of magazine publishing in Australia.* Sydney, 1947. [Lists current and defunct periodicals.]

Pitt (E. B.). *Union catalogue of the scientific and technical periodicals in the libraries of Australia.* 2nd edn, Melbourne, 1951; supplement, new titles, 1946–52, Melbourne, 1954.

Press Directory of Australia and New Zealand. 13th edn, Sydney, 1954.

CANADA

Boone (M. P.), ed. *Union list of scientific and technical periodicals in libraries of the Maritime Provinces and Newfoundland.* Halifax, N.S., 1951.

Goggio (E.), Corrigan (B.) and Parker (J. H.). *A bibliography of Canadian cultural periodicals (English and French from colonial times to 1950) in Canadian libraries.* University of Toronto, 1955. Processed.

McKim's *Directory of Canadian publications* (newspapers and periodicals). Montreal, issued at irregular intervals since 1899.

Manitoba Library Association. *Union list of serials in the libraries of Winnipeg.* The Association, Winnipeg, 1953. Mimeographed.

Montreal Special Libraries Association. *Union list of periodicals in Montreal libraries.* Montreal, 1953. Mimeographed.

Stuntz (S. C.). *List of the agricultural periodicals of the United States and Canada, 1810 to 1910.* E. B. Hawks, ed. Washington, 1941.

Toronto, University Library. *A joint catalogue of the serials in the libraries of the City of Toronto.* Toronto, 1953.

MAURITIUS

Toussaint (A.). *Bibliography of Mauritius, 1502 to 1954.* Port Louis, 1956. [Includes a section devoted to periodicals, newspapers and serials.]

NEW ZEALAND

General Assembly Library. *Copyright periodicals currently received.* 2nd rev. edn, Wellington, 1952.

National Library Service. *Union list of serials in New Zealand libraries.* Wellington, 1953, with suppls.

Press Directory of Australia and New Zealand. 13th edn, Sydney, 1954.

Indexing in Libraries

There is no comprehensive index to periodical literature of the Commonwealth. Some libraries maintain indexes in their particular subject or undertake selective indexing of periodicals for inclusion in their library catalogues. Indexing of periodicals is undertaken by, *inter alia*, the following libraries:

Imperial Institute (Libraries of Colonial Products Laboratory and Mineral Resources Division of the Colonial Geological Survey). A vast index is maintained covering sixty years in the plant and animal sections and thirty years in the mineral section. It is estimated that the indexes together contain over half a million entries.

Institute of Bankers. A card-index of many of the periodicals in the library is maintained.

International African Institute. A bibliographical card-index of books, reports and articles relating to a wide range of African studies, mainly south of the Sahara, is maintained. A quarterly bibliography is published in *Africa*.

London, University: School of Oriental and African Studies. A comprehensive index has been compiled of periodical literature relating to the far East and South East Asia from 1920 to date. Since 1954 lists of references have been issued monthly, and cumulated annually.

Ministry of Agriculture. A selective index to current periodicals appropriate to the libraries' fields is maintained.

Oxford, University: Imperial Forestry Institute. A comprehensive card-index of world forestry literature has been maintained from 1934 onwards, from which entries for *Forestry Abstracts* are selected.

Oxford, University: Indian Institute. An index of articles in approximately twenty periodicals is maintained; it will eventually be extended to cover about eighty periodicals.

Oxford, University: Institute of Commonwealth Studies. A selective index of periodical articles is compiled and issued in duplicated form each quarter.

Royal Empire Society. All important periodical articles were, to 1939, indexed and included in the library's printed and card catalogues. The work of indexing has now been resumed and it is hoped eventually to fill the gaps.

Royal Geographical Society. A selective index to periodicals is maintained.

Royal Institute of International Affairs. A selective index to periodicals is maintained.

Published Indexes

International Index to Periodicals. Chiefly humanities and sciences. 1907 onwards, with frequent cumulations. New York, 1916 in progress.

Library Association. *Subject Index to Periodicals.* 1915 onwards. London, 1919 in progress.

Poole's *Index to Periodical Literature,* 1802 to 1906. 6 vols., Boston, 1882–1907.

Public Affairs Information Service, Bulletin. New York, 1915 in progress.

Ragatz (L. J.). *Bibliography of articles . . . on Colonies and other dependent territories, appearing in American geographical and kindred journals.* To the year 1950. 2nd edn, 2 vols., Washington, 1951.

Readers' Guide to periodical literature. 1900 onwards. New York, 1905 in progress.

AUSTRALIA

Public Affairs Information Service. Subject index to current literature. Monthly, 1945 onwards; annual cumulations 1955 onwards. Canberra.

New South Wales Public Library. The Mitchell Library. *Index to periodicals.* 1944 to June 1949; July 1949 to Dec. 1951. 2 vols. Sydney, 1950–5.

New South Wales Public Library. *Monthly catalogue of new books, Australian sup-*

plement. [Includes subject entries of articles in Australian and Pacific periodicals; a continuation of the *Index*, above.]

CANADA

Canada, Mines and Technical Surveys Dept. *Bibliography of periodical literature on Canadian geography, 1940–50.* Ottawa, 1952.

Canadian Periodical Index, 1938–47. 10 vols., Toronto, 1939–49.

Canadian Index, 1948 onwards. Ottawa, 1949 in progress.

NEW ZEALAND

Index to New Zealand Periodicals. 1940, 1941–6, 1947 onwards. Wellington, 1947 in progress.

SOUTH AFRICA

Johannesburg Public Library. *Index to South African Periodicals,* 1940–9, 1950 onwards. Johannesburg, 1953 in progress.

INDEXES IN SPECIAL FIELDS

In addition to the foregoing, indexes to periodicals in special fields are published by the H. W. Wilson Company of New York as follows:

Agricultural Index	*Education Index*
Art Index	*Industrial Arts Index*
Bibliographical Index	*Index to Legal Periodicals*
Biography Index	

Some journals regularly include lists, bibliographies, etc., of articles in periodicals, *Africa,* the *Canadian Historical Review,* the *Economic History Review* and the *Middle East Journal* being good examples.

Ulrich's *Periodicals Directory,* to which reference has already been made, is not only a classified guide to a select list of current periodicals but is also a guide to where the individual periodicals are indexed or abstracted.

Location of Indexes

The best collections of printed indexes in London are in the University Library, the London School of Economics Library and the Westminster Central Reference Library. Those of Commonwealth interest are all in the Institute of Commonwealth Studies.

Abstracting

Information on abstracting services may be obtained from the following publications:

Index Bibliographicus. Directory of current periodical abstracts and bibliographies.

T. Besterman, comp. Unesco. 3rd edn, Paris, 1952 in progress. [Vol. i, Science and technology; vol. ii, Social sciences, education, humanistic studies.]
Royal Society, Abstracting Services Consultative Committee. *List of periodicals and bulletins containing abstracts published in Great Britain, with appendix giving partial list . . . published in the British Commonwealth.* 2nd edn, London, 1950.

Abstracting periodicals include the following:

Abstracts of published papers and list of transactions. C.S.I.R., Australia. Monthly, 1952 onwards. Melbourne, 1952 in progress.
Australian Social Science Abstracts, Nos. 1–18. Melbourne, 1946–54.
African Abstracts. London, 1950 onwards.
Colonial Review. London, 1939 onwards.
Economic Abstracts. The Hague, 1953 onwards.
Empire Cotton Growing Review. London, 1924 onwards.
Historical Abstracts. 1775–1945. Vienna, 1955 onwards.
International Political Science Abstracts. Paris, later Oxford, 1951 onwards.
South Asia Social Science Abstracts, 1952 onwards, Unesco. New Delhi, 1954 in progress.

See also the several abstracts issued by the Commonwealth Agricultural Bureaux, listed at p. 196.

B: NEWSPAPERS

The British Museum maintains a vast collection of newspapers published since 1800, British, Commonwealth and foreign; they are housed in the newspaper repository at Colindale. No other library attempts to collect papers on a similar scale. A separate newspaper Catalogue is maintained, a photographic copy of which is in the Institute of Commonwealth Studies.

Some 190 daily and weekly newspapers are taken in the Colonial Office; of these Commonwealth countries are represented selectively (approximately one from each country), for Colonial territories an adequate selection is available. Issues are, at present, retained for about three years and then destroyed. The Public Record Office has some of the early Colonial newspapers, a record of which is maintained in the P.R.O. and the Colonial Office. Newspapers to the year 1900 are also noted in the P.R.O. *Lists and Indexes,* No. 36.

Rhodes House Library, Oxford, takes the more important Commonwealth newspapers some of which are retained for permanent reference; the library is building up a collection on microfilm of early South African and Canadian papers (see p. 170).

The Royal Empire Society has available approximately 100 current newspapers, none of which is kept for permanent reference.

Indian newspapers in the English language are well represented in the India Office Library where they are kept for permanent reference. The

Indian Institute, Oxford, has a few papers from 1950 onwards. Current English language papers are available in the reading room of India House (some of which are received by air mail).

The Guildhall Library, City of London, also takes a number of Commonwealth newspapers (some being received by air mail) but they are retained only for short periods.

All the most important Commonwealth newspapers are available for short periods in the London offices of the several High Commissioners and Agents-General. The London offices of agents of most newspapers published overseas maintain files but few are kept for more than a few weeks. Addresses of agents are to be found in the *Newspaper Press Directory*.

The Times

Files of *The Times* are available, complete, in the British Museum, the University Library, Cambridge, and the Westminster Public Library, in the last two cases some being on microfilm. Other files available include those in the Bodleian (defective in early years), the Institute of Historical Research (from 1800 to date, a few issues missing), the Guildhall Library, City of London (from 1806), the University of London Library (from 1830), and the London School of Economics library (from 1813).

Palmer's Index to *The Times*, covering the years 1790 to date, has been published since 1868; an Official Index has also been published since 1906.

Lists of Newspapers

The Institute of Commonwealth Studies maintains (on cards) a union list of newspapers in libraries in London, Oxford and Cambridge.

Lists of newspapers are to be found in the *Newspaper Press Directory* and *Willings Press Guide* as well as in other press directories and some of the lists of periodicals referred to on pp. 42–3.

Other printed sources of information include the following:

Arnot's *Bibliography of the newspapers filed in the Mitchell Library and the general reference collection of the Public Library of New South Wales*. Sydney, 1944.
Australian Advertising Rates and Data Service (NAARDS). Sydney, 1953. [Lists newspapers.]
British Museum. *Catalogue of printed books—supplement. Newspapers published in Great Britain and Ireland, 1801–1900*. London, 1905.
Johannesburg Public Library. *List of serial publications available*. J. B. Brown, ed. Johannesburg, 1947. [Includes newspapers.]
Moid and Siddiqui's *Guide to periodical publications and newspapers of Pakistan*. Karachi, n.d.[? 1954].

E

New Zealand. General Assembly Library. *Union catalogue of New Zealand News-papers.* G. H. Scholefield, ed. Wellington, 1938.
New Zealand. General Assembly Library. *Newspapers currently received.* Welling-ton, 1953.
Press in Africa. H. Kitchen, ed. Washington, 1956.
South African Library. *Union list of South African Newspapers, November, 1949.* (Grey Bibliographies No. 3.) Cape Town, 1950.
Toussaint's *Bibliography of Mauritius, 1502–1954.* Port Louis, 1956. [Contains section devoted to periodicals and newspapers.]
University College, Ibadan. *Nigerian periodicals and newspapers, 1950–55.* Ibadan, 1955.

VII. CONCISE SURVEY OF LIBRARY RESOURCES BY SUBJECT

Further information on each of the institutions listed in this section will be found in Part II, below, except in the case of institutions marked †. The British Museum, the Bodleian, Oxford, and the University Library, Cambridge, are not always specifically referred to under the various subject headings since these great libraries contain material in practically every field of study. See also the Subject Index.

History

See also Public Archives, p. 7; Private Papers, p. 12; Chartered and other Companies' Papers, p. 17; Parliamentary Papers and Official Publications, p. 25.
For Bibliographies, *see* pp. 73–5; Periodicals, *see* pp. 40–8.

i. GENERALLY

London: British Museum.
      Institute of Historical Research.
      London School of Economics library.
      University College, London.
      University of London Library.

      Bedford College Library.
      King's College Library.

Oxford: Bodleian.
      History Faculty Library.†
      Codrington Library, All Souls College.†

Cambridge: University Library.
      Seeley Historical Library.

ii. NAVAL AND MARITIME HISTORY

Admiralty Library. [Naval history and naval science, as well as material relating to events in which the Royal Navy has participated.]

Imperial War Museum.
Institute of Historical Research.
King's College, London.
National Maritime Museum, Greenwich.†
Royal United Services Institution.

iii. MILITARY HISTORY

War Office Library. [Probably the most comprehensive collection. It contains, *inter alia*, an almost complete collection of Commonwealth Regimental and Unit histories as well as histories of Colonial campaigns and military intelligence reports on Colonial territories.]

Royal United Services Institution. [Historical material relating to the three services throughout the Commonwealth and to defence and military history in general.]

Imperial War Museum.

iv. COMMONWEALTH IN GENERAL

(*See also* i, above. *For* Naval and Military History *see* ii and iii above)

Colonial Office and Commonwealth Relations Office libraries.
Institute of Commonwealth Studies.
Rhodes House Library, Oxford. (Except India and Pakistan.)
Royal Empire Society.

Institute of Historical Research.
King's College, London.
London School of Economics library.

Historical periodicals, societies' transactions and publications and printed archival material of Commonwealth countries are particularly well represented in the Royal Empire Society and the Institute of Historical Research.

The libraries maintained in the headquarters of the various Christian Missionary Societies contain material, not only dealing with missionary activities and the Church overseas, but much devoted to general history, description, exploration and travel.

v. AFRICA

Colonial Office and Commonwealth Relations Office libraries.
Rhodes House Library, Oxford.
Royal Empire Society.
School of Oriental and African Studies.

International African Institute.
Institute of Commonwealth Studies.
Oxford Institute of Commonwealth Studies.

East Africa House library.
London Missionary Society. [Includes a collection of pamphlets on South African affairs, covering the period 1800 to 1860, and works on exploration, description and travel.]
Northern Rhodesia House library.
Rhodesia House library.
Royal Anthropological Institute. [Possesses the Sir Richard Burton library of 2,000 books and pamphlets, mainly on Africa.]

Society for the Propagation of the Gospel. [Includes diocesan magazines from
many parts of the world dealing with historical events.]
South Africa House library.
Universities Mission to Central Africa.

vi. ASIAN COUNTRIES

British Museum. [A collection of approximately 250,000 volumes and 50,000
manuscripts devoted to India, Pakistan and Ceylon.]
India Office Library. [One of the most outstanding collections.]
India House library.
Indian Institute, Oxford.
Royal Empire Society.
School of Oriental and African Studies.

Ceylon Association.
Goldsmiths' Library, University of London. [Includes a collection of pamphlets on
the East India Company.]
Institute of Historical Research.
London Missionary Society.
Office of the High Commissioner for Ceylon.
Royal Anthropological Institute.
Royal Asiatic Society. (Members only.)
Royal Central Asia Society. (Members only.)

vii. AUSTRALASIA

Australia House library.
Colonial Office and Commonwealth Relations Office libraries.
Institute of Commonwealth Studies.
London Missionary Society.
New Zealand House library.
Rhodes House Library, Oxford.
Royal Empire Society.
School of Oriental and African Studies. [Includes a collection of material on the
languages and ethnology of the peoples of the Pacific.]
Offices of the Agents-General in London.

viii. CANADA

Canada House library.
Colonial Office and Commonwealth Relations Office libraries.
Institute of Commonwealth Studies.
Quebec House, Westerham. [Contains a small library on the life and times of
Wolfe and early history of Quebec and Canada generally.]
Rhodes House Library, Oxford.
Royal Empire Society.
University of London Library. [Possesses the Biggar collection of pamphlets of the
nineteenth and twentieth centuries on Canadian history.]
Offices of the Agents-General in London (Alberta, British Columbia, Ontario,
Saskatchewan).

ix. OVERSEAS TERRITORIES

Colonial Office Library.
Institute of Commonwealth Studies.
Oxford Institute of Commonwealth Studies.
Rhodes House Library, Oxford. [Includes a fine collection of material on Malta.]
Royal Empire Society.

Cyprus Government Office.
Malta Government Office.
Methodist Missionary Society.
University College Library, London. [Includes the Hume tracts 1810 to 1850,
many of which relate to Africa and the West Indies, and material on the Ameri-
can Colonial period.]
West India Committee.

x. FOREIGN OVERSEAS TERRITORIES

King's College Library, London. [Possesses the Prestage library of Portuguese
Colonial material.]
Oxford Institute of Commonwealth Studies. [Particularly material relating to the
French Union.]
Royal Empire Society.

xi. SLAVERY AND THE SLAVE TRADE

Anti-Slavery and Aborigines Protection Society. [The Society's archives are at
Rhodes House, Oxford.]
Admiralty Library.
Goldsmiths' Library, University of London.
London School of Economics library. [Includes a collection of the Anti-Slavery
Society's reports, petitions, etc., 23 parts, in 1 vol., c. 1815–1900.]
Rhodes House Library, Oxford.
Royal Empire Society. [A large collection, including 60 volumes of pamphlets.]
University College Library, London.
West India Committee.

Libraries of the several Missionary Societies, particularly the Church Missionary
Society and the Methodist Missionary Society.

xii. MISSIONS AND MISSIONARIES

Libraries of the several Missionary Societies, particularly the London Missionary
Society, the Methodist Missionary Society, and the Society for the Propagation of
the Gospel. The Scottish Missionary Societies also possess records and printed
material.

Political Science and Public Administration

For Bibliographies *see* pp. 73–85; Periodicals *see* pp. 40–8

i. GENERALLY

London School of Economics library. [The best collection, not only for the United
Kingdom but also the Commonwealth as a whole.]

Royal Institute of Public Administration library. [Includes works on all aspects of public administration.]

Board of Trade library.
Nuffield College, Oxford.
Rhodes House Library, Oxford.
School of Oriental and African Studies.
Seeley Historical Library, Cambridge.
University College Library, London.
University of London Library.

Colonial Office and Commonwealth Relations Office libraries.
India Office Library.
Indian Institute, Oxford.
Institute of Commonwealth Studies.
Oxford Institute of Commonwealth Studies.
Royal Empire Society.

Fabian Colonial Bureau. [A small collection from approximately 1939, including press cuttings—accommodation is very limited and reference to the library should be by appointment.]

ii. INTERNATIONAL AND INTER-COMMONWEALTH AFFAIRS

Royal Institute of International Affairs. [The principal library on international affairs generally; it includes material on inter-Commonwealth relations. Chatham House also maintains a press library of cuttings from British, foreign and some Commonwealth newspapers from 1924 (for further information see p. 144).]
Foreign Office library.
London School of Economics library.

A guide to *Resources on international affairs in London Libraries*, by Barbara Kyle, appeared in *International Affairs*, 32, pp. 190–8, April 1956.
(Note: The Library of Congress has published a *Guide to bibliographic tools for research in foreign affairs* (H. F. Conover, comp. Washington, 1956).)

Economics and Statistics

For Bibliographies *see* pp. 72–85; Periodicals *see* pp. 40–8

i. ECONOMICS GENERALLY

London School of Economics library. [An outstanding collection.]
Goldsmiths' Library of Economic Literature, University of London Library. [Also outstanding, especially for material to the year 1850 approximately.]

Barnett House Library, Oxford.† [Economics, sociology and related subjects.]
Bedford College, London.
Board of Trade Library. [Mainly current material but includes some economic history.]
Codrington Library, All Souls College, Oxford.†
Institute of Bankers. [Includes works on economics, banking, finance and economic conditions in many Commonwealth and foreign countries.]
Institute of Export. [Economics and business law and administration.]

Ministry of Agriculture, etc., Food Section. [Coffee, cocoa, tea, rice and sugar.]
Marshall Library, Cambridge.
National Institute of Economic and Social Research. [A good collection of material on economics, economic theory and income and wealth.]
Nuffield College, Oxford.
Science Museum Library.

The Bank of England maintains a valuable library but it is private and applications for general admission will not be entertained. Permission to consult *individual* items, not available elsewhere, may be granted under certain circumstances. It possesses a set of the *Course of Exchange* and its successor the *Stock Exchange Gazette* from the 1690's, and sets of bulletins of all Commonwealth Reserve Banks, Central Banks, etc., as well as statistical bulletins.

ii. COMMONWEALTH ECONOMICS

Colonial Office and Commonwealth Relations Office libraries.
Fabian Colonial Bureau [but see note on p. 54].
India House Library.
India Office Library.
Indian Institute, Oxford.
Institute of Bankers.
Institute of Commonwealth Studies.
London School of Economics library. [Includes a collection of pamphlets, reports, etc., on Alberta Social Credit, 89 parts in 6 vols., 1934–8.]
Oxford Institute of Commonwealth Studies.
Rhodes House Library, Oxford.
Royal Empire Society.

Libraries in the offices of the various High Commissioners and Agents-General in London also maintain economic sections, mainly of current material.

Material on the Commonwealth is also to be found in the libraries listed under i, above.

iii. STATISTICS

Royal Statistical Society library. [Probably the most comprehensive collection in the country, from earliest times to the present day.]
Board of Trade library. [Particularly the Board's Statistics Library which attempts complete coverage of statistical publications on trade and production and material in related fields for the whole of the Commonwealth from 1929— earlier material has been transferred to the British Museum. It also possesses statistical publications of the United Nations and its Specialized Agencies and of other international organizations.]
London School of Economics library.

Commonwealth Economic Committee.
Guildhall Library, City of London.
Imperial Institute libraries.
Institute of Commonwealth Studies.
Institute of Historical Research.
Institute of Statistics, Oxford. [Statistical analysis and the application of statistical method to economic and social problems.]
National Institute of Economic and Social Research.

Royal Empire Society.
Science Museum Library. [Particularly the theory of statistics.]
University College Library, London. [Particularly the theory of statistics.]
University Library, Cambridge.
University of London Library.
Westminster Central Reference Library.

Libraries in the offices of the various High Commissioners and Agents-General in London also include statistical material appropriate to their countries, states or provinces. The collection in Australia House reference library is particularly comprehensive, a hand-list to which has been prepared.

The British Bureau of Non-Ferrous Metal Statistics, Birmingham (p. 197) collects and publishes statistics relating to non-ferrous metals and manufacturers of the United Kingdom, the Commonwealth and foreign countries.

Statistical information in the form of blue-books, year-books, registers, abstracts, digests, etc., is available in several libraries. Particular attention is drawn to sets and collections of such publications in the Board of Trade, the Commonwealth Economic Committee, the Guildhall Library, City of London, the Imperial Institute libraries, the India Office library, the Institute of Commonwealth Studies, the Institute of Historical Research, the Institute of Statistics, Oxford, the London School of Economics, Rhodes House Library, Oxford, the Royal Empire Society (which possesses a valuable and extensive collection of early Colonial blue-books from the 1820's) and the Royal Statistical Society.

Statistical Bibliographies

Australia, High Commissioner's Office, London. *Australian statistical publications.* London, 1953. [A mimeograph list of sources of statistical information covering Australia and its territories received in the Library.]

Buros (O. K.). *Research and statistical methodology; books and reviews of 1933–1938. Second yearbook of research and methodology; books and reviews* [1938–41]. *Statistical methodology reviews, 1941–1950.* 3 vols., New Brunswick, Highland Park, N.J., and New York, 1938, 1941, 1951.

Guide to Current Official Statistics, 1922–38. H.M.S.O., London. [No. 17 (1938) was the last issue to appear.]

Government Statistical Services. Published for H.M. Treasury by H.M.S.O. London, 1953. [Briefly describes the work of British Government statistical services; it includes a list of the principal statistical publications.]

India. Office of the Economic Adviser. *Guide to current official statistics.* 3 vols., Delhi, 1943–9.

Institut International de Statique. *Bibliographie Statistique Internationale.* Issued quarterly in the *Revue,* The Hague, 1933 onwards. [Unfortunately the quarterly issues are neither cumulated nor indexed.]

Interdepartmental Committee on Social and Economic Research. *Guide to Official Sources,* No. 1, Labour Statistics. Revised and re-issued, H.M.S.O. London, 1950.

International Statistical Institute. *Bibliography of basic texts and monographs on statistical methods.* The Hague, 1951.

Kendall (M. G.) and Hill (A. B.), eds. *Sources and nature of the Statistics of the United Kingdom.* Royal Statistical Society. Vol. 1. London, 1952. [Contains bibliographies on, *inter alia*, overseas trade and commodities, including rubber, cotton, tobacco and sugar.]

Library of Congress. *Statistical yearbooks*: an annotated bibliography of the general statistical yearbooks of major political subdivisions of the world. Prepared by P. G. Carter. Washington, 1953.

Library of Congress. *Statistical bulletins*: an annotated bibliography of the general statistical bulletins of major political subdivisions of the world. Prepared by P. G. Carter. Washington, 1954. [Both these publications of the Library of Congress include Commonwealth countries and territories.]

Neale (E. P.). *Guide to New Zealand official statistics*. 3rd edn, Christchurch, N.Z., 1955.

United Nations. *Analytical bibliography of international migration statistics, selected countries, 1925–1950*. New York, 1955. [U.N. Population Studies, No. 24. Includes U.K., Australia, Canada, New Zealand and South Africa.]

Westminster Public Libraries. *Statistics: a guide to current material*. London, 1951.

iv. TRADE, PROCESSING AND MANUFACTURING
See also Commodities; Agriculture, *below*; Statistics, *above*.

Board of Trade library.

London School of Economics library.

[Both of these libraries possess outstanding collections devoted to trade, commerce and industry.]

Colonial Office and Commonwealth Relations Office libraries.

Institute of Commonwealth Studies.

Patent Office library. [Contains a large section devoted to industrial property.]

Rhodes House Library, Oxford.

Royal Empire Society. [Includes reports of Commonwealth Chambers of trade and trading organizations.]

University of London Library. [Early history of English trade, companies, mercantile and Colonial policy, navigation laws, rise of the East Indian and American trade, growth of foreign trade, international monetary policy, etc.]

V. COMMODITIES
See also Forestry, *below*

Ceylon Association. [Tea in particular; rubber.]

Colonial Office and Commonwealth Relations Office libraries.

Commonwealth Economic Committee.

Empire Cotton Growing Corporation. [Technical books and pamphlets on cotton growing in the Commonwealth and foreign countries; annual reports on cotton and other official publications; file of the *Quarterly Statistical Bulletin* of the International Advisory Committee, Washington.]

Imperial Institute libraries. [Commodities in general, as well as oils, fats and textiles; include a wide range of periodicals with an extensive index.]

Indian Jute Mills Association. [Jute and other fibres.]

International Sugar Council. [Industrial, economic and commercial aspects of sugar, sugar beet and sugar cane.]

International Wool Secretariat. [Economics, history, science and technology of wool, including wool-producing and wool-manufacturing industries of Australia, Canada, India, Pakistan, South Africa and New Zealand.]

Ministry of Agriculture, etc., Food Section. [Coffee, cocoa, tea, rice and sugar.]

Northern Polytechnic (National College of Rubber Technology).† [Rubber.]

Queensland, Agent-General's Office, London. [Historical material on the sugar trade.]

Research Association of British Rubber Manufacturers, see p. 199. [Devoted to the whole field of rubber, including planting and the use of rubber throughout the Commonwealth.]

Royal Empire Society.

Science Museum library. [Cocoa, coffee, cotton, rubber, rice, sugar, tea, timber, tin.]

Tea Bureau. [History of tea and the tea industry (production and manufacture).]

West India Committee. [Citrus industry and sugar in particular; cocoa, coffee, cotton, tea and tobacco.]

vi. AGRICULTURE, FISHERIES AND FORESTRY
(INCLUDING SOIL SCIENCE)
See also Trade, etc., *above*

Board of Trade library. [Economic aspects.]

Cambridge, University. School of Agriculture library.

Commonwealth Agricultural Bureaux. [Most of the bureaux possess, or share, libraries devoted to various aspects of agriculture and animal husbandry.]

Goldsmiths' Library, University of London.

Imperial Institute libraries.

London School of Economics library. [Economic aspects.]

Ministry of Agriculture, Fisheries and Food. [Commonwealth material is limited to those countries which have a system of agriculture similar to that of the United Kingdom; it includes works on soil science, forestry and timber.]

Oxford, University. Agricultural Economics Research Institute library.

Oxford, University. Department of Agriculture library.

Rothamsted Experimental Station, see p. 195. [Soil science.]

Science Museum library.

Some material is also available in the London Offices of Commonwealth Representatives, particularly India, Queensland, and East Africa.

Information on library resources is also to be found in *Library Resources in the Greater London area, No. 5: Agricultural libraries* (Library Association, Reference and Special Libraries Section). London, 1956.

Forestry

Empire Forestry Association.

Forestry Commission. [Mainly the United Kingdom but there is some material of Commonwealth interest.]

Imperial Institute libraries.

Ministry of Agriculture, Fisheries and Food.

Oxford, University. Imperial Forestry Institute. [A large collection on forestry and ancillary subjects.]

Science Museum library.

Timber Development Association. [Forestry and timber, mainly technical, but some material devoted to economic aspects.]

Bibliographies

Agricultural Index, 1916 onwards. New York, 1919 in progress (with regular cumulations).

Bernstein (E. H.). *Farming in Southern Rhodesia: a bibliography*. (Univ. of Cape Town, School of Librarianship). Cape Town, 1949.

Bibliography [of Agriculture and Forestry]. Issued quarterly in *Colonial Plant and Animal Products*. London, 1950 in progress.

Canada, Dept. of Mines and Technical Surveys. *Bibliography of pedogeography of Canada*. (Bibliographical series No. 12.) Ottawa, 1953.

Commonwealth Bureau of Soil Science. *Bibliography of Soil Science, etc.* Issued approximately every four years. [Harpenden], 1935 onwards.

Hubbard (J.). *South African forestry since 1913: a bibliography*. (Univ. of Cape Town, School of Librarianship). Cape Town, 1949.

Knight (R. L.) and Boyns (B. M.). *Agricultural science in the Sudan: a bibliography with abstracts*. Arbroath, 1950.

Luscombe (M.). *Soil: a bibliography*. (Univ. of Cape Town, School of Librarianship.) Cape Town, 1945.

Maule (J. P.). *A bibliography of tropical agriculture*. In *British Book News*, 1949, pp. 65–9. London, 1949.

Munns (E. N.). *A selected bibliography of North American Forestry*. 2 vols., Washington, 1940. [Includes Canada.]

Oxford, University. Imperial Forestry Institute. *Basic library list for forestry*. Oxford, 1952.

United Nations, F.A.O. *Bibliography of forestry and forest products*, 1950; 1951. Washington, Rome, 1950–1.

United States, Dept. of Agriculture. *Bibliography of agriculture*, 1942 onwards. Washington, 1942 in progress (with regular cumulations).

See also the publications of the Commonwealth Agricultural Bureaux, a list of which appears at p. 196.

vii. DEMOGRAPHY

See also Statistics, *above*

Board of Trade Statistics library.
Goldsmiths' Library, University of London.
Institute of Statistics, Oxford.
London School of Economics library.
Royal Statistical Society library.
Science Museum library.

Colonial Office and Commonwealth Relations Office libraries.
India Office Library.
Indian Institute library, Oxford.
Institute of Commonwealth Studies.
Rhodes House Library, Oxford.
Royal Empire Society.

Censuses and similar material are also to be found in the libraries maintained in the offices of the several High Commissioners in London.

Bibliographies

Dubester (H. J.). *Population censuses and other Official demographic statistics of Africa* (not including British Africa). (United States, Department of Commerce and the Library of Congress.) Washington, 1950.

Dubester (H. J.). *Population censuses and other Official demographic statistics of British Africa*. (United States, Department of Commerce and the Library of Congress.) Washington, 1950.

Kuczynski (R. R.). *The Cameroons and Togoland: a demographic study*. London, 1939. [Contains an extensive bibliography of 'sources quoted'.]

Kuczynski (R. R.). *Demographic survey of the British Colonial Empire*, vol. i, West Africa; vol. ii, S.A. High Commission territories, East Africa, Mauritius and Seychelles; vol. iii, West Indian and American territories. London, 1948–53. [Each of the volumes contains extensive bibliographies of 'sources quoted'.]

Princeton University (School of Public Affairs) and the Population Association of America. *Population Index*, 1935 onwards. Princeton, N.J., 1935 (quarterly) in progress.

Shock (N. W.). *A classified bibliography of gerontology and geriatrics*. Stanford, Calif., 1951. [Includes section on demography.]

United Nations. *Demographic Year-book*, 1948 onwards. New York, 1949 in progress. [Regularly includes a bibliography of recent official demographic statistics; the issue for 1953 included a revised cumulative bibliography which was also issued separately under the title of *Bibliography of recent official demographic statistics* (U.N. Stat. Papers, Ser. M., No. 18). New York, 1954.]

viii. MINING AND METALS

Colonial Office, Mineral Resources Division library (Imperial Institute). [A very extensive collection.]

Institution of Mining and Metallurgy. [Possesses a large library of material including geology and mining throughout the Commonwealth.]

London School of Economics Library.

Science Museum Library. [Includes a specialized collection covering mineralogy, geology, mining and economic geology and metallurgy.]

Aluminium Development Association. [Bauxite and aluminium.]

British Iron and Steel Federation.

British Non-Ferrous Metals Research Association.

Copper Development Association, Radlett. [Possesses a small library devoted to mining, processing and economics of copper, see p. 197.]

India House Library. [A small collection including an almost complete set of the Memoirs and Records of the Geological Survey of India.]

Iron and Steel Institute and Institute of Metals Joint Library. [Production of iron and steel and the properties and treatment of both ferrous and non-ferrous metals and kindred subjects.]

Royal School of Mines† (Imperial College of Science and Technology).

Tin Research Association. [Includes material on the economics, history and technology of tin and on metallurgy in general.]

Zinc Development Association. [Metallurgy in general and zinc in particular as well as statistical material on non-ferrous metal production and consumption.]

Statistical material is also to be found in the libraries mentioned under Statistics, above, p. 55.

Bibliographies

(containing material on mining and metals)

Allen (R. S.) and Collins (B. W.). *Bibliography of New Zealand geology since 1908.* Christchurch, n.p., 1951–4 (typescript). (Dept. of Scientific and Industrial Research.)

Canada, Dept. of Mines and Technical Surveys. Geological Survey of Canada. *Publications of the Geological Survey of Canada, 1845–1917, 1917–1952.* 2 vols., Ottawa, 1920, 1952.

Commission for Technical Co-operation in Africa south of the Sahara. *Geological bibliography of Africa south of the Sahara, I, the Karroo system.* London, 1957.

Select bibliography on Geology and the Mineral Industry. Issued quarterly in *Colonial Geology and Mineral Resources,* London, 1949 in progress.

South Africa, Geological Survey. *Bibliography of South African geology,* to 1920; 1921 to 1935; with subject indexes. Pretoria, 1922–39.

United States, Dept. of the Interior. Geological survey. *Bibliography of North American geology, 1785–1918, 1919 onwards.* Washington, 1923 in progress.

ix. TRANSPORT AND COMMUNICATIONS

There are no 'collections' on the subject of Commonwealth transport and communications as such but some material is available in the following:

Colonial Office and Commonwealth Relations Office libraries.

Rhodes House Library, Oxford.

Royal Empire Society.

Material is also available in:

Canadian National Railway, London Office.† [The Research and Development Department maintains a small library.]

Institute of Navigation. [Possesses technical works, not accessible elsewhere, devoted to sea and air navigation.]

Institute of Transport. [Contains works on the economics and administration of transport by land, sea and air, including Commonwealth material.]

Institution of Electrical Engineers.† [Contains material on telecommunications.]

Institution of Mechanical Engineers. [The library contains material on Imperial communications (land, sea, air and radio).]

Bibliographies

Joubert (E.). *Road transportation in South Africa in the 19th century: bibliography.* (Univ. of Cape Town, School of Librarianship.) Cape Town, 1955.

Lewin (E.). *Select list of publications in the library of the Royal Colonial Institute illustrating the communications of the overseas British Empire with spec. ref. to Africa generally and the Baghdad railway.* London, 1927. (Royal Colonial Institute bibliographies, No. 4.)

Geography and Collections of Maps, Charts, Atlases and Gazetteers

Royal Geographical Society. [An outstanding collection of approximately 100,000 volumes, mainly on geography and the geographical sciences, travel and exploration, as well as works on economics, sociology, anthropology, agriculture, demography and law in so far as they impinge on the geographic field.]

Cambridge, University. Department of Geography library. [Contains some 5,000 volumes devoted to geography and allied subjects.]

King's College, London. [The College houses the Joint Library of the School of Geography of the College and the London School of Economics.]

Oxford, University. School of Geography library. [Contains some 20,000 volumes devoted mainly to geography and allied subjects (historical, political, social, economic and physical geography) of the United Kingdom, the Commonwealth and foreign countries.]

Colonial Office and Commonwealth Relations Office libraries.

Imperial Institute libraries.

India Office Library.

Indian Institute, Oxford.

Rhodes House Library, Oxford.

Royal Empire Society.

University of London Library.

The libraries of the several Missionary societies also have representative collections.

Bibliographies

American Geographical Society. *Current Geographical Publications*. New York, 1938 in progress. [A classified index to current books, pamphlets, official publications and periodical articles.]

Behavior Science Bibliographies. *Selected bibliography of the geography of Southeast Asia*. K. J. Pelzer. (Southeast Asia Studies, Yale University.) New Haven, Conn., 1949 in progress. (Pt. i, Southeast Asia as a whole; pt. ii, the Philippines; pt. iii, Malaya.)

Bibliographie géographique internationale. Paris, 1891 in progress. [An annual classified bibliography, with annotations.]

Canada, Dept. of Mines and Technical Surveys. Geographical Branch. Geographical series:

Selected bibliography of Canadian geography, 1949 onwards. Ottawa, 1950 in progress.

University dissertations, theses and essays on Canadian geography. Ottawa, 1950.

Annotated bibliography of Saskatchewan geology, 1823–1951. Ottawa, 1952.

Bibliography of periodical literature on Canadian geography for the period 1940–1950. Ottawa, 1952.

Canadian urban geography. Ottawa, 1954.

Royal Geographical Society. *Recent Geographical Literature*, 1918–39. Class supplements to the *Geographical Journal*.

Royal Geographical Society. *New Geographical Literature and Maps*. Published about twice a year.

Royal Geographical Society. Bibliography of Geographical Bibliographies. [A comprehensive bibliography maintained on cards.]

Wright (J. K.) and Platt (E. T.). *Aids to Geographical Research*. New York, 1947.

MAPS, ETC.

Admiralty Library. [Contains between 80,000 and 100,000 maps, charts and atlases. The Admiralty Hydrographic Department has a very large number of surveys and maps and an historic collection of original charts covering the sixteenth to the nineteenth centuries. *A survey of selected manuscript documents [maps and charts] of historic importance preserved in the Department* was printed (but not published) in 1950.]

Bodleian Library, Oxford. [Possesses a very large collection, including survey material, although maps of historical interest are not plentiful.]

British Museum. [The map resources are vast and cover the whole world. The Map Room contains official maps issued in the Commonwealth, maps published by the Directorate of Colonial Surveys and those published by individual Colonial Survey Departments. It also possesses the George III topographical collection which is particularly strong in overseas material.]

Cambridge, University Library. [Possesses about 250,000 maps and atlases.]

Oxford, University. School of Geography. [Maps and atlases of the world, including Colonial survey maps and large selections of Australian and Canadian material. Commonwealth gazetteers are also available—the Indian collection is particularly fine. The School issued, in 1956, a union list of *Special Maps in Oxford Libraries*.]

Royal Geographical Society. [Possesses approximately 500,000 maps, atlases and gazetteers.]

Colonial Office library. [The Colonial Office's collection of early maps is now deposited in the Public Record Office (*C.O. 700*); a catalogue was compiled and printed in 1910 entitled *Catalogue of the Maps, Plans and Charts in the Library of the Colonial Office*. An earlier *List of Maps, Plans, &c. belonging to the Rt. Hon. the Lords Commissioners for Trade and Plantations* was prepared, in manuscript, in 1780, a photographic copy of which is in the British Museum.]

Imperial War Museum. [Contains a large collection of maps and air photographs.]

India Office Library. [A good collection of Indian material, including the Survey of India and gazetteers.]

Indian Institute, Oxford.

London School of Economics, Department of Geography. [Contains maps of all parts of the world although Commonwealth material is not particularly comprehensive.]

London School of Hygiene and Tropical Medicine. [Possesses maps showing the distribution of diseases in tropical areas.]

Rhodes House Library, Oxford. [Possesses a collection of early Colonial maps and atlases.]

Royal United Service Institution. [Contains approximately 7,000 maps and 52,000 charts.]

School of Oriental and African Studies. [Possesses a collection of gazetteers.]

University of London Library. [Possesses a general collection of about 20,000 maps and charts and a good collection of modern atlases.]

Westminster Central Reference Library. [Contains a world coverage of maps amounting to about 10,000 items and a representative collection of gazetteers.]

Summary of Map Collections

Historical

British Museum.

Admiralty Hydrographic Department.

Colonial Office (deposited in the P.R.O.).

India Office Library.

Royal Geographical Society.

Printed Historical
  Bodleian Library.
  Cambridge, University Library.
  Colonial Office.
  Rhodes House Library.
  Royal Geographical Society.

Current material
  Admiralty.
  British Museum.
  Bodleian Library.
  Cambridge, University Library.
  Cambridge, University. Department of Geography library.
  Imperial War Museum.
  London School of Economics.
  Oxford, University. School of Geography.
  Royal Geographical Society.
  Royal United Services Institution.
  University of London Library.
  Westminster Central Reference Library.

Maps are also available in the Offices of the High Commissioners in London, particularly Australia House, which has a selection of special and general maps, including the Australian Geographical Series, the Australian Aeronautical Series and some State maps; Canada House, which possesses the Survey Maps of Canada; and India House, which has the Survey of India, special maps and a valuable collection of gazetteers.

Bibliographies

Bibliographie cartographique internationale. Paris, 1949 in progress.
Canada, Dept. of Mines and Technical Surveys, Geographical Branch. *Canadian maps, 1949–54*. Ottawa, 1956. (Biblio. series, No. 16.)
Canada, Public Archives. *Sixteenth-century maps relating to Canada: a check list and bibliography*. Ottawa, 1956.
de Paris (P. M.). *Maps*. London, 1954. ('Library Resources in the Greater London Area' series, Library Association (Reference and Special Libraries Section, S.E. Group).)
Geographisches Taschenbuch. Wiesbaden, 1949 in progress.
Royal Geographical Society. *New Geographical Literature and Maps*. London, 1951 in progress. [Published about twice a year, it includes new map additions to the Library.]
Scientific Council for Africa South of the Sahara. *Topographical Maps of Africa South of the Sahara* (Pub. No. 15); *Maps of Africa South of the Sahara* (Pub. No. 17). London, 1955.
United Nations. *World Cartography*. New York, 1951 in progress.

New Colonial maps are also listed in the Monthly Lists of Colonial Official Publications (Colonial Office).

See also lists mentioned under Admiralty Library, Colonial Office library and Oxford University School of Geography, above.

Law

The great law libraries are those of the Inns of Court—Gray's Inn, Inner Temple, Lincoln's Inn and Middle Temple. With the exception, possibly, of Gray's Inn, which is still making good losses suffered in the second World War, they all possess large collections of treatises, statutes, reports, digests, encyclopaedias and periodicals. The Bar Library in the Royal Courts of Justice and the Law Society's library also have good collections but of them all the Middle Temple has, probably, the most comprehensive library of Commonwealth law, with Lincoln's Inn and the Inner Temple following very closely. Current law reports and statutes are generally to be found in all these libraries but for early law reports the Middle Temple has the best collection; it also possesses an outstanding collection of Roman-Dutch and South African law.

Use of these libraries, however, is normally restricted to members. Other persons, on suitable recommendation, are permitted to consult individual works not available elsewhere.

Other law libraries and collections include the following:

Institute of Advanced Legal Studies. [An outstanding collection. Contains the Nuffield Library of Commonwealth Law which is becoming comprehensive and includes material not in the Inns of Court, principally a few treatises, annotated collections of statutes and some law reports.]

Colonial Office library. [A complete collection of Colonial laws is maintained and indexed in the library.]

Commonwealth Relations Office library. [A collection of the laws of Australia, Canada, Ceylon, New Zealand and South Africa is available, an index to which is maintained.]

Squire Law Library, Cambridge. [Current law; earlier material is returned to the University Library.]

Board of Trade library.
Codrington Library, All Souls' College, Oxford.†
India House library. [Indian law.]
India Office Library. [Indian law.]
Indian Institute, Oxford. [Indian law.]
King's College library, London.
London School of Economics library.
Rhodes House Library, Oxford.
Royal Empire Society.
School of Oriental and African Studies. [African, Indian and Pakistani law.]
University College library, London.

Statutes and some reports and treatises are also available in the Offices of the various High Commissioners and Agents-General in London.

F

JUDICIAL COMMITTEE OF THE PRIVY COUNCIL, APPEAL PAPERS

A set of the printed papers in Appeals heard by the Judicial Committee of the Privy Council is available for consultation by accredited research workers in the Privy Council Office, Downing Street, London, S.W.1. Normally the papers consist of Appellant's case, Respondent's case, Record of Proceedings, Judgment and the Order-in-Council. Other sets are in the Bar Library, Royal Courts of Justice, and in the libraries of the Inns of Court. They are, however, not all easily accessible and in any case admission to the libraries is restricted. The Institute of Advanced Legal Studies is building up a collection; it possesses at present Canadian Appeals from 1892 to 1955, Australian Appeals from 1945 to 1955 and Ceylon Appeals from 1945 to 1955; Appeals from the Colonies include some between the years 1930 and 1944, and from 1945 to date.

Bibliographies

Index to Legal Periodical Literature (to 1937). 6 vols. Boston, etc., 1888–1939.

Index to Legal Periodicals, 1908 onwards. New York, 1908 in progress. [Monthly, with annual and three-year cumulations.]

Institute of Advanced Legal Studies. *Survey of Legal Periodicals: union catalogue of holdings in British libraries.* 2nd edn, London, 1957.

Institute of Advanced Legal Studies. *Union list of Commonwealth Law Literature in the Libraries of Oxford, Cambridge and London.* London, 1952. [Copies of both these publications are kept up to date in the Institute of Advanced Legal Studies where they may be consulted.]

Institute of Advanced Legal Studies. *Bibliographical guide to the law of the United Kingdom, &c.* (U.K. National Committee of Comparative Law and the Institute.) London, 1956. [Contains a section on the Commonwealth listing works 'concerned primarily with the judicial character of the Commonwealth association, and with the status and interrelationship of the countries of the Commonwealth considered in terms of constitutional law.']

Legal Periodical Digest, 1928 onwards. New York, 1928 in progress.

Meek (C. K.). *Colonial law: a bibliography with special reference to native African systems of law and land tenure.* (Nuffield College Reading lists.) Oxford, 1948.

Middle Temple. *A Catalogue of the printed books in the Library.* 3 vols. London, 1914; supplement (to 1924), 1925. [A valuable bibliography up to the year 1924.]

Maxwell (W. H.) and Brown (C. R.). *Complete list of British and Colonial law reports and legal periodicals.* London, 1937; supplement, 1946.

Roberts (A. A.). *A South African Legal Bibliography.* Pretoria, 1942.

Sweet and Maxwell's *Legal Bibliography.* 7 vols. London, 1925–49. [Includes Commonwealth law literature—vol. 6 (Australia, New Zealand, Fiji and the Western Pacific) and vol. 7 (British Colonies, Protected and Mandated territories) to both of which a supplement was issued in 1954. A revised edition is in preparation, vol. 3 of which, published 1957, is entirely new and is devoted to Canada and British-American Colonial law to Dec. 1956.]

Sociology

i. SOCIAL ANTHROPOLOGY

Institute of Social Anthropology, Oxford.
International African Institute.
London School of Economics library.
London School of Hygiene and Tropical Medicine.
Royal Anthropological Institute.
Science Museum library.
For Bibliographies, *see* pp. 72–85.

ii. EDUCATION

Colonial Office library.
India Office Library.
Institute of Education, Department of Education in Tropical Areas. [Probably the most comprehensive collection.]
Rhodes House Library, Oxford.
Royal Empire Society.

Bibliographies

Drake (K. H.). *Bibliography of African education.* Aberdeen, 1942.
Levy (G.). *European education in South Africa: bibliography.* (Univ. of Cape Town, School of Librarianship.) Cape Town, 1946.
Mules (M.) and Butchers (A. G.). *Bibliography of New Zealand education.* 2nd edn, Wellington, 1947.

iii. RACE RELATIONS

There is no comprehensive 'collection' of material on race relations although many libraries include some literature on the subject. The Institute of Commonwealth Studies does, however, set out to acquire all material of significance. The Department of Racial Studies, Royal Institute of International Affairs, has a small library devoted to racial questions. Mention should also be made of the libraries of the Church Missionary Society, the Colonial Office, the London School of Economics, the Royal Anthropological Institute, the Royal Empire Society, and the Society for the Propagation of the Gospel.

Bibliographies

Jacobson (E.). *The Cape Coloured: Bibliography.* (Univ. of Cape Town, School of Librarianship.) Cape Town, 1945.
Lewin (E.). *Select bibliography of recent publications in the library of the Royal Colonial Institute illustrating the relations between Europeans and coloured races.* (Royal Colonial Institute bibliographies No. 3.) London, 1926.
Manuel (G.). *The Coloured people: bibliography.* (Univ. of Cape Town, School of Librarianship.) Cape Town, 1943.
Morris (G. R.). *The Indian question in South Africa: bibliography.* (Univ. of Cape Town, School of Bibliography.) Cape Town, 1946.

South Africa, Union. Library of Parliament. *Europeans and Coloured Races. Guide to publications in the Library . . . dealing with relations between Europeans and coloured and backward races.* Cape Town, 1927.

Thompson (E. T. and A. M.). *Race and region: a descriptive bibliography compiled with spec. ref. to the relations between whites and negroes in the United States.* Chapel Hill, N.C., 1949.

Tropical Medicine and Hygiene

Works on tropical medicine and hygiene in general and on entomology, parasitology and trypanosomiasis in particular are to be found in the following libraries:

London School of Hygiene and Tropical Medicine.
Imperial College of Science and Technology.†
King's College Hospital Medical School, London.†
Middlesex Hospital Medical School.†

Entomological literature is also available in the libraries of the following:

British Museum (Natural History).†
Commonwealth Institute of Entomology.
East Malling Research Station.
Rothamsted Experimental Station.

Bibliography

Barnard (C. C.). *Tropical medicine and hygiene: a selection of British publications.* In *British Book News*, 1949, pp. 31–7. London, 1949.

VIII. THESES AND RESEARCH IN PROGRESS

United Kingdom

Only in recent years have attempts been made to compile and publish consolidated lists and indexes of university theses. In 1952 Unesco issued *Theses in the Social Sciences*: an international analytical catalogue of unpublished doctorate theses, 1940–50 (printed in English and French). Ten British universities contributed. In addition, information from some of the universities in six other countries of the Commonwealth is included.

In 1953 appeared the first volume of a new serial publication, *Index to Theses accepted for higher degrees in the Universities of Great Britain and*

Ireland, 1950–1 (London, Aslib). The second volume (1951–2) was issued in 1955 and the third (1952–3) in 1956. The Colonial Office (Colonial Social Science Research Council) issues lists of theses on Colonial historical and administrative subjects; the lists first appeared in 1955.

The only reasonably comprehensive compilation is the card-index maintained by the Institute of Commonwealth Studies. It contains references to United Kingdom university theses on Commonwealth studies which have been extracted from printed lists and other material published since the 1920's and from other sources. It does not claim to be complete but the number of entries is very considerable. The index is arranged under authors, subjects and territories and is kept up to date.

Generally British universities require that at least one copy of every thesis shall be deposited with the university authorities, usually the Librarian; they are normally available for inspection with certain safeguards regarding their use. Detailed information on university requirements as to deposit, inter-library loans and microfilming of theses is to be found in *A Survey of Thesis Literature in British Libraries* by P. D. Record (London, the Library Association), 1950; more up-to-date information is to be found in the *Indexes to Theses*, published by Aslib and referred to above. Some universities regularly issue, or have issued, lists or abstracts of theses. Those available include the following:

Aberdeen. Titles (listed in the University Calendar).
    Abstracts, 1931/32 to 1936/37.
Birmingham. Annual Reports, 1938/39 onwards.
Bristol. List, 1923–51 [unpublished; a copy is in the Library of the Institute of Commonwealth Studies].
Cambridge. Lists (in the *Cambridge Historical Jl.*)
    Annual Reports of the Board of Research Studies (*University Reporter*).
    Abstracts, 1938/39 onwards.
Durham. Abstracts, 1931/32 to 1938/39.
Edinburgh. Lists, 1930/31 onwards.
Glasgow. Titles (listed in the University Calendar), to 1946.
Leeds. Abstracts, 1927/28 to 1937/38.
    Titles, 1950/51 onwards.
Liverpool. Titles, 1950 to 1952/53.
    Annual Reports, 1953/54 onwards.
London. Lists (in the University Calendar) from 1929/30 to 1936.
    Subjects, 1937 to 1944, 1945 onwards.
Oxford. Abstracts, 1925 to 1940.
    Titles, 1940–49, 1949 onwards.
    Subjects, etc. (Supplements to the University Gazette.)
    'Colonial Studies' theses (duplicated lists, issued by the Oxford Institute of Commonwealth Studies), covering the period 1940 onwards.
Reading. Lists (in University Gazette).

Sheffield. Summaries, 1926/27 to 1937/38.
  Summaries and titles (in the Annual Reports), 1926/27 to 1936/37, 1949/50
    onwards.
Southampton. Abstracts, 1953/54 onwards.
Wales. Summaries, 1933 to 1941.
  Titles (listed in the University Calendar).

University theses in the field of history were listed in the journal *History* from 1911 to 1928 when the listing was taken over by the *Bulletin* of the Institute of Historical Research. The *Theses Supplements* to the *Bulletin* record all historical theses completed or in progress in the Universities of the United Kingdom. Those relating to British Imperial history can readily be ascertained from the subject indexes. Doctoral dissertations on subjects in the social sciences have also been noted in the *Register of Research in the Social Sciences* (National Institute of Social and Economic Research) since 1947/48.

Research in progress is noted in the *Register of Research in the Social Sciences*, 1943 onwards.

Other lists containing information on completed theses and research in progress are:

Association of British Orientalists. *Bulletin of Near Eastern and Indian Studies* (later *Oriental Studies*). Oxford, 1951 in progress.
International Register of current team research in the social sciences (1950–1952): a tentative survey. (Unesco, 1955.)
Institute of Advanced Legal Studies (University of London). *Legal research topics in British universities*, duplicated lists, first issued in 1950.
List of researches in education and educational psychology presented for higher degrees in the Universities of the U.K., Northern Ireland and the Irish Republic from 1918 to 1948, by A. M. Blackwell, London, 1950. A second list, 1949, 1950 and 1951 (1952). Supplement I, 1952 and 1953 (1954).
List of studies in progress on British territories in Tropical Africa, by Charlotte Leubuscher. (London, R.I.I.A., 1951.)
Royal Institute of Public Administration. *Survey of research in progress in the Universities into public administration and allied fields.* Lists issued annually since March 1951.

Various other organizations exist to foster and encourage research in specific fields and information as to work in progress may be obtained on application to the headquarters of each, a list of which appears at pp. 195–200.

Commonwealth

Colonial research is reported annually in the reports of the several Colonial Office Research Committees and Councils which have been issued since 1943 as Command Papers (H.M.S.O.). They appear together in one Paper annually, now entitled *Colonial Research*, which also lists theses on Colonial subjects. The Colonial Office (Information Department) also issues from time to time in duplicated form *Notes on Colonial Research*.

Information regarding theses and research in progress in Commonwealth universities and other organizations overseas has been assembled in the Institute of Commonwealth Studies in the form of published and unpublished lists and other material, together with some information relating to research in the United States on Commonwealth affairs. Some American lists are also available in the Institute.

Several universities in the Commonwealth issue their own lists of theses and research in progress. Comprehensive lists have also been published including the following:

AUSTRALIA

Historical Studies, Australia and New Zealand, Melbourne: annual lists of theses have appeared since 1950 (vol. iv onwards).
Social Science Research Council. *Australian Social Science Abstracts*, Melbourne: lists of unpublished theses, 1949–54 (Nos. 8–18).

CANADA

Canadian Historical Review, Toronto: Annual lists of graduate theses in Canadian history and related subjects.
Dept. of Citizenship, etc., Canadian Citizenship Branch. *Research on immigrant adjustment and ethnic groups*, unpublished theses, 1920–53. Ottawa, 1955.
Dept. of Mines, etc., Geographical Branch. *University dissertations, theses and essays on . . . Geography* (Bibliog. Ser. No. 3). Ottawa, 1950.
Doctoral dissertations accepted by American Universities, 1933 onwards. New York, 1934 in progress. [Includes Canadian Universities.]
National Library. *Canadian graduate theses in the humanities and social sciences*, 1921–1946. Ottawa, 1951.
National Library. *Canadian Theses*, 1952 onwards. Ottawa, 1953 in progress.

INDIA

Inter-University Board. *Bibliography of doctorate theses in science and arts accepted by Indian Universities*. Madras, 1930 onwards. [The last issue appears to be that for the period 1946–8.]
National Archives. *Bulletin of research theses and dissertations*, January 1955 onwards. New Delhi, 1955 in progress.

NEW ZEALAND

National Historical Committee. New Zealand Centennial, 1940: *List of theses.* n.p.
University of New Zealand. *List of theses submitted for degrees, 1920–1948 (Provisional list)*. n.p.

University of New Zealand. *Research in the University*, 1946–9, 1949–52. Wellington, 1950–3.
Historical Studies, mentioned under Australia, see above.

SOUTH AFRICA

Catalogue of theses and dissertations accepted for degrees by the South African Universities, 1918–41, by A. M. L. Robinson, Cape Town, 1943. A continuation to cover the period 1942 to 1955 is in course of preparation by S. J. Malan of Potchefstroom University.
South Africa, Union. Dept. of Education, etc. *Archives Year Book for South African History*, Cape Town, 1938 in progress. [They include theses submitted for M.A. and doctoral degrees.]

IX. BIBLIOGRAPHIES AND WORKS OF REFERENCE

A: BIBLIOGRAPHIES

The best collections of bibliographies are to be found in the three National libraries, the University of London library, the library of the London School of Economics, the Institute of Historical Research and, in the field of Commonwealth bibliography, the libraries of the Colonial Office, the Royal Empire Society, the Institute of Commonwealth Studies and Rhodes House, Oxford. Asian material is available in the India Office Library and the library of India House, London.

Many individual bibliographies have appeared over the years—subject, territorial and regional—which may be identified by reference to various 'bibliographies of bibliographies', the most important of which are listed below:

Bibliographies of Bibliographies

Besterman (T.). *World bibliography of bibliographies*. 3rd edn, 4 vols. Geneva, 1955–1956. [Although not entirely comprehensive it is a monumental and invaluable work.]
Bibliographic Index. New York, 1936 in progress. [Published quarterly with regular cumulations; the last issued, covering the period 1951–5, was published in 1956.]
Collison (R. L.). *Bibliographies, subject and national*. London, 1951.
Harries (J. M.). *Union list of bibliographies*. London, 1950. [Although compiled for the use of students of librarianship it is of value to research workers in locating

400 bibliographies in Metropolitan and Greater London libraries. A new edition is in preparation.]

Institute of Commonwealth Studies. A bibliography of bibliographies in the Institute's Library. n.p. [Loose leaf; it includes individual bibliographies and bibliographies and major reading lists in other works.]

Leeson (Ida). *Bibliography of bibliographies of the South Pacific.* London, 1954.

Library of Congress. *Current national bibliographies.* H. F. Conover, comp. Washington, 1955.

McGill University, Library School. *Bibliography of Canadian bibliographies.* Montreal, 1930. [Includes general, regional, local and subject bibliographies.]

Malclès (L. N.). *Les sources du travail bibliographique.* Geneva, 1950 in progress. [Three volumes have been published to date.]

Royal Empire Society. A bibliography of bibliographies in the Library. n.p. [Maintained on cards; includes individual bibliographies and bibliographies and major reading lists in other works.]

Royal Geographical Society. Bibliography of geographical bibliographies. n.p. [Maintained on cards.]

South African Library. *Bibliography of African bibliographies.* (Grey Bibliographies, No. 6.) 3rd edn, Cape Town, 1955.

Bibliographies—a Select List

See also under Agriculture and Forestry, p. 59; Demography, p. 60; Education, p. 67; Geography and Maps, pp. 62, 64; Law, p. 66; Mining and Metals, p. 61; Newspapers, p. 49; Parliamentary Papers and Official Publications, pp. 28, 35; Periodicals, pp. 42–5; Race Relations, p. 67; Reference Works, p. 87; Statistics, p. 56; Theses, pp. 69–72; Transport and Communications, p. 61; Tropical Medicine, p. 68.

Albion (R. G.). *Maritime and naval history: an annotated bibliography.* Revised edn, Mystic, Conn., 1955.

British Library of Political and Economic Science (London School of Economics). *London bibliography of the Social Sciences, being the subject catalogue of the . . . . Library . . .* [and of some other libraries]. London, 4 vols., 1931–2, with supplements to date.

British Museum. *Subject index of modern books acquired 1881–1945.* London, 1902 in progress. [Other catalogues of the British Museum are noted at p. 99.]

British National Bibliography. London, 1950 in progress. [A general bibliography. Weekly with quarterly and annual cumulations.]

Cambridge History of the British Empire. Cambridge, 1929 in progress. [To date 8 volumes have been issued, each of which includes an extensive bibliography —vol. i, Old Empire to 1783; vol. ii, New Empire, 1783–1870; vol. iii, in preparation; vol. iv, British India, 1497–1858; vol. v, Indian Empire, 1858–1918; vol. vi, Canada; vol. vii, pt. i, Australia; vol. vii, pt. ii, New Zealand; vol. viii, South Africa.]

Colonial Office. Administrative Reports on individual Colonies and territories, mostly annual. [The latest reports include reading lists.]

Colonial Office. *Catalogue of books in the library.* London, 1896. Supplement, 1st Aug. 1907.

Colonial Office and Commonwealth Relations Office. *Select list of Accessions* (formerly entitled 'Digest of books and pamphlets'). London, bi-monthly, 1946 in progress.

Dutcher (G. M.) and others. *A guide to historical literature.* New York, 1949. [Chapters on Colonial expansion, India, Oceania, Africa and British North America. Includes material to 1930 only.]

English Catalogue of Books. London, 1835 onwards. [A general bibliography. Annually with regular cumulations.]

Frewer (L. B.). *Bibliography of historical writings published in Great Britain and the Empire, 1940–45.* Oxford 1947.

Hazlewood (A.). *Economics of 'under-developed' areas: an annotated reading list of books, articles and official publications.* (Oxford Institute of Commonwealth Studies Reading Lists.). Oxford, 1954.

Historical Association. *Annual bulletins of historical literature.* London, 1911 (No. 1–), in progress. [The earlier issues contain chapters on Colonial history; the later issues on Asia, Africa and the New World.]

Institute of Historical Research. *Bibliography of historical works issued in the U.K.,* 1946–56. Joan Lancaster, comp. 1957. [Includes Africa, Asia, Canada, Australasia, and W. Indies.]

International Association for Research in Income and Wealth. *Bibliography on income and wealth,* 1937–47, 1948/49 onwards. Cambridge, 1952 in progress.

Keesing (F. M.). *Culture change: an analysis and bibliography of anthropological sources to 1952.* Stanford, Cal., 1953.

Morrell (W. P.). *Select list of books relating to the history of the British Commonwealth and Empire overseas.* (Hist. Assoc., Pamphlet No. 130, revised.) London, 1948.

Royal Empire Society. *Subject Catalogue of the Library.* 4 vols. London, 1930–7.

Royal Empire Society. *Bibliographies:*

1. *Foreign colonization.* W. C. Hill. 1915.
2. *Recent publications in the library illustrating constitutional relations between parts of the British Empire.* E. Lewin. 1926.
5. *Warren Hastings.* V. Ward. 1932.
6. *Constitutional relations of the British Empire* (publications 1926–32). E. Lewin. 1933. [Also issued as joint publication by the Society and the Royal Institute of International Affairs, 1933.]
10. *Best books on the British Empire: a guide for students.* E. Lewin. 1943. 2nd edn, 1945.

[Other bibliographies in the series are referred to under appropriate subjects]

Royal Historical Society. *Writings on British history,* 1934 onwards. A. T. Milne comp. London, 1937 in progress. [Include material on the Commonwealth.]

UNESCO. *Current sociology.* International bibliography of sociology, 1952 onwards, about four issues per annum. Paris, 1952 in progress.

UNESCO. *Education for community development—a selected bibliography.* Paris, 1954.

UNESCO. *International bibliography of economics,* 1952, vol. i onwards. Paris, 1955 in progress.

UNESCO. *International bibliography of political science,* 1952, vol. i onwards. Paris, 1954 in progress.

United Nations. *Bibliography on the processes and problems of industrialization in under-developed countries.* New York, 1954.

United Nations. *Bibliography on industrialization in under-developed countries.* New York, 1956.

United States. State Department. *Point Four, Latin America and European depen-*

dencies in the Western hemisphere—a select bibliography of studies on economically under-developed countries. Washington, 1950.

Whitaker's Cumulative Book List. London, 1924 onwards. [A general bibliography. Quarterly, with annual cumulationsl]

Whitaker's Reference Catalogue of Current Literature. London, irregular issues since 1874. Current issue (1951), 1952. [A general bibliography.]

AFRICA

See also Other Territories, *below*

Cambridge History of the British Empire. Vol. viii, South Africa. 1936.

Cape Town, University. School of Librarianship. *Bibliographical Series.* [These bibliographies are the work of students for the Diploma in Librarianship; they have not been edited or amended and none claims to be exhaustive in treatment.] Those issued include the following titles (in abbreviated form):

Amyot. *Tercentenary of landing of van Riebeck.* 1950.

Appleyard. *Livingstone.* 1949.

Arnheim. *Swaziland.* 1950.

Baker. *Sir B. d'Urban's administration . . . Eastern frontier of the Cape . . . 1834–38.* 1946.

Bee. *Hist. biblio. of . . . Durban, or Port Natal.* 1946.

Bernstein. *Farming in S. Rhodesia.* 1949.

Bielschowsky. *List of books in German on South Africa.* 1949.

Blum. *Union Native policy in Govt. legislation and publications, 1910–48.* 1950.

Bosman. *Afrikaanse kleuterboeke.* 1945.

Brownlee: *South African missionaries.* 1952.

Burgher. *General Hertzog.* 1953.

Carpenter. *Development of S. Rhodesia.* 1946.

Cox. *Federation of the Rhodesias and Nyasaland up to June, 1949.*

Cross. *Bibliography of Pretoria.* 1948.

du Toit. *Bibliografie van Totius.* 1949.

du Toit. *C. F. L. Leipoldt.* 1947.

Ehlers. *Vertalings in Afrikaans, 1919–1940.* 1943.

Farmer. *Social security.* 1944.

Feinstein. *Nutrition and nutritional deficiences, with spec. ref. to the non-European.* 1952.

Flinn. *Cereals in South Africa.* 1948.

Fox. *Prisons and penal reform.* 1949.

Galloway. *Zululand and the Zulus.* 1944.

Ginsberg and Schwartz. *Medical research on the Bantu, 1920–52.* 1952.

Greshoff. *English writings by South African Bantu.* 1943.

Griessel. *Jan F. E. Celliers.* 1951.

Holden and Jacoby. *Suppl. to Schapera's Select bibliography of S. African Native life.* 1950.

Hubbard. *South African Forestry since 1913.* 1949.

Hutton. *Constitution of the Union.* 1946.

Jacobsen. *Cape Coloured.* 1945.

Joubert. *Road Transportation in S. Africa in the 19th Century.* 1955.

Kamp. *C. M. van den Heever.* 1953.

Kilgour. *Sir George Grey.* 1950.

Levy. *European education in South Africa*. 1946.

Loeming. *Bibliography of the Status of S.W. Africa to June 1951*. 1951.

Louw. *Nederlandse en Afrikaanse Boeke gedruk en uitgegee duer D.F. du Toit & Co*. 1951.

Luscombe. *Soil*. 1945.

Malan. *C. J. Langenhoven*. 1951.

Mandelbrote. *The Cape Press, 1838–1850*. 1945.

Manuel. *The Coloured People*. 1943.

Moreland. *Bilingualism*. 1948.

Morris. *The Indian question in South Africa*. 1946.

Muller. *Military strategy and tactics*. 1951.

Muller. *The Orange River*. 1953.

Plaat. *List of books and pamphlets in German on South Africa and S.W. Africa after 1914 in the South African Public Library*. 1951.

Price. *Port Elizabeth*. 1949.

Rabe. *Merino wool production and wool research*. 1952.

Rossouw. *African languages (1858–1900) in the Grey Collection, South African Library*. 1947.

Rowley. *Sugar*. 1947.

Saul. *South African periodical publications, 1800–1875*. 1949.

Scott. *J. C. Smuts*. 1953.

Smith. *Deciduous fruit*. 1947. [Relates to the industry.]

Southey. *Kimberley and the diamond fields of Griqualand West, 1869–1900*. 1946.

Spohr. *German Africana*. 1948.

Stevens. *Bechuanaland*. 1947.

Stevens. *Zimbabwe culture*. 1950.

te Groen. *Basutoland*. 1946.

Thomson. *Cecil John Rhodes*. 1947.

Turest. *National Health Services in South Africa*. 1945. [Articles from periodicals, etc.]

van Heerden. *Bibliografie van boeke oor Afrikaanse taalkunde*. 1943.

van Heerden. *Closer Union movement, 1902–1910*. 1952.

Verster. *Olive Schreiner*. 1946.

Vowles. *City of Pietermaritzburg*. 1946.

Wagner. *The first British occupation of the Cape 1795–1803*. 1946.

Watts. *Gold Mining in the Eastern Transvaal*. 1954.

Webb. *Citrus fruit industry in South Africa*. 1951.

Welch. *South West Africa*. 1946.

Whyte. *Works of Sarah Gertrude Millin*. 1952.

Wookey. *Physical anthropology in South Africa*. 1947.

Central African Archives: *Bibliography of Cecil John Rhodes*. Salisbury, 1952.

Comhaire (J.). *Urban conditions in Africa: select reading list on urban problems in Africa*. (Oxford Institute of Commonwealth Studies Reading Lists.) Oxford, 1952.

Doke (C. M.). *Bantu modern grammatical, phonetical and lexicographical studies since 1860*. London, 1945.

Gross (F.). *Bibliography of Rhodes of Africa*. Typescript, 1956. [Copies have been deposited in the British Museum and the Bodleian.]

Hambly (W. D.). *Bibliography of African anthropology, 1936–49*. Chicago, 1952. (Suppl. to *Source Book for African Anthropology*, 2 vols. Chicago, 1937.)

Institut Française d'Afrique Noire: Instructions summaires iii: *Conseils aux chercheurs.* 4th edn, Dakar, 1953. [Includes selective bibliographies arranged under subjects.]

International African Institute, London. Bibliographical card-index of books, reports and articles relating to a wide range of African studies mainly south of the Sahara. n.p.

International African Institute. *Select annotated bibliography of Tropical Africa.* N.Y. (Twentieth Century Fund), London (The Institute), 1956.

Johannesburg Public Library. *Catalogue of Bantu, Khoisan and Malagasy in the Strange Collection.* Johannesburg, 1942 (duplicated).

Library of Congress. *British East and Central Africa: a selected list of references.* H. F. Conover, comp. Washington, 1942.

Library of Congress. *British West Africa: a selected list of references.* H. F. Conover, comp. Washington, 1942.

Library of Congress. *Introduction to Africa: a selective guide to background reading.* Washington, 1952.

Library of Congress. *The British Empire in Africa.* H. F. Conover, comp. Washington, 1942–3.

Library of Congress. *Union of South Africa—a selected list of references.* H. F. Conover, comp. Washington, 1943.

Long (U.). *Index to authors of privately owned manuscripts relating to the history of South Africa, 1812–1920.* London, 1947 (mimeographed).

Mendelssohn (S.). *South African Bibliography.* 2 vols. London, 1910. Reprint, 1957. Additions 1910–14 (1914). [Kept up to date by unpublished supplements at the Library of Parliament and, from 1938, by an 'Annual List of Africana added to the Mendelssohn Collection' (Library of Parliament).]

Nienaber (P. J.). *Bibliografie van Afrikaanse Boeke* (from 1861). 3 vols. Johannesburg, 1943–54.

Perry (R.). *A preliminary bibliography of the literature of nationalism in Nigeria.* (International African Institute.) London, 1956.

Royal Empire Society. *Subject catalogue of the Library.* Vol. 1, Africa, 1930.

Royal Empire Society. *Bibliographies:*
  7. *Italian colonization in Africa* by D. H. Varley. 1936. o.p.
  8. *African Native Music* by D. H. Varley. 1936.
  9. *Recent publications on Africa, south of the Sahara* by E. Lewin, 1943.

Santandrea (P. S.). *Bibliografia di studi Africani della Missione dell' Africa centrale.* Verona, 1948.

Schapera (I.). *Select bibliography of South African native life and problems.* London, 1941. [Supplement by A. Holden and A. Jacoby has been issued by the University of Cape Town School of Librarianship, Cape Town, 1950.]

South African Library. *Quarterly Bulletin.* Cape Town, 1946 onwards.

South African Library. *South Africa in Print, a catalogue of exhibition of books, etc., van Riebeeck Festival.* Cape Town, 1952.

South African Catalogue of Books, 1900–1950. 4th edn, 2 vols., Johannesburg, 1950.

State Library, Pretoria. *Lists of publications received in terms of copyright.* Monthly and annual lists. Pretoria, 1933 onwards.

Theal (G. McC.). *Catalogue of books, etc., Africa south of the Zambesi, in English, Dutch, French and Portuguese in the G. McC. Theal Collection.* Cape Town, 1912.

Uganda, Ministry of Land Tenure. *Bibliography of land tenure.* Entebbe, 1957.

Venter (R. J.). *Bibliography of regional meteorological literature, vol. 1 (Southern Africa), 1486–1948.* Pretoria, 1950.

Whitley (W. H.) and Gutkind (A. E.). *Linguistic bibliography of East Africa.* Kampala, 1954, with suppls.

Wieschhoff (H. A.). *Anthropological bibliography of Negro Africa (American Oriental Studies,* vol. 23). New Haven, Conn., 1948.

ASIA

(including Middle East and Far East)

See also Ceylon; India and Pakistan. *For* Malaya *see under* Other Territories, *below*

Association of British Orientalists. *Select list of books on the civilizations of the Orient.* (ed. W. A. C. H. Dobson.) Oxford, 1955.

Baqai (I. A.). *Books on Asia.* Issued under auspices of Asian Relations Conference. New Delhi, 1947.

Colonial Office. *Annotated bibliography on land tenure in British and British protected territories in S.E. Asia and Pacific.* (Colonial Office Research Study No. 6.) London, 1952.

Embree (J. F.). *Select bibliography of S.E. Asia.* New York, 1950.

Embree (J. F.) and Dotson (L. A.). *Bibliography of peoples and culture of mainland S.E. Asia.* New Haven, 1950.

Ettinghausen (R.), ed. *Select and. annotated bibliography of books and periodicals in Western languages dealing with the near and middle East.* (Middle East Institute). Washington, 1954.

Far Eastern Bibliography, Bulletin. 1936–40. Continued in *Far Eastern Quarterly,* vol. i, 1941 onwards. Ann Arbor, Mich., 1941 in progress.

Field (H.). *Bibliography on Southwestern Asia.* 3 vols. Coral Gables, Florida, 1953–1956.

Library of Congress. *Southern Asia, publications in Western languages,* a quarterly list. Washington, 1952 in progress.

Library of Congress. *Select list of books (with references to periodicals) relating to the Far East.* Washington, 1904.

Library of Congress. *Southeast Asia, an annotated bibliography of selected reference sources.* C. Hobbs, comp. Washington, 1952.

Library of Congress. *Southeast Asia, 1935–45, a select list of references.* C. Hobbs, comp. Washington, 1952.

Orientalische Bibliographie, annually, covering years 1887 to 1911, 25 vols. Berlin, 1888–1922.

Quan (L. King.). *Introduction to Asia, a selective guide to background reading.* Library of Congress, Washington, 1955.

Royal Empire Society. *Subject catalogue of the Library.* Vol. 4, Middle East, Far East, 1937.

U.N. (Ecafe). *Asian bibliography,* half-yearly. Bankok, 1952 in progress.

UNESCO. South Asia Co-operation Office (New Delhi). *Social science bibliography, India,* 1952 in progress. New Delhi, 1954 onwards.

AUSTRALIA

Australia, Library of Parliament. *Catalogue of the books . . . in the Library.* 1911 Melbourne, 1912.

Australia, National Development Ministry, Regional Development Division. *Classified and select bibliography on Australia for regional development purposes.* K. M. Hedburg, comp. Canberra, 1948 in progress. [Parts issued: ii, N.S.W.; iii, Victoria; v, W. Australia; vii, S. Australia.]

Cambridge History of the British Empire. Vol. 7, pt. i. Australia. 1933.

Commonwealth National Library, Canberra:
Annual Catalogue of Australian Publications, issued since 1936 (No. 1).
Australian Books, a select list (formerly *Select List of representative works dealing with Australia*), annually, 1934 onwards.
Books published in Australia, a monthly leaflet issued since Jan.–Mar. 1946.
Monthly lists of Australian Government Publications. Issued since Jan. 1952 (in duplicated form).
Select Bibliographies (Australian Series), issued since 1952 (in duplicated form).
Select Bibliographies (general series), issued since 1952 (in duplicated form).

Crowley (F. K.). *Records of Western Australia.* Perth, 1953.

Ferguson (J. A.). *Bibliography of Australia, from 1784* [to 1850]. 4 vols. Sydney, 1941–55.

Foxcroft (A. B.). *Australian Catalogue; a reference index to the books and periodicals published and still current in the Commonwealth of Australia.* Melbourne, 1911.

Francis Edwards Ltd. *Catalogue of books relating to Australasia.* London, 1899.

Francis Edwards Ltd. *Catalogue of the Australasian collection formed by the late J. E. Partington.* London, 1934.

Gill (T.). *Bibliography of South Australia.* Adelaide, 1886. [Out of date, but still useful.]

Gill (T.). *Bibliography of the Northern Territory of South Australia.* Adelaide, 1903, continued to 1933 by C. H. Hannaford. Supplement 1934–7 compiled by C. H. Hannaford [1938?] (typescript).

Library of Congress. *Selected list of references on Australia.* G. H. Fuller, comp. Washington, 1942.

Mackaness (G.) and Stone (W. W.). *Books of the bulletin, 1880–1952, an annotated bibliography.* Sydney, 1955.

Miller (E. M.). *Australian Literature, 1810–1938,* extended to 1950. 2nd edn (ed. Macarthy). 2 vols., Melbourne, 1956.

Politzer (L. L.). *Bibliography of German literature on Australia, 1770–1947.* Melbourne, 1952; ditto, French literature, 1595–1946, 1953; ditto, Dutch literature, 1953.

Royal Empire Society. *Subject catalogue of the Library.* Vol. 2, Australia, 1931.

Royal Empire Society. *Bibliographies,* No. 13. *Best Books on Australia and New Zealand,* by E. Lewin. 1946.

Spence (S. A.). *A Bibliography of Early Books and pamphlets relating to Australia 1610–1880.* London, 1952. Supplement to 1610–1880 and extension from 1881–1900, London, 1955. [Contains 'material which up to the present has failed to appear in any single volume relating to Australia'.]

Steere (F. G.). *Bibliography of books, articles, etc., dealing with Western Australia issued since discovery in 1616.* Perth, 1923.

Sydney, Public Library. *Catalogue of the books in the Free Public Library, Sydney, relating to, or published in, Australasia.* Sydney, 1893.

Sydney, University. *Bibliography of public administration in Australia (1850–1947).* Joan Craig, comp. Sydney, 1955.

CANADA

Brown (G. W.), ed. *Canada*. (U.N. Series.) Berkeley, California, 1950. [Contains an extensive bibliographic chapter on various aspects of Canadian history and affairs.]

Cambridge History of the British Empire, vol. 6, Canada. 1930.

Canada, Citizenship and Immigration Department. *Research on immigrant adjustment and ethnic groups; a bibliography of published material, 1920–53*, 1953–4 onwards. Continued annually. Ottawa, 1954 in progress.

Canada, Library of Parliament:
    Catalogue of books in the library of the Legislative Assembly of Canada. Montreal, 1846.
    Catalogue. 2 vols., Toronto, 1857–58.
    Catalogue of the Library of Parliament, General Library. Toronto, 1857.
    Alphabetical catalogue . . . being an index to the classified catalogues printed in 1857–58 and to the books added to the library up to the first of March, 1862. Quebec, 1862.
    Supplement to the alphabetical catalogue . . . containing all books and pamphlets added . . . 1885–April, 1886. Ottawa, 1886. *Annual Supplements, 1887–1925*.
    Index to the catalogue to the Library of Parliament. Ottawa, 1879–80. 2 vols.

Canada, Mines and Technical Surveys Department. Geographical Branch. *Bibliographical series*. Ottawa, 1950 in progress.

Canadian Historical Review, Toronto. [Quarterly issues, contain lists of *Recent publications relating to Canada*. The *Bibliography of Canadian Anthropology*, prepared by Prof. McIlwraith, is now published in the *Bulletin* of the National Museum, 1954–55 onwards.]

Dionne (N. E.). *Inventaire chronologique des livres, etc., 1764–1905*, and Supplement. Quebec, 1908–12.

Gagnon (P.). *Essai de bibliographie Canadienne*. 2 vols. (vol. 1 published Quebec, vol. 2 published Montreal), 1895–1913.

Garigue's *Bibliographical introduction to the study of French Canada*. (McGill University.) Montreal, 1956.

Haight (W. R.). *Canadian Catalogue of books, 1791–1897*. 3 vols., Toronto, 1896–1904.

National Library of Canada. *Canadiana*. Ottawa, monthly and annually, 1951 onwards.

Maggs Bros. *Canada, Newfoundland, Labrador and the Canadian Arctic, a selection o, 650 books*. London, 1939.

Manitoba, Legislative Library. *A bibliography of Manitoba selected from holdings in the Legislative Library of Manitoba*. M. Morley, comp. Winnipeg, 1948. Another edition, Winnipeg, 1953 (mimeograph).

Morgan (H. J.). *Bibliotheca Canadensis*. Ottawa, 1867.

Murdock (G. P.). *Ethnographic bibliography of North America*. New Haven, 1953. [North American Indians.]

Peel (B. B.). *A Bibliography of the Prairie Provinces to 1953*. Toronto, 1956.

Queen's University, Kingston. *Canadiana, 1698–1900, in the possession of the Douglas Library, Queen's University, Kingston, Ontario*. Kingston, Ont., 1932.

Review of Historical Publications relating to Canada (University of Toronto), 1896–1917/18; superseded by the *Canadian Historical Review*, quarterly. Toronto.

Royal Empire Society. *Subject catalogue of the Library*. Vol. 3, Canada and Newfoundland, 1932.

Société des Ecrivains. *Bulletin Bibliographique*. Montreal, 1937 onwards. [French Canadian literature.]

Staton (F. M.) and Tremaine (M.). *Bibliography of Canadiana*. Toronto, 1934.

Tod (D. D.) and Cordingley (A.). *Check list of Canadian Imprints, 1900–1925* Ottawa, 1950.

Toronto Public Library. *Canadian catalogue of books published in Canada, about Canada, as well as those by Canadians*. Toronto, annually 1921 to 1950. Continued by *Canadiana* (National Library of Canada).

Toronto Public Library. *The Canadian North-west, a bibliography of the sources of information in the . . . Library*. Toronto, 1931.

Tremaine (M.). *Bibliography of Canadian Imprints, 1751–1800*. Toronto, 1952.

Trotter (R. G.). *Canadian history, a syllabus and guide to reading*. Revised edn, Toronto, 1934.

Sir George Williams College, Montreal. *Bibliography of Canadiana*. J. B. Crombie and M. A. Webb, comps. Montreal, 1944 (mimeograph). Supplement 1944–6. Montreal, 1946 (mimeograph).

Winnipeg Public Library. *Select bibliography of Canadiana of the Prairie Provinces, publications relating to Western Canada, etc*. Winnipeg, 1949.

CEYLON
See also Asia

Ceylon, Information Department. *Bibliography on land tenure and related problems in Ceylon*. Colombo, 1952.

Ceylon, Office of Registrar of Books and Newspapers. *Statement of Books printed in Ceylon*, 1885 onwards, quarterly. [Contained in the Ceylon Official Gazette, part v.]

Library of Congress, Reference Dept. *India, Tibet and Ceylon*. Washington, 1942.

Royal Empire Society. *Subject catalogue of the Library*. Vol. 4, Ceylon, 1937.

INDIA AND PAKISTAN
See also Asia

Bombay Historical Society. *Annual bibliography of Indian history and Indology, 1938 to 1942*. Bombay. [Vol. v appears to be the last issued; it was published in 1949.]

Calcutta National Library. *Tentative Bibliography of Basic Publications on all aspects of Indian Culture*. Sect. I, Indian Anthropology. Calcutta, 1955.

Cambridge History of the British Empire. Vol. 4, British India 1497–1858. 1929. Vol. 5, Indian Empire 1858–1918. 1932.

Cambridge History of India. Cambridge, 1922 in progress.

Campbell (F. B. F.). *An index-catalogue of bibliographical works chiefly in the English language relating to India*. London, 1897.

Deshpande (P. G.). *Gandhiana*. Ahmedabad [1953?]. [A bibliography of Gandhian literature.]

Ghani (A. R.). *Pakistan—a select bibliography*. Lahore, 1951.

India, Government. *Quarterly Catalogues*, 1867 to 1947.

India, Ministry of Food and Agriculture. *Bibliography of Indian agricultural economics*. Delhi [1953].

India, National Library. Monthly lists of additions, 1953 onwards.

G

India, High Commissioner's Office. *India House Library, a short catalogue*. London, 1933.

India, High Commissioner's Office. *Monthly list of [official] publications received in the Publications Branch and Library, and of [unofficial] books, pamphlets and periodicals received in the Library*. London, 1928 in progress.

India Office. *Catalogue of the Library*. London, 1888, with supplementary volumes.

Library of Congress, Reference Department. *India, Tibet and Ceylon*. Washington, 1942.

Morae (G. M.). *Bibliography of Indological studies, 1942*. Bombay, 1945.

North (R.). *Literature of the N.W. Frontier of India. A select bibliography*. Peshawar, 1946.

Royal Empire Society. *Subject catalogue of the Library*. Vol. 4, India, East Indies, 1937.

Sharma (J. S.). *Mahatma Gandhi, a descriptive bibliography*. Delhi, 1955.

Wilson (P.), comp. *Government and politics of India and Pakistan, 1885–1955:* a bibliography of works in western languages. (Institute of East Asiatic Studies, University of California.) Berkeley, Cal. [1956].

NEW ZEALAND

Allen (R. S.) and Collins (B. W.). *Bibliography of New Zealand geology since 1908*. Christchurch, 1951–4 (n.p., typescript).

Anderson (J. C.). *One hundred representative New Zealand books*. (Alex. Turnbull Library Bulletin No. 1), Wellington, 1925.

Auckland Free Public Library. *General Catalogue*. 2 vols. in 1. Auckland, 1888, Supplement to vol. 1, 1891; Supplement to catalogue, 1892.

Auckland University College. Department of Economics. *Bibliography of New Zealand Economics and Economic History*. B. G. Hardie, comp. Auckland, 1953 (duplicated).

Bagnall (A. G.). *Reference list of books, etc., associated with the New Zealand Centennial, 1840–1940*. Wellington, 1942.

Cambridge History of the British Empire. Vol. 7, pt. ii, New Zealand. 1933.

Carter (C. R.). *Catalogue of books on or relating to New Zealand*. [Wellington?] 1887.

Chapple (J. B.). *Bibliographical brochure containing addenda and corrigenda to extant bibliographies of New Zealand literature*. Dunedin, 1938.

Collier (J.). *Literature relating to New Zealand, a bibliography*. Wellington, 1889.

Harris (J.). *Guide to New Zealand reference material and other sources of information*. 2nd edn, Wellington, 1950; supplement, 1951.

Hocken (T. M.). *Bibliography of the literature relating to New Zealand*. Wellington, 1909; supplement by A. H. Johnstone, 1927.

Hocken Library, Dunedin. *Catalogue*. Dunedin, 1917.

Holmes (M.). *Captain Cook, a bibliographical excursion*. London, 1952.

Johnstone (A. H.), comp. *Canterbury books, 1847–1955: a bibliography*. Christchurch, N.Z., 1956.

New South Wales, Public Library. *Bibliography of Captain James Cook*. Sydney, 1928.

New Zealand, Authors' Week Committee. *Annals of New Zealand literature, a preliminary list of New Zealand authors and their works*. [Wellington], 1936.

New Zealand, Dept. of Scientific and Industrial Research. *Bibliography of New*

Zealand Geology since 1908. R. S. Allen, comp.; with subject index by A. P. and D. L. Jenkins. Christchurch, 1951–4 (duplicated).

New Zealand, General Assembly Library. *Catalogue.* Wellington, 1897; supplement, 1899, 3 vols.

New Zealand, General Assembly Library. *Copyright lists*, monthly; *Official publications*, annually.

New Zealand National Library Service. *New Zealand Catalogue of books, 1948–1952.* Wellington. Printed on cards, service now incorporated in the *National Bibliography of New Zealand*, a part of the *Index to New Zealand Periodicals.*

New Zealand National Library Service. *Union catalogue of non-fiction books in New Zealand Libraries.* Wellington, 1941 in progress.

New Zealand Official Year Book. Current issues contain lists of notable works published annually since 1950. [Earlier works are listed in the 1932 and 1947/49 issues.]

Olsson (A. L.). *Bibliography of the historical, political and commercial relations between New Zealand and Oceania, 1840–1947.* Wellington, 1947 (typescript).

Royal Empire Society. *Subject catalogue of the Library.* Vol. 2, New Zealand, 1931.

Taylor (C. R. H.). *Select list of books relating to New Zealand and certain Pacific Islands, 1912–1945.* 2nd edn, Wellington, 1949.

Williams (H. W.). *Bibliography of printed Maori to 1900.* Wellington, 1924; supplement, 1928.

PACIFIC

See also Australia; New Zealand

Allied Pacific High Commission, Allied Geographical Section (S.W. Pacific Area). *An annotated bibliography of the S.W. Pacific and adjacent areas, 1944–1945,* 4 vols. [i. Netherlands and British East Indies and the Philippines; ii, New Guinea, Papua, Solomons, New Hebrides and Micronesia; iii, Malaya and some non-British areas; iv, Supplement to vols. i–iii.]

Australia, Defence Department. *Handbook of selected reference material—Pacific.* 1948 (duplicated). [Includes agriculture, economic conditions, industry, politics, sociology.]

Kennedy (R.). *Bibliography of Indonesian peoples and cultures.* (Behavior Science Bibliographies; South-east Asia Studies, Yale University.) 2 vols., New Haven, Connecticut, 1955. [Includes Borneo.]

Klienberger (H. R.). *Bibliography of Oceanic linguistics* (in the press, due 1957).

Library of Congress. *Islands of the Pacific: a select list of references.* H. F. Conover, comp. Washington, 1943; supplement, 1945.

O'Reilly (P.). *Bibliographie méthodique, analytique et critique de la Nouvelle-Caledonie.* Paris, 1955.

Royal Empire Society. *Subject catalogue of the Library.* Vol. 2, South Pacific, 1931.

Royal Empire Society. *Bibliographies.* No. 11, *Pacific Regions*, by E. Lewin. London, 1944.

Société des Océanistes. *Bibliographie de l'Océanie.* 1939–44, 1945 annually. Paris, 1945 onwards.

South Pacific Commission (Soc. Development Section). *Cargo cults and other Nativistic movements in the South Pacific.* I. Leeson, comp. Sydney, 1952.

Bibliography of co-operation in the South Pacific, Dec. 1953. Noumea, 1953.

Bibliography of bibliographies in the South Pacific. I. Leeson, comp. London, 1954.

Taylor (C. R. H.). *A Pacific bibliography; printed matter relating to the native peoples of Polynesia, Melanesia and Micronesia.* Wellington, 1951.

Utinomi (H.). *Bibliography of Micronesia.* [Honolulu], 1952.

OTHER TERRITORIES
British Somaliland

Viney (N. M.). *A bibliography.* [Burao], 1947 (mimeograph).

Caribbean

Caribbean Commission, Trinidad. *Current Caribbean Bibliography.* Quarterly, Port of Spain, 1951 onwards. [An alphabetical list of publications issued in the Caribbean territories of the United Kingdom, U.S.A., France and Holland.

Cundall (F.). *Bibliography of the West Indies (ex. Jamaica).* Kingston, Jamaica, 1909; *Bibliotheca Jamaicensis.* (Some account of the principal works on Jamaica in the Library of the Institute of Jamaica.) Kingston, Jamaica, 1895.

Edwards Bros. *West Indies: a catalogue of books, maps, etc.* London, 1929.

Hiss (P. H.). *Selective guide to the English literature on the Netherlands West Indies, with a supplement on British Guiana.* New York, 1943.

Library of Congress. *British possessions in the Caribbean area: a select list of references.* A. D. Brown, comp. Washington, 1943.

Ragatz (L. J.). *Guide for the study of British Caribbean history, 1763–1834, including the abolition and emancipation movements.* Washington, 1942.

Roth (V.). *Bibliography of British Guiana*, 1948 (typescript).

Royal Empire Society. *Subject catalogue of the Library.* Vol. 3, West Indies, 1932.

West India Committee, London. *Catalogue of the Library.* London, 1941.

Ghana

Cardinall (A. W.). *A bibliography of the Gold Coast.* Accra, 1932.

Howe (G. N.). *A select bibliography of recent literature on the Gold Coast, 1955 onwards.* Accra, 1955 in progress.

Malaya
See also Asia; Pacific, above

Daniel's *Descriptive catalogue of the books relating to Malaysia in the Raffles Museum and Library*, Singapore, 1941. (*Jo. Royal Asiatic Society*, Malayan Branch, vol. 19, pt. 3.)

Government Gazette. *Quarterly lists of books registered under the Preservation of Books Ordinance*, since 1950.

Library of Congress. *British Malaya and British North Borneo: a select list of references.* F. S. Hellman, comp. Washington, 1943.

Pelzer (K. J.). *Selected bibliography of the geography of Southeast Asia*, Part III, Malaya. New Haven, 1956.

Robson (J. H. M.). *Bibliography of Malaya; also a short list of books relating to North Borneo and Sarawak.* Kuala Lumpur, 1938.

Royal Empire Society. *Subject catalogue of the Library.* Vol. 4, Malaya, 1937.

Malta

Melita historica, vol. I, 1952 onwards. Valletta, 1952 in progress. [Appears at irregular intervals, approximately one issue per annum; each number contains a bibliography devoted to some aspect of Maltese affairs.]

Mauritius

Archives Department. *Annual Reports*, 1949 onwards. [Containing lists of publications printed in Mauritius during the year.]

Toussaint (A.). *A select bibliography*. Port Louis, 1951.

Toussaint (A.). *Bibliography of Mauritius (1502–1954)*. Port Louis, 1956. [To be kept up to date by supplements issued as annexures to the Annual Reports of the Archives Department.]

Nigeria

Ibadan, University College. *Nigerian Publications*, 1950–2, 1953 onwards. [Lists of works received under the Publications Ordinance by the Library. Issued quarterly and annually.]

Northern Rhodesia

Publications Bureau. *Annual Reports*, 1949 onwards. [Contain lists of books published each year.]

St. Helena

[Kitching.] *A St. Helena bibliography*. [St. Helena], 1937.

Sierra Leone

Luke (H. C.). *A bibliography of Sierra Leone*. 2nd edn, London, 1925.

Sudan

Hill (R. L.). *Bibliography of the Anglo-Egyptian Sudan to 1937*. London, 1939.

Sudan Notes and Records. [Contain annual Sudan bibliographies.] Khartoum, 1918 in progress.

B: REFERENCE WORKS

Location

Works of reference in general and those of the Commonwealth in particular are available in abundance. In addition to the three National libraries such works, including biographical material, are well represented in the University of London Library and the library of the London School of Economics, as well as in the Guildhall Library, City of London, and the Westminster Central Reference Library. The Guildhall claims to possess an unrivalled collection; it includes, in addition to the familiar almanacs, calendars, year-books, etc., a very comprehensive collection of British, Commonwealth and foreign commercial and trade directories, specialist directories and lists, town and local directories, telephone directories and time-tables. The Westminster Reference Library is much the same; in addition, it includes many dictionaries, vernacular and technical. The Board of Trade library possesses a collection similar to that in the Guildhall.

Libraries concentrating on Commonwealth material are those of the Colonial Office, the Royal Empire Society, the Institute of Commonwealth Studies and Rhodes House, Oxford. Works relating to Asian countries of the Commonwealth are available in the India Office Library, which secures all standard works of reference and biographies available, the School of Oriental and African Studies and the Indian Institute, Oxford. Appropriate works of reference are also available in the offices of the High Commissioners and Agents-General in London. Reference should be made to the various entries in Part II, below.

Selections of similar material are to be found in many other libraries but such works and the libraries in which they are available are too numerous to mention individually, except in the case of Official *Yearbooks*, complete sets of which are in the University of London Library, the London School of Economics library, the Institute of Commonwealth Studies, the Royal Statistical Society's library and the appropriate offices of the various High Commissioners. The University of London Library and the London School of Economics library also have some issues of the Australian States and Canadian Provinces yearbooks; they will also be found in the appropriate offices of the Agents-General. The Guildhall Library and the Westminster Central Reference Library have good collections of current and recent issues.

It may be useful to record here the location of some important British works of reference, namely:

Annual Register. Sets are in the Colonial Office Library, the Institute of Historical Research, the London School of Economics library (but for three issues), the Royal Empire Society, the School of Oriental and African Studies, the University of London Library, the Bodleian and the University Library, Cambridge. Bedford College Library, London, possesses a set complete except for one volume.

Bankers Almanac. The Institute of Bankers possesses a complete set; the University Library, Cambridge, contains a set from 1845.

British Almanac and Companion and the *Royal Calendar.* Good runs are available in the University Library, Cambridge (from 1767 and 1828 respectively) and in the Institute of Historical Research.

British Imperial Calendar and Civil Service List. Sets are in the Colonial Office Library and the Bodleian. The University Library, Cambridge, possesses a set from 1847 with a few gaps. The London School of Economics library has a set from 1810 (with gaps). The University of London Library has a complete set from 1947 with a few earlier issues. Issues from 1951 are in the Institute of Commonwealth Studies.

Colonial Office List, Dominions Office and Commonwealth Relations Office List. Complete sets are to be found in the Colonial Office Library, the University Library, Cambridge, and Rhodes House library, Oxford. Good runs are available in the University of London Library, the London School of Economics library and the Royal Empire Society. Various issues from 1879 and from 1948 onwards are in the Institute of Commonwealth Studies.

India Office List. Complete sets are in the India Office Library (where the earlier list, the *Indian Register*, is also available), the Bodleian and the University Library, Cambridge (which also possesses earlier and similar lists, namely, the *Indian List, Civil and Military*, 1877–95, the *Indian Army and Civil Service List*, 1861–76, and the *East India Register*, 1806–60, with some gaps). India House Library possesses a set from 1826, with some gaps in earlier years. Good runs are also in the University of London Library and the Institute of Historical Research.

Statesman's Year Book. Complete sets are in the London School of Economics library, the Bodleian and the University Library, Cambridge. Good runs are available in the University of London Library, the Institute of Historical Research, the Royal Empire Society, the Westminster Reference Library and Rhodes House library, Oxford.

Stock Exchange List. A complete set from 1889 is in the Guildhall Library.

Whitaker's Almanack. Complete sets are available in the University of London Library, the Royal Empire Society and the Bodleian. Good runs are also in the London School of Economics library (from 1869), the Colonial Office Library (from 1870), the Institute of Historical Research, the Westminster Reference Library, the University Library, Cambridge, and Rhodes House library, Oxford.

Who was Who and *Who's Who.* Complete sets are to be found in the University of London Library, the London School of Economics library, the Royal Empire Society, the Bodleian and the University Library, Cambridge. Runs are also available in the Institute of Commonwealth Studies and the Westminster Reference Library.

Bibliographies of Reference Works

Information on reference books in general is to be found in the following works:

Besterman (T.). *British sources of reference and information: a guide to societies, works of reference and libraries.* London, 1947.

Cape Town, University. School of Librarianship, Booklist series No. 1: *Guide to South African Reference Books.* R. Musiker, comp. Cape Town, 1955.

Elahi (K. N.), Moid (A.) and Siddiqui (A. H.). *Guide to works of Reference published in Pakistan.* Karachi, 1953.

Garde (P. K.). *Directory of reference works published in Asia.* (Unesco.) Paris, 1956.

Harris (J.). *Guide to New Zealand reference material and other sources of information.* 2nd edn, Wellington, 1950; supplement, 1951.

Henderson (G. P.), comp. *Reference manual of directories*: an annotated list, index and guide to the directories of all countries. London, 1957 in progress. [To be published in parts and will include Canada (pt. 7), the Middle East (pt. 10),

India, Pakistan, Burma, Ceylon (pt. 11), the Far East (pt. 12), Africa (pt. 13), and Australasia (pt. 14). Australasia, was published 1957.]

Minto (J.). *Reference books.* 2 vols., London, 1929–31. [Although nearly thirty years old it is still of value. A new guide to succeed Minto is in preparation by the Library Association, under the editorship of Dr. A. J. Walford.]

Roberts (A. D.). *Guide to reference books.* New edn, London, 1956.

South African Library. *Classified list of South African annual publications as at Mar. 31, 1951.* (Grey Bibliographies No. 4.) Cape Town, 1951.

Walford (A. J.). *Union list of reference books.* London, 1954. [Compiled for the use of students of librarianship, but valuable to research workers in locating 400 works of reference in some Greater London libraries. A new edition is in preparation.]

Winchell (C. M.). *Guide to reference works.* Chicago, 1951; Supplements, Chicago, 1954, 1956. [A standard work covering the whole world; it gives information on guides and manuals, bibliographies, indexes and abstracts, encyclopaedias, handbooks, dictionaries of special terms, annuals and directories, histories, biographical works, atlases and serial publications.]

Select Bibliography of Biographical Works

GENERAL

Chambers' *Biographical dictionary.* London, 1949.

Colonial Office Lists. London.

Commonwealth Relations Office Lists. London.

Dictionary of National Biography. London.

International Who's Who. London.

International Year-book and Statesman's Who's Who. London.

Men of the Reign—a biographical dictionary of eminent persons of British and Colonial birth, who have died during the reign of Queen Victoria. T. H. Ward, ed. London, 1885.

Men of the Time—biographical sketches of eminent living characters. Various issues. London, 1856–99.

Who was Who. London.

Who's Who. London.

World Biography. New York.

AFRICA

Central and East African Who's Who for 1956. Salisbury, S. Rhodesia, 1956.

Hill (R.). *Biographical Dictionary of the Anglo-Egyptian Sudan.* Oxford, 1951.

Men of the Times: Old Colonists of the Cape Colony and Orange River Colony. Johannesburg, 1906.

Men of the Times: Pioneers of the Transvaal and glimpses of South Africa. Johannesburg, 1905.

South African Who's Who, 1956. Johannesburg.

Who's Who in Nigeria: a biographical dictionary. Lagos, 1956.

Year Book and Guide to the Rhodesias and Nyasaland. Annually, Salisbury, S. Rhodesia.

[Biographical collections in Afrikaans are noted in the *Guide to South African Reference Books* (University of Cape Town, School of Librarianship, Booklist series No. 1.) Cape Town, 1955.]

AUSTRALIA

Australian Encyclopaedia, 2 vols., Sydney, 1926–7. [Contains biographies.]
Heaton (Sir J. H.). *Australian dictionary of dates and Men of the time.* Sydney, 1879.
Humphreys (H. R. M.). *Men of the time in Australia.* Melbourne, 1882.
Johns (F.). *Australian biographical dictionary.* Adelaide, 1934.
Johns (F.). *Notable Australians, who they are and what they do.* Melbourne, 1906.
Mennell (P.). *Dictionary of Australasian Biography.* London, 1892.
Serle (P.). *Dictionary of Australian Biography,* 2 vols., Sydney, 1949.
Who's Who in Australia, 1955. J. A. Alexander, ed. Melbourne.

CANADA

Canadian Who's Who. Toronto, 1954.
Encyclopaedia of Canada. W. S. Wallace, ed. 6 vols., Toronto, 1935–7. [Contains
    biographies; a new edition is in preparation.]
Les Biographies Françaises d'Amerique. Sherbrooke, Que., 1950.
Morgan (H. J.). *Canadian men and women of the time.* Toronto, 1912.
Morice (A. G.). *Dictionnaire historique des Canadiens.* Quebec, 1908.
Newfoundland Who's Who. St. John's, 1952.
Standard Dictionary of Biography. C. G. D. Roberts and A. L. Tunnell, eds. 2 vols.,
    Toronto, 1934–8.
Wallace (W. S.). *Dictionary of Canadian Biography.* 2 vols., Toronto, 1945.
Who's Who in Canada. B. M. Greene, ed. Toronto, 1954.

HONG KONG

Asia Who's Who. Hong Kong, 1957.

INDIA AND PAKISTAN

Asia Who's Who. Hong Kong, 1957.
Buckland (C. E.). *Dictionary of Indian Biography.* London, 1906.
Government of India. *House of the People [Lok Sabha] Who's Who.* New Delhi,
    1952.
India and Pakistan Year-book and Who's Who. Bombay, 1951. [Superseded by the
    Times of India Directory and Year-book and Who's Who, which does not now in-
    clude Pakistan.]
India Office Lists, to 1947. London.
Indian Who's Who, 1937–8. Bombay. [Includes a separate section on the Rulers of
    the Princely States.]
Lethbridge (Sir R.). *Golden Book of India.* London, 1900.
Parliament of India. *Rajya Sabha [Council of States] Who's Who.* New Delhi, 1955.
Peters' *Who's Who in India, Burma and Ceylon.* Poona, 1938.
Rao (C. H.). *Indian Biographical Dictionary.* Madras [1915?].
Times of India Directory and Year-book and Who's Who, 1956–57. Bombay, 1957.
Who's Who in India. Lucknow, 1911–14.
Year Book and Who's Who. Lahore, 1951.
Yearbook, Who's Who and Directory. Karachi, 1950.

MALAYA

Leaders of Malaya and Who's Who, 1956. J. V. Morais, ed. Kuala Lumpur, 1956.

MAURITIUS

Dictionary of Mauritian Biography. Port Louis, 1941 in progress.

NEW ZEALAND

Mennell (P.). *Dictionary of Australasian Biography.* London, 1892.
Scholefield (G. H.). *Dictionary of New Zealand Biography.* 2 vols., Wellington, 1940.
Who's Who in New Zealand. 6th edn. F. A. Simpson, ed. Wellington, 1956.

WEST INDIES

Advocates Year-book and Who's Who. Bridgetown, 1951.
British Caribbean: Who, What, Why. Glasgow, [1956].
Trinidad: Who, What, Why. Port of Spain, 1950.
Who is Who in British Guiana. 4th edn, 1945–8. Georgetown, 1948.
Who's Who, Jamaica, 1954. Kingston, Jamaica.

Part II

INDIVIDUAL COLLECTIONS

I. COLLECTIONS IN LONDON

The Admiralty
Archway (Block South), Whitehall, S.W.1

The Admiralty library contains more than 140,000 volumes mainly devoted to naval history and science, together with some 80,000 to 100,000 maps, charts and atlases. Its manuscript collection is small as most of its papers have been deposited with the Public Record Office, the British Museum and the National Maritime Museum at Greenwich which possesses an immense collection of original papers. The library does, however, possess some original documents relating to early voyages of discovery and exploration sponsored by the Royal Navy.

The value of the library to the Commonwealth research worker lies in its collections of material relating to naval and imperial history and events in which the Royal Navy has participated, the slave trade and its suppression, and voyages and travels. Its collection of nautical surveys and maps is unique. It also possesses sets of the *Navy List* since 1814 (and some of its predecessors) to date and of the publications of the Navy Record Society.

Information is being assembled on the location of collections of naval papers in private hands.

Accredited research workers may be granted access to the library on prior application in writing addressed to the Archivist. It is open from 10.0 a.m. until 5.0 p.m., Monday to Friday, and from 10.0 a.m. until 12.30 p.m. on Saturdays.

The Hydrographic Department, Oxgate Lane, Cricklewood, N.W.2, also possesses a very large number of surveys and maps and an historic collection of original charts covering the sixteenth to the nineteenth centuries.

Alberta
Office of the Agent-General in London
Alberta House, 37 Hill Street, W.1

A small general library is maintained. It contains a selection of Government departmental reports, the Government Gazette and Statutes since 1948. Efforts will be made to secure earlier material when required by research workers.

Aluminium Development Association
33 Grosvenor Street, W.1

The Association's library contains approximately 1,500 books and many thousands of pamphlets devoted to aluminium and metallurgy in general as well as on bauxite deposits. It also subscribes to 175 current periodicals to which a consolidated index of articles relating to aluminium is maintained.

The library is open to research workers from 9.30 a.m. to 5.30 p.m., Monday to Friday.

Anti-slavery and Aborigines Protection Society
Denison House, 296 Vauxhall Bridge Road, S.W.1

The Society's library consists of approximately 1,350 volumes dealing with slavery and native races and allied subjects throughout the world.

The library is intended for the use of members but non-members are permitted access on personal application.

The Society's Archives are deposited in Rhodes House, Oxford, see p. 168.

Aslib
(Association of Special Libraries and Information Bureaux)
4 Palace Gate, W.8

This organization exists to facilitate co-operation among, and systematic use of, sources of knowledge and information in industry and commerce and in the arts and sciences and to promote the development of special libraries and information departments. Services are normally restricted to members but individual enquirers may obtain assistance through member institutions.

It maintains the British copy of the Commonwealth Index to unpublished Scientific and Technical translations as well as a panel of specialist translators and indexers. A document reproduction service will supply microfilms and photocopies of published material. It will also undertake the location of publications, documents and papers.

A *Journal of Documentation* is published quarterly and a classified list of university theses annually; a new and enlarged edition of the *Aslib Directory of Sources of Information* is in course of preparation.

Australia
Office of the High Commissioner
Australia House, Strand, W.C.2

The Australian Reference library at Australia House contains some

5,000 volumes about Australia or by Australians, including history and law, of which there is a good representative collection, as well as pamphlets, press cuttings and other material. In addition it contains sets of Official reports, Parliamentary Papers, Debates and Gazettes of the Commonwealth of Australia complete from 1901. Many State reports are currently available but are retained for two years only. The collection of current statistical material is particularly valuable—a *List of Sources* of statistical information covering Australia and its Territories is issued by the library from time to time. Periodicals and other serial publications in many fields are received but they are, generally, retained for two years only; a few Australian periodicals of permanent value are retained, e.g. the *Australian Quarterly* has been bound and is available from 1935. Works of reference are abundant. A *List* of periodical and serial publications and reference works in the library has been issued.

The *Melbourne Herald* and the *Sydney Morning Herald* are regularly taken; the former is retained for approximately two months but the latter has been bound and kept for permanent reference since 1912—the Index is also available from 1927.

The map collection contains a selection of general and special maps, including the Australian Geographical Series (in progress) and the Australian Aeronautical Series, together with a selection of State maps.

The library is open to all readers without restriction from 9.0 a.m. until 5.15 p.m. daily, and from 9.0 a.m. until 12.0 noon on Saturdays; it is closed on British and Australian public holidays.

Baptist Missionary Society
93 Gloucester Place, W.1

The archives and library of the Society suffered some damage during the late war and the collections are not at present accessible. Restoration work is going forward and it is expected that they will again be available to research workers in the near future.

Bedford College
(University of London)
Regent's Park, N.W.1

The College library contains some 110,000 books, pamphlets and volumes of periodicals. In addition to serving the needs of undergraduates it includes material useful for post-graduate research workers in the faculties of arts and science. The collections in the fields of history, geography, sociology, social science and economics contain much of Commonwealth interest. Current periodicals number some 535 series,

Commonwealth geographical journals being particularly well represented.

United Kingdom Parliamentary papers are taken in the library selectively. Some Parliamentary debates and Journals of both Houses of Parliament are also available but the sets are incomplete. Calendars of State Papers are almost complete. It possesses good runs of British and Foreign State Papers, a set of Hertslet's treaties and, except for one year, a set of the Annual Register.

Accredited research workers are admitted to the library between 9 a.m. and 7 p.m., Monday to Friday, and between 9 a.m. and 4 p.m. on Saturdays. (During vacation the hours are shorter.)

Board of Trade
Library: Horse Guards Avenue, London, S.W.1
Statistics Library: Lacon House, Theobalds Road, W.C.1
Export Services Branch: Lacon House, W.C.1

The Board of Trade library contains more than 150,000 books and pamphlets, mainly of current material in the field of the social sciences, with emphasis on trade and economics, and sections devoted to public administration, economic history, labour, and the economic aspects of agriculture, fisheries and forestry. It also possesses a collection of laws of the Commonwealth, consisting of the latest revisions and succeeding sessional volumes.

Official publications of the United Kingdom include a nearly complete set of Parliamentary papers from 1801, a selection of Non-Parliamentary papers within the Library's field of interest, Hansard complete from 1803 (with some earlier material), Journals of the House of Commons complete to date, and Journals of the House of Lords (but with some gaps). Official publications of the Commonwealth are selected according to subject matter. Most Commonwealth Gazettes are available, but they are retained for two years only. Sets of *Official Year Books* of Australia, Canada, New Zealand and South Africa are fairly complete; some of India and Ceylon are also available.

More than 2,300 current periodicals are received by the Library, including many of those published in the Commonwealth within its field. Sets of the *Board of Trade Journal* are complete from 1886. Both the American and Australian *Bulletins of the Public Affairs Information Services* are on the shelves.

The statistics collection is one of the best available. The Statistics Library at Lacon House attempts a complete coverage of statistical publications on trade and production, and material in related fields, for the whole of the Commonwealth (including Colonial Blue Books) from 1929 to date—all the earlier material has been transferred to the British Museum. It also possesses statistical publications issued by the United Nations and its Specialized Agencies, and by other international organizations. Both the Statistics Library and the H.Q. Library hold complete sets of such United Kingdom statistical series as Tables of the Revenue, Annual Statement of Trade, Trade and Navigation Accounts, Annual Abstract of Statistics, Commonwealth Abstract of Statistics, etc.

The Export Services Branch maintains a collection of trade directories, manufacturers' catalogues and telephone directories of the Commonwealth.

The Library is open from 9.0 a.m. until 6.0 p.m., Monday to Friday, and from 9.0 a.m. until noon on Saturdays. Accredited research workers may be admitted on prior application in writing to the Librarian. The Statistics Library and Export Services Branch at Lacon House are open to the public without restriction.

British Columbia
Office of the Agent-General in London
1 Regent Street, S.W.1

British Columbia House possesses a small library of approximately 700 volumes for general reference, consisting mainly of government publications and laws. It has a fine collection of British Columbia Sessional Papers complete from 1876 to date, the Journals of the Legislative Assembly since 1881, a set of the Laws of British Columbia, Public Accounts from 1925, department annual reports since 1949 and vital statistics since 1949. It is particularly strong in material relating to mines and materials, including Annual Reports of the Mines Department since 1911 and Reports of the Geological Survey, and to forestry and fisheries.

The library is available for reference during normal office hours, Monday to Friday.

British Iron and Steel Federation
Steel House, Tothill Street, S.W.1

The library of the Federation contains some 2,800 books, including a number on the mining, processing and economics of iron and steel, about 3,000 pamphlets and 300 current periodicals. It also maintains a union list of periodicals on metallurgy.

Research workers are admitted to the library between 9.30 a.m. and 5.30 p.m., Monday to Friday.

H

British Museum
Great Russell Street, W.C.1

The British Museum contains the national library. Since the middle of the eighteenth century it has enjoyed the right under the Copyright Acts to receive copies of every book published in the United Kingdom and its collection, now numbering between five and six million books, is unrivalled in the country. It is, therefore, quite impossible to attempt to assess the collection under various subject headings. In addition to British material, foreign books, periodicals and newspapers are also purchased in fairly large numbers. For many years the Museum has also regularly purchased a wide selection of Commonwealth material to supplement that received under overseas Copyright legislation. The provisions of the South African Act have been well observed from the beginning. The Canadian Act was observed until it was repealed in 1921 and for two years afterwards. The Indian Books Registration Act conferred the right of selection until 1939, a right which the Museum exercised fairly liberally. In the case of Australia and New Zealand some publishers, although under no statutory obligation, have sent their more important publications to the British Museum which, however, has always set out to purchase works published in these two countries. In Ceylon the law requiring deposit with the British Museum is no longer in force but it still permits the Museum to select material, which is done with regularity. Cyprus, Hong Kong, Malta, Mauritius, Singapore and the Malayan Federation have all been depositing their publications in the Museum for many years, not comprehensively, but in sufficient quantity to ensure useful collections. The position with regard to official publications is quite different. As a result of arrangements made by the Colonial Office, and international exchange agreements between Governments of the Commonwealth, the State Paper room has a fine and comprehensive collection from all parts of the Commonwealth; it is staffed by specialists at the disposition of readers.

Material on India, Pakistan, Ceylon and Burma in oriental languages is housed in the Department of Oriental Books and Manuscripts and consists of approximately 250,000 volumes and 50,000 manuscripts.

MANUSCRIPTS

The Department of Manuscripts contains probably 60,000 volumes in addition to many thousands of Charters and rolls. Material for the history of India includes the Ripon Papers, the Warren Hastings Papers, the Wellesley correspondence and Papers and the Broughton correspondence and Papers. Most of the extant records of British rule in India are in the custody of either the British Museum or the Commonwealth Relations Office, as successor to the India Office. The correspondence of General Haldimand, which includes records of his commands in Canada, and the Khartoum Journal and other papers of General Gordon are also available.

NEWSPAPERS

Newspapers, including Commonwealth papers, published after 1800 are now stored in the Newspaper Library at Colindale to which there is a separate Catalogue. A copy of the Catalogue is also available in the Library of the Institute of Commonwealth Studies. A complete file of *The Times* is available in the Newspaper Library at Colindale; another set, with some imperfections in the early years, is available for consultation at Bloomsbury. No other library attempts to collect newspapers on anything like the same scale.

MAPS

The Museum's very large collection of maps includes official maps issued in the Commonwealth, maps published by the Directorate of Colonial Surveys and maps published by individual Colonial survey departments. The collection is housed in the Map room. Manuscript maps are preserved in the Department of Manuscripts and oriental maps are kept in the Department of Oriental Printed Books.

CATALOGUES

Of the printed Catalogues the early issues may not be of great practical value to the research worker, but the last complete edition commenced publication in 1881 and ended, with a supplement, in 1905. It was issued in 437 parts and represents the contents of the library as at the end of the nineteenth century. (A photo-offset lithographic edition of this Catalogue was issued by Edwards Bros. of Ann Arbor, Michigan, in 1946.) A new edition is in course of publication, the first volume appeared in 1931 and at the present time has reached the letter D (Vol. 51, to 'Dez', 1954). A completely new work, however, is proposed consisting of approximately 300 volumes. The 51 volumes of the edition already issued will be brought up to date and re-issued after the remainder of the new catalogue has been published.

Printed subject indexes have been issued since 1902 covering the periods 1881–1900, 1901–5, 1906–10, 1911–15, 1914–18 (works on the Great War), 1916–20, 1921–5, 1926–30, 1931–5, 1936–40, and 1941–5.

Catalogues of books and manuscripts and of oriental books and manuscripts have been published over a long period; information concerning them is to be found in three papers originally contributed to the *Journal of Documentation* but available from the Museum as reprints in pamphlet form. They are:

The Catalogues of the British Museum: printed books, by F. C. Francis, 1948.

The Catalogues of the Manuscript collections, by T. C. Skeat, 1951.

The Catalogues of the Oriental printed books and manuscripts, by F. C. Francis, 1951.

The Catalogues are also mentioned individually in the appropriate chapters in Esdaile's work, referred to below.

ADMISSION AND USE

A collection of reference works and certain sets of learned periodicals is on open access in the Reading Rooms, otherwise requests for all books and periodicals must be made on printed forms provided for the purpose and handed in to the staff on duty in the Reading Room.

The main purpose of the British Museum library is to provide material for research and reference *not readily available in other libraries* normally accessible to readers who are recommended to try other sources before seeking admission to the Museum. Admission is by ticket only. Tickets are of two kinds; long-period, valid in the first instance for a period not exceeding one year, but normally renewable; and short-period, valid for a period not exceeding three days. Application for long-period tickets must be made in writing to the Director, giving full name and permanent address and stating the specific purpose for which the application is made, adding particulars necessary to show that the use of the Reading Room is required for research. Applications should be accompanied by a written recommendation from a person of recognized position based upon personal knowledge of the applicant and certifying that he or she is a fit and proper person to use the Reading Room. Applications from students attending a university or other educational institution must be accompanied by a recommendation from a member of staff of the institution who can certify that the applicant is an advanced student who needs to make use of the resources of the library. (Recommendations from hotel keepers, etc., are not accepted.) Short-period tickets are intended for persons desiring to make only temporary use of the Reading Room and they may be obtained either on personal application at the Museum or on written application to the Director. Applicants must state the purpose for which they seek admission and give a permanent address. A written recommendation may also be required. Printed forms of application are available.

The Library is open every week-day including bank holidays (except Good Friday, Christmas Day, and the week beginning with the first Monday in May) from 9 a.m. to 5 p.m.

Much has been written on the British Museum and its Library but one of the most recent and useful reference works is *The British Museum Library*, by Arundell Esdaile (Allen and Unwin), 1946. See also Rye's *Guide* and *The Libraries of London* (ed. Irwin), 1949, ch. I, referred to at pp. 5, 6.

British Non-ferrous Metals Research Association
81–91 Euston Road, N.W.1

The Association maintains a library containing some 5,000 volumes, over 30,000 pamphlets and 300 current periodicals covering all aspects of non-ferrous metallurgy. The library serves the member companies of the Association and Government departments but it may also be used by others by special arrangement (either by letter or telephone).

Canada
Office of the High Commissioner
Canada House, Trafalgar Square, S.W.1

The library of Canada House contains some 2,000 volumes. In addition to official publications it contains works on most aspects of Canadian life—history, political science, constitutional history, Canada international affairs and economics. There are also small sections on literature, the fine arts, description and travel and biography. Official publications include departmental reports, most of which commence between 1935 and 1940; Reports of the Department of External Affairs from 1927; Public Accounts from 1927; publications of the Dominion Bureau of Statistics from the 1940's; Canadian Treaty series complete from 1933; Canada Gazette and Canadian Labour Gazette, both from 1930; Debates and Journals of the House of Commons complete from 1879 and 1916 respectively; Debates and Journals of the Senate from 1876 and 1924 respectively (with some gaps); and Reports of Committees of the Senate complete from 1945, Gazettes of New Brunswick, Nova Scotia, Prince Edward Island and Quebec are available for one year. Collections of statutes include the Revised Statutes of Canada and sessional volumes from 1907, together with revised editions of Provincial statutes and sessional volumes from varying dates. Geological Survey maps (and some others) of Canada are also available.

Works of reference are particularly well represented; the collection includes the *Canadian Almanac* and *Legal and Court Directory* from 1849 to date; the *Year Book and Almanac of Canada*, 1870–9; the *Dominion Annual Register*, 1878–86; the *Canadian Annual Review of Public Affairs*, 1902–38; the *Canada Year Book* from 1905 to date; and the *Canada Who's Who*, 1936/37 to date, together with some other early and current specialist directories.

The Library also possesses a large and miscellaneous collection of papers and pamphlets on many subjects, maintained in filing cabinets. A file of bibliographies compiled by the Librarian is maintained for reference. The more important Canadian daily newspapers are available for two or three months, although the Montreal and Toronto papers are kept for longer periods. Files of the Financial Post and the Montreal Gazette are retained for permanent reference from 1946.

The Library endeavours to cater for those Provinces not represented in London, namely, New Brunswick, Newfoundland, Nova Scotia, Prince Edward Island and Quebec. (*See also under* Alberta, British Columbia, Manitoba, Ontario and Saskatchewan (Offices of the Agents-General).)

The Library is open to the public between the hours of 9.30 a.m. and 5.30 p.m. daily, except Saturdays.

Ceylon
Office of the High Commissioner in London:
13 Hyde Park Gardens, W.2

A small library is maintained containing some 300 works on history, constitutional development and law of Ceylon. The historical section is particularly valuable; it contains works in English and other languages which are not readily available elsewhere. Official publications include debates of the Senate and House of Representatives from 1947 and departmental annual reports from 1950, together with the Ceylon Year Book from 1948. A selection of newspapers is available for about three months.

The Library is open for reference from 9.30 a.m. to 5.0 p.m., Monday to Friday, and from 9.30 a.m. to 12.0 noon on Saturdays.

Ceylon Association in London
2 Crosby Square, E.C.2

The Association maintains a small library of between 400 and 500 books mainly on Ceylon history and on tea and rubber together with some statistical material and works of reference.

A catalogue is included in the Annual Report.

Non-members of the Association are not permitted to borrow books but are admitted to the library on suitable recommendation and applications should be made by letter addressed to the Association.

Chatham House
See Royal Institute of International Affairs, p. 144.

Church Missionary Society
6 Salisbury Square, Fleet Street, E.C.4

The Library of the Society contains some 25,000 volumes. It specializes in material relating to the spread of missionary work and the history of missionary societies in general. Material relating to Africa, India, Pakistan, Ceylon and the Mediterranean and to China and the Middle and Far East is particularly well represented but material on Australia, Canada and New Zealand is scanty. It also possesses a small but valuable collection on slavery and emancipation. Other fields covered are those of history, anthropology, geography, economics, education, current race problems and comparative religion. Biography is well represented. The Library contains complete sets of the scarce *Missionary Register*, 1813–55, the *C.M.S. Intelligencer*, 1850–1906, and the *Church Missionary Review*, 1850–1927 (which incorporates the *Intelligencer*). It also possesses an interesting collection of pamphlets which includes many dealing with historical matters and missionary affairs throughout the Commonwealth.

The Library is open to the public daily from 10.0 a.m. to 12.30 p.m. and from 1.30 p.m. to 5.0 p.m., Saturdays excepted. It is desirable to give notice if an appointment with the Librarian is required. Under certain circumstances books may be borrowed by non-members.

The Society was established in 1799 and its archives from that date until 1914 are available for consultation by accredited research workers. The archives include Minute Books, Incoming Letters, Missionaries' Journals and 'Annual Letters', Outgoing Letters and Mission Books. The latter contain copies of incoming letters, journals and 'annual letters' up to the year 1848; from that date until 1880 brief particulars only are noted but from 1880 until 1934 the entries consist of précis of the various documents. The originals, however, have been retained over the whole period.

Descriptive lists have been prepared of the contents of various volumes of records, boxes of papers, etc., relating to Africa and Mediterranean missions to the year 1880. There are also indexes to the Minutes of the Society and a hand-list of other archives from 1799 to 1880. There is a large number of general papers on miscellaneous matters, together with a few collections of Personal Letters and Papers, including those of Archdeacon Walker (Uganda), Bishop Tucker (India and Dr. Pennell (India). The Society also possesses the Journal of Alexander MacKay, the East African explorer, and Krapf's Journals and sketch maps.

The archives are available for consultation on Mondays, Wednesdays and Fridays between 10.0 a.m. and 4.30 p.m. Prior application for permission to use them should be made by letter.

There is a Photographic Library containing a number of photographs relating to the work and personnel of the Society from 1799 to the present day. The material may be consulted daily, Monday to Friday, between 9.30 a.m. and 5.30 p.m.

Colonial Geological Survey
(Resources Division)
See p. 111.

Colonial Office and Commonwealth Relations Office Libraries
C.O.: 3 Sanctuary Buildings, Great Smith Street, S.W.1
C.R.O.: Downing Street, S.W.1

Although there was a division of business within the Colonial Office to deal with affairs of the Dominions and of the non-self-governing territories before 1907, that year saw the formation of two such main sections. In 1925 a separate Secretaryship of State for Dominions Affairs, with a distinct department, was established which later became the Commonwealth Relations Office. These offices shared a common building until 1947 when the Colonial Office moved to Great Smith Street; its library, however, remained in Downing Street until 1953, the year it moved to Sanctuary Buildings. The Commonwealth Relations Office, Downing Street, possesses a small library of material relating almost exclusively to the self-governing countries of the Commonwealth published after 1925. It includes sets of official publications of those countries, both before and after self-government. The early and modern historical works (except for the period 1920 to 1945 approximately, which was somewhat neglected) on the Empire as a whole and of the dependent territories in particular, together with statistical and descriptive material, are to be found only in the Colonial Office.

The Colonial Office Library has a fine collection of official publications. Except for a few minor gaps it contains complete collections of laws, ordinances, gazettes, legislative debates and journals, blue books, official and departmental reports and sessional papers of the Colonies. Transfers of this material are regularly made to the Public Record Office (where it is available for consultation) about fifteen years in arrears of the current date. Legislative debates and journals, official gazettes, Parliamentary papers (but not the non-Parliamentary series) issued by self-governing countries of the Commonwealth are also available. The law section is particularly good.

Of British official publications the Colonial Office has all those of Commonwealth interest, the numbered series and the annual (administrative) reports on individual Colonies. Most of the official Year Books (Federal, State and Provincial) of the Commonwealth are available; the Australian set is complete but gaps exist in other series.

Periodicals of the Commonwealth are well represented—of the Colonies all official and a wide selection of non-official periodicals are taken; of the self-governing countries a selection only is available. Altogether about 1,500 current serials are received in the Colonial Office Library, most of which are bound and permanently retained. The library is not strong in printed indexes to periodical literature.

Some 190 daily and weekly newspapers are taken; of these the self-governing countries are represented selectively (approximately one from each) but for the Colonies an adequate selection is available. Issues are retained for about three years and then destroyed.

Maps, atlases and gazetteers of the self-governing countries are available to a reasonable extent; of the Colonies, however, all standard maps, etc., including those issued by the Directorate of Colonial Surveys and by local Survey departments are to be found in the library. Early maps and charts have been transferred to the P.R.O. where they may be consulted.

Bibliographies and general works of reference published in or about the various parts of the Commonwealth are well represented, particularly Colonial publications.

No catalogue has been published since 1896 (Supplement, 1907), but there are up-to-date author catalogues and subject indexes maintained in the libraries. A bi-monthly *Selective List of Accessions* (formerly *Digest of books and pamphlets received in the Library*) has been regularly issued in duplicated form since 1946. A Catalogue of maps, etc., was printed in 1910. A particularly valuable note on the Colonial Office and the Commonwealth Relations Office and their libraries, including detailed information on official publications, by A. B. Mitchell, is to be found in *Government Information and the Research Worker* (chapter xxiv), 1952.

The libraries of the Colonial Office and Commonwealth Relations Office are open to the public for reference to published material *not readily available elsewhere*—they are not available as public reference libraries for general use. Application for admission may be made in person to the library staff or by letter addressed to the Librarian. They are open from 9.30 a.m. to 5.30 p.m., Monday to Friday; they do not open on Saturdays.

Colonial Products Laboratory

See p. 111.

Commonwealth Agricultural Bureaux
Farnham House, Farnham Royal, Bucks.

For information as to organization, library facilities and publications see pp. 194–6.

Commonwealth Economic Committee
2 Queen Anne's Gate Buildings, Dartmouth Street, S.W.1

The Library contains nearly 3,000 volumes consisting mainly of Commonwealth statistical material and official reports on trade, agriculture, dairy produce, fruit, sugar, vegetable oils, rubber, grain, wool, jute, cotton, tobacco and other commodities, some from 1934 onwards, with similar material in respect of many foreign countries. The collection of statistical bulletins and abstracts is particularly good although it dates only from 1947/48. Current periodicals and serials number 1,550, many of which are retained for several years. In addition to official publications the Library also possesses a variety of market reports and trade papers.

Accredited research workers are permitted to use the Library, which is open between 10.0 a.m. and 5.0 p.m., Monday to Friday.

Commonwealth Institute of Entomology

See p. 195.

Commonwealth Mycological Institute

See p. 195.

Commonwealth Relations Office
See p. 104.

Cyprus Government Office
15 Victoria Street, S.W.1

A small collection of books of a general nature on Cyprus is maintained. Current government publications, the Official Gazette and the Laws are available but are retained for two to three years only. The library is open to the public from 9.30 a.m. to 1.0 p.m. and from 2.15 to 4.30 p.m., Monday to Friday, and from 9.30 a.m. to 12.0 noon on Saturdays.

East African Office
(East Africa High Commission and Governments of Kenya, Tanganyika, Uganda and Zanzibar)
Grand Buildings, Trafalgar Square, W.C.2

The library contains some 400 volumes of a general nature dealing with East Africa including history, anthropology, ethnography and agriculture as well as works of reference and directories. It also possesses complete collections of official publications of the territories represented; Official Gazettes of Kenya from 1926, of Zanzibar from 1926, of Uganda from 1911 and of Tanganyika from 1921. Debates of Kenya from 1932, of Tanganyika from 1926, of Uganda from 1939 and of Zanzibar from 1929; Statutes of Kenya from 1914, of Tanganyika from 1923, of Uganda from 1951 and of Zanzibar from 1917; the Statistical Bulletin from 1948 and some Blue Books for the period 1914 to 1945 approximately.

The library is open to accredited research workers, on presentation of a letter of introduction, from 10 a.m. to 5 p.m., Monday to Friday, and from 10 a.m. to 12 noon on Saturdays.

Empire Cotton Growing Corporation
12 Chantrey House, Eccleston Street, S.W.1

The Corporation maintains a small library of technical books and pamphlets on cotton growing in Commonwealth and foreign countries. The material includes Agricultural department reports dealing with cotton and other official publications and a file of the *Quarterly Statistical Bulletin* of the International Cotton Advisory Committee, Washington. Not all material going into the Corporation is retained for permanent reference as much of it is sent to the Corporation's Research Station in Uganda. The Library is primarily for the use of the

Corporation's staff but other persons are permitted to use it in certain circumstances. Application for permission should be made by letter addressed to the Secretary.

Empire Forestry Association
Royal Empire Society
Northumberland Avenue, London, W.C.2

The Association maintains a reference library of over 4,000 publications relating to forestry and timber including Commonwealth material, as well as 368 Commonwealth and 272 foreign current periodicals.

The Association publishes the *Empire Forestry Handbook*, the *Empire Forestry Review* (quarterly) and *British Commonwealth Forest Terminology*.

The library is open to accredited research workers from 10 a.m. to 5 p.m., Monday to Friday.

Fabian Colonial Bureau
Fabian Society
11 Dartmouth Street, S.W.1

The Bureau has a small library of approximately 1,500 books and pamphlets mainly in the field of the political and economic sciences. It includes official publications of the United Kingdom dealing with Colonial affairs and similar material issued in Overseas territories from about the year 1939 onwards. Since 1940 the Bureau has assembled a large collection of cuttings from the Colonial press.

The Bureau is extremely limited in working space and staff and does not normally provide facilities for reference to its material by non-members. In special cases, however, by prior appointment, access might be arranged for accredited research workers between 10 a.m. and 5.30 p.m., Monday to Friday only.

Foreign Office
Cornwall House, Stamford Street, S.E.1

The printed library of the Foreign Office contains some 100,000 volumes on international relations and on the diplomatic, political and economic history of individual foreign countries and countries of the Commonwealth, although the latter are not covered quite so well as the former.

It is a closed library and admission by persons not of the Foreign Office can be obtained only by special application addressed to the Librarian. It will, of course, assist research workers wherever possible when material is not available elsewhere. Books are not normally available for loan.

A *Catalogue of Printed Books in the Library* was published in 1926. Weekly Accessions Lists are issued.

Forestry Commission
Forest Research Station
Alice Holt Lodge, Wrecclesham, Farnham, Surrey

The Commission maintains a library of some 3,750 volumes and 150 current periodicals mainly relating to the United Kingdom but also containing some material of Commonwealth interest. The library is open to research workers from 9 a.m. to 5 p.m., Monday to Friday, and from 9 a.m. to 12 noon on Saturdays but previous notice must be given to the Librarian by persons wishing to avail themselves of the privilege of using it.

Guildhall Library
(City of London)
Guildhall, E.C.2

The library of the Guildhall contains approximately 120,000 volumes. It is the public reference library for the City and, as such, possesses good collections of works on history, economics, commerce, industry and law as well as on other subjects. Its value to the Commonwealth research worker lies not only in its sets of official publications and general works of reference but in its London collection.

The collection of parliamentary papers is complete from 1835 to date but it also has an extensive selection of earlier House of Commons papers. It also possesses sets of the Debates and Journals of both Houses of Parliament, the *London Gazette* from the first issue in 1665 and the *Calendars of State Papers*. A set of the *Stock Exchange List* is complete from 1889. Current issues of official and unofficial year books and digests of statistics from all parts of the Commonwealth are available as well as the Official Year-books of Australia, Canada, New Zealand and South Africa (Federal, State and Provincial). For the Commonwealth and foreign countries its collection of commercial and trade directories, handbooks, guides, Who's Who, specialist directories and lists, local directories, telephone directories and time-tables is unrivalled in the country.

In addition to daily British newspapers, the more important of those published in the Commonwealth are available (some being received by air mail)—they are normally retained for varying periods from six weeks to three years. Files of *The Times* are kept from 1806, and of the *Financial Times* from 1921, as well as extensive files of nineteenth century, and later, periodicals and newspapers. The library also possesses an interesting collection of seventeenth-century newspapers.

The collection of trade, financial and professional periodicals (British and some overseas) is vast, most of which, however, are retained only for limited periods, some up to three years. Amongst those kept permanently are the *Board of Trade Journal* (from 1927), the *Economic Journal* (from 1891, with some gaps), the *Economist* (from 1848, with some gaps), the *Ministry of Labour Gazette* (from 1893) and the *Statist* (from 1920).

The Library contains parish, ward and diocesan records and the archives of most of the City livery companies. The records of the New England Company are complete from 1650 to 1941 and the collection of business and trading company records includes a few papers of the South Sea, East India and Canada Companies. In addition it possesses the papers of Thomas Bowrey (1650–1713), sea captain and merchant, dealing, *inter alia*, with trading in the East Indies and the South Seas. Some City firms and insurance companies have also deposited their early business papers in the Muniment Room.

In the Guildhall Records Office are preserved records originating in the business of the Corporation of the City—charters, administrative records, judicial records and financial records.

The Guildhall Library is open daily from Monday to Saturday inclusive from 9.30 a.m. until 5 p.m. Admission is unrestricted. Books are lent only through the National Central Library to other libraries.

Information regarding the contents of the Library is available in the following:

Guildhall *Library Bulletin*, issued about three times a year.
Guildhall *Miscellany*, twice yearly.
Handlist of seventeenth century newspapers, Feb. 1954.
List of the British and Oversea Newspapers in the Commercial Reference Room, June 1954.
List of the Trade, Financial and Professional Periodicals in the Commercial Reference Room, Nov. 1954.
The C.R.R. Courier (containing particulars of directories and other reference works added to the stock), issued about six times a year.
Jones (P. E.) and Smith (Raymond). *A guide to the records at Guildhall London*, London (English Universities Press), 1951.
The Libraries of London (ed. Irwin), 1949, ch. xv.

House of Commons
Houses of Parliament
S.W.1

The Library of the House of Commons contains about 100,000 volumes. It is not open to the public. Under exceptional circumstances accredited research workers may be admitted and applications should be submitted in writing addressed to the Librarian.

Further information may be obtained from *The Libraries of London* (ed. Irwin), 1949, ch. vii (The House of Commons Library, by N. W. Wilding) although it is somewhat out of date.

House of Lords Record Office
See p. 10.

Imperial Institute
(Colonial Office: Libraries of the Colonial Products Laboratory and the Mineral Resources Division of the Colonial Geological Survey)
Imperial Institute Road, South Kensington, S.W.7

For convenience the library is still known as the Imperial Institute library but it was, in fact, taken over by the Secretary of State for the Colonies in 1949 when he assumed responsibility for the scientific and technical activities of the Institute. It is a joint library shared by the Colonial Products Laboratory and the Mineral Resources Division but, in the near future, it will be physically divided between these two bodies.

The Library, as it is now constituted, contains over 150,000 items exclusive of periodical literature. Special attention has been paid to the assembly of material relating to tropical agriculture, forestry, mineral resources and the production and utilization of raw materials. In addition to a comprehensive collection of Commonwealth Official Publications, it possesses an outstanding series of publications issued by the United States Department of Agriculture and the United States Department of the Interior.

The Library has a world coverage of periodicals in its particular fields, including the most important Commonwealth series. Altogether some 1,200 periodicals are available.

In addition to the normal library catalogues both the Mineral Resources Division and the Colonial Products Laboratory maintain vast indexes to periodical literature in the Library but these are not available for consultation by the public.

The Library is open from 10 a.m. to 5 p.m. from Monday to Friday. Every facility for borrowing is available to government departments, public corporations, research institutions and academic bodies. Books are not available for loan to individuals.

Imperial War Museum
Lambeth Road, S.E.1

The Imperial War Museum Library contains over 70,000 books and pamphlets and receives over 300 current periodicals devoted to all aspects and effects of the two great wars and the naval, military and air operations since 1914 in which the British Commonwealth and Empire Forces have been engaged. The collection of regimental and ships' histories however date from a much earlier period. It includes material relating to the Armed Forces, the social, political and economic life of the Commonwealth countries and also many hundreds of wartime magazines, service journals and newsletters.

The Photographic Library contains over 3,000,000 photographs covering the same period and aspects as the Library. A very large collection of maps and air photographs is also available.

The Reference sections are open between 10 a.m. and 5 p.m. on Monday to Friday.

India
Office of the High Commissioner
India House, Aldwych, W.C.2

The Library at India House came into existence, with the High Commissioner's Office, in 1920. From then until August, 1947, it received a copy of all English language publications of the Central and Provincial Governments in India (including Burma to 1940 and the area which later became Pakistan to 1947). It also received copies of all British official publications relating to India and it purchased the most important of commercially published works in the country. Since partition and independence publications of the Central Government and Part A States (i.e. the former Provinces) have been received but few only from Part B and C States (i.e. the former Princely States and Estates). Books published in the U.K. and in India continue to be added with a greater proportion from India than was the case before 1947. In this way some 70,000 volumes have been collected, the main emphasis being in the field of sociology, especially economics, although agriculture, forestry and history are also well represented.

Important sets available include the proceedings of the Legislative

Council of India and its successors from 1854 to date, the Gazette of India from 1920, Central and Provincial/State Acts, censuses, trade returns and statistical abstracts. Most of the District Gazetteers are also available as well as many thousands of Survey of India Maps and special maps of India.

The *Eastern Economist* from vol. iii (1946) and the *Reserve Bank of India Bulletin* from vol. i (1947) are two of the unofficial journals which are filed. Current Indian newspapers (in the English language) are available in the Reading Room; they are retained only for a few weeks. A good selection of general works of reference is regularly acquired.

A *Short Catalogue* of India House Library, arranged under classes, was published in 1933. Monthly accession lists are issued (gratis).

The Library is open to everyone without restriction both for reference purposes and borrowing, on personal application to the Librarian. It is open from 9 a.m. to 5.30 p.m. on Mondays to Thursdays, and from 9 a.m. to 5 p.m. on Fridays (it is closed on Saturdays).

India Office Library
(Commonwealth Relations Office)
King Charles Street, S.W.1

The India Office Library was established in 1801 by the East India Company and in 1858 it came under the administration of the newly created India Office. That Office was abolished in 1947 but the Library has retained its name, so well established, although it is now under the control of the Secretary of State for Commonwealth Relations. It possesses more than a quarter of a million printed books of which about 75,000 are in English and other European languages and which form probably the largest collection of books on Indian studies. The scope of the Library may be described as Indological; its sources cover every aspect of India, Pakistan, Burma and neighbouring countries. It may be mentioned that the Library today acquires little material in the natural sciences.

The Library possesses about 1,500 periodicals of which some 350 Indian and oriental series are current. A list of current periodicals and other serials issued annually, and a detailed catalogue of all holdings, both current and those which have ceased publication, is being compiled for publication. Indian newspapers in the English language are particularly well represented, including some of the eighteenth and nineteenth centuries. Files are kept for permanent reference.

All standard British, Indian and Pakistani works of reference and bibliographies are available, including a complete set of the *India Office*

I

List and of its predecessor the *India Register*. A set of the *Quarterly Catalogues* of publications registered in the various Provinces of British India since 1867, constituting in effect a 'national bibliography' of India since that year, is maintained. Since 1947 these Catalogues have been issued only for certain territories.

The Library's manuscript collections are particularly valuable. Manuscripts in English and other European languages number perhaps 10,000; of manuscripts in oriental languages there are some 20,000. Numerous catalogues of manuscripts have been published; others are in preparation. The manuscripts in each oriental language are classed as one unit, with its own catalogue. The European manuscripts form a separate unit, also with its own catalogue. A handlist of the principal manuscript collections, both oriental and European, is to be found in Sutton's *Guide*, which also records published catalogues. Manuscript accessions are constantly received, particulars of which are recorded in the Librarian's *Annual Reports*. The European manuscripts include many large collections of value in historical research. Such collections as were received before 1938 are fully described in the five printed volumes of the Library's *Catalogue of European Manuscripts*. The more notable collections acquired since that date are as follows:

Bell. Papers relating to Tibet collected by Sir Charles Bell (1870–1945).
Nicholson. Letters of John Nicholson and other prominent British officials and
    soldiers in India during the Mutiny period.
Ampthill. Papers relating to Lord Ampthill's period of office as Governor of Madras
    (1900–6) and Governor-General of India (1904).
Lawrence. Papers of Sir Henry Montgomery Lawrence (1806–57).
Clerk. Correspondence of Sir George Russell Clerk (1800–89).
Hamilton. Correspondence of Lord George Hamilton, Secretary of State for India
    in Council, 1895–1903, with the Viceroys of India.
Fergusson. Correspondence of Sir James Fergusson of Kilkerran as Governor of
    Bombay, 1880–5.
Clive. Papers of Robert, first Baron Clive (1725–74).
Halifax. Papers of Sir Charles Wood, first Viscount Halifax, as President of the
    Board of Control, 1852–5, and Secretary of State for India in Council, 1859–66.
Lytton. Papers of the first Earl of Lytton as Viceroy of India, 1876–80.
Elgin. Papers of the eighth Earl of Elgin as Viceroy and Governor-General of India
    1862–3, and of the ninth Earl as Viceroy and Governor-General, 1894–9.

Other collections include the papers collected by Col. Colin Mackenzie (1753?–1821) dealing with Java and the Dutch East Indies and with the history, literature and antiquities of South India, and letters and papers of Sir Thomas Stamford Raffles relating mainly to Java and Malaya.

In 1950 the Library embarked on a project for microfilming all its unique, rare and important manuscripts. Up to the end of March 1956,

2,502 manuscripts and many hundreds of manuscript fragments had been filmed.

Other material in the Library includes drawings, photographs, prints, gramophone records, slides, coins and textile specimens.

The Indian Records Section of the Commonwealth Relations Office contains the official records of the East India Company from 1600 to 1858, of the Board of Control (the 'India Board') from 1784 to 1858 and of the Secretary of State for India from 1858 to 1947. Records after 1902 are not available for consultation. The remainder are in the custody of the Librarian of the India Office Library, and may be consulted in the Library's Reading Room. Sir W. Foster's *Guide to the India Office Records*, 1919, covers the East India Company; there are also various lists of the India Office records. The Indian Records Section also has a virtually complete collection of the official publications of the Indian Central Provincial and State governments down to 1947. Since that date every effort has been made to acquire such publications, as well as those of Pakistan, but not all have so far been secured. The collection includes departmental reports, returns, statistics, reports of Royal Commissions and Committees, Official gazettes, debates and journals. The Library itself also possesses a large collection of such publications but those not filed in the Library may be obtained from the Records Section for consultation in the Library Reading Room. A collection of some 5,000 Indian maps is also housed in the Section; the collection, however, is not kept up to date.

Information on the Library and its resources is to be found in *The Library of the India Office: a historical sketch* by A. J. Arberry, 1938; *A Guide to the India Office Library* by S. C. Sutton, 1952; and in a leaflet, available on application to the Librarian, entitled *The India Office Library: its functions, scope and resources*.

The Library may be used by certain officials, listed in the Library *Rules*, and by readers recommended to the Secretary of State by persons of recognized position. Applications should, in the first instance, be addressed to the Librarian. It is open daily from 9.30 a.m. to 6 p.m., except on Saturdays when it is closed at 1 p.m. Books are available on loan but no person may have more than eight volumes on loan at one time.

Indian Jute Mills Association
Baltic House, Leadenhall Street, E.C.3

The London Office of the Association possesses a small library of approximately 300 volumes devoted mainly to the growing, processing and economics of jute and other fibres together with statistical material on the subject. Some 2,000 periodicals are taken annually but only a few are retained for permanent reference. A long run of the Association's Annual Reports is also available.

Accredited research workers are permitted to use the library between the hours of 10 a.m. and 5 p.m., Monday to Friday. Applications for admission should be addressed to the Association's Representative in the U.K., at the above address.

Institute of Advanced Legal Studies
(University of London)
25 Russell Square, W.C.1

The library of the Institute contains some 47,000 volumes devoted to the law of the United Kingdom, the Commonwealth, the United States and other foreign countries as well as to Public and Private International law. The Nuffield Library of Commonwealth Law contains a comprehensive holding for all parts of the Commonwealth (other than India and Pakistan) consisting of statutes (consolidations, annual volumes and subsidiary legislation), law reports, digests of cases, legal encyclopaedias, treatises and legal periodicals. A selective policy has to some extent been followed in building up the collection and, in addition to basic series, priority has been given to material not readily available elsewhere in London. Subscriptions to all important series are now maintained currently and good progress has been made in obtaining the majority of earlier volumes.

The Institute collects from British universities particulars of legal research being currently undertaken, as well as abstracts of approved theses and dissertations. A list of topics approved over the period 1935 to 1954 has been published and an annual list of topics in progress is issued. Information is kept up to date on cards.

The Institute has compiled and published several union catalogues of material available in libraries in London, Oxford and Cambridge and elsewhere. To date catalogues issued include the following:

Survey of legal periodicals; union catalogue of holdings in British libraries, 2nd edn. 1957.
Union list of Commonwealth law literature in libraries of Oxford, Cambridge and London. 1952. [Includes statutes, reports, digests and treatises.]

The information in these publications is kept up to date in the library.

A *Readers' Guide* to the library has been issued, 1955 (reprinted June, 1956).

The library is open from 10 a.m. until 8 p.m. (Fridays 6 p.m., Saturdays 12.30 p.m.) in term; there are some variations in vacations. Admission may be granted without fee to teachers of law in Universities and University Colleges of the Commonwealth, postgraduate students engaged on approved research and other persons by permission of the Director. Applications for admission should be addressed to the Secretary and Librarian.

Institute of Bankers
10 Lombard Street, E.C.3

The Library of the Institute contains some 36,000 books on banking, economics, finance, law, current affairs and economic conditions in about sixty Commonwealth and foreign countries. There are over 600 periodicals, commercial reports, returns and market circulars available together with a representative collection of Parliamentary papers on commerce, economics and finance from the beginning of the nineteenth century. Bulletins and other publications of central banking institutions of Commonwealth countries are complete. There is also a good collection of reference works including the *Annual Register* from 1758 to date and the Bankers' *Almanac* from the first issue. Catalogues of banking and central bank reports, of periodicals, proceedings and reports of organizations and of Parliamentary papers have been compiled and issued. A card-index of periodical articles is maintained.

Advanced students and research workers may use the Library on suitable recommendation. Application should be made to the Librarian. The Library is open daily from 9 a.m. until 5 p.m., Saturdays from 9 a.m. until 12 noon. Books are not available on loan to non-members.

Institute of Commonwealth Studies
(University of London)
27 Russell Square, W.C.1

The Institute exists to promote advanced study of the Commonwealth and its field of interest is primarily, but not exclusively, that of the social sciences. Its library, now numbering approximately 18,000 volumes, is in the process of building up a collection of primary material on Commonwealth relations, history, political, economic and social development, particularly in tropical areas, demography and race relations. With this object in view it regularly acquires official publications, statistics, guides to archives, etc. The collection of British Parliamentary papers and official publications on Commonwealth affairs includes all those of significance of the twentieth century; in addition the most important papers from about 1850 have also been acquired, particularly those relating to Africa. Official publications and Parliamentary papers of the Commonwealth include the following:

Australia, from 1901 to 1950, thereafter a selection is made within the Institute's field of interest; Victoria, from 1859 to 1891; South Australia and New South Wales, miscellaneous papers issued in the 1860's and 70's.

Canada, from 1894 to 1915 and from 1920 to 1925; from 1950 a good selection is available and kept up to date.

Ceylon, a selection from 1950 only.

India and Pakistan, a limited selection only.

New Zealand, from 1862 to 1873, since 1950 a selection only.

South Africa, a selection from the end of the nineteenth century to date.

Colonies, Protectorates, etc., a wide selection from 1950 but much earlier material is still being acquired.

(Parliamentary proceedings and journals and Official gazettes are not taken.)

It also possesses a good collection of *F.O. Prints* dealing with Colonial affairs before 1902.

A good collection of statistical material in the form of censuses, year-books, abstracts, digests, blue-books, etc., has been acquired.

Sets of the Official Year-books of Australia, Canada, New Zealand and South Africa are available, together with many earlier 'unofficial' year-books, as well as current issues of some Colonial year-books, guides, etc. Commonwealth dictionaries of biography, current Who's Who and other works of reference are regularly acquired.

The Library acquires nearly 200 current periodicals and statistical bulletins and some bank reviews. It also possesses many union lists of periodicals and indexes to periodical literature; the latter include *Poole's Index* to 1902; the *International Index*, 1907–14 and from 1924 onwards; the *Subject Index to Periodicals* from 1941; and those of Australia from 1946, Canada from 1938, New Zealand from 1941, South Africa from 1940.

A very strong bibliographical section is being assembled—in addition to union lists and indexes referred to above, it acquires all bibliographies of consequence within its field of interest as well as guides and indexes to Parliamentary papers and official publications of the United Kingdom and Commonwealth countries and other aids to research. A union list of Commonwealth newspapers is maintained; it also possesses a photographic copy of the British Museum newspaper catalogue. A 'bibliography of bibliographies' in the library and a Register of Research and of deposited Theses in British Universities are also maintained.

Apart from primary material of the nature already referred to the library has a good selection of principal secondary works on Common-wealth development over the last century.

Published archives and records of the Cape, the Orange Free State and the Transvaal (with the Archives Year-book of South Africa), of Canada, Ontario and Quebec and of some other countries and Colonies, as well as the Historical Records of Australia, are in the Library.

Books and papers are for reference only and may not be borrowed. Members of the academic and senior administrative staffs and graduate research workers of Commonwealth Universities, University Colleges and Research Institutions may use the Library, which is open daily from 9.30 a.m. until 5.30 p.m., Saturdays, until 12.30 p.m. Application for admission to the Institute and Library should be made to the Secretary/Librarian.

Institute of Education
Department of Education in Tropical Areas
(University of London)
Malet Street, W.C.1

The departmental library is housed in the Institute of Education and contains some 7,000 volumes and 8,000 pamphlets, mainly on education and its background in tropical areas of the world. History, anthropology and race relations are also well represented. Official publications of the United Kingdom and Colonies devoted to education, community development, medicine and agriculture are available from about the year 1926. There is also a good range of periodicals which are selectively indexed and included in the Library catalogue.

The Library is available to all university students on personal application to the Librarian. It is open daily from 9.30 a.m. until 6 p.m. on weekdays (Fridays until 5 p.m.) and from 9.30 a.m. until 12.30 p.m. on Saturdays.

The Institute's Division of Overseas Students also maintains a small reference library of comparative education in Commonwealth countries, particularly India, and America, in which official publications predominate.

Institute of Export
14 Hallam Street, S.W.1

The Institute possesses a small library of volumes mainly on economics and business law and administration which include representative collections of material relating to the British Commonwealth. Periodicals of significance in the field are taken including bank reviews and journals of Chambers of Commerce throughout the Commonwealth; they are retained for twelve months and thereafter selectively.

Accredited research workers may be permitted to use the Library between the hours of 10 a.m. and 5 p.m., Monday to Friday.

Institute of Historical Research
(University of London)
Senate House, W.C.1

The Institute of Historical Research serves as the University's centre for advanced work in history and the library of over 80,000 volumes is designed for teaching purposes as well as study. It contains the principal printed records of British and foreign history, together with bibliographies, guides to archives and libraries, and other secondary works essential for the study of original sources. There are complete sets of the various *Calendars of State Papers* and other publications of the Public Record Office, the Record Commissions and the Historical Manuscripts Commission. There are also sets of archival publications of Australia, Canada and South Africa. The file of Hansard is almost complete, and there are most of the earlier unofficial records of Parliamentary debates, sets of the Journals of both houses to 1936, and long runs of *Votes and Proceedings*. The collection of Parliamentary papers on open shelves lacks most of the House of Lords series and some of the Commons. Nearly all the papers relating to colonial affairs up to the year 1900 are, however, present. Among important serials taken are the *London Gazette* (to 1899, with a few gaps in the seventeenth century), the *Annual Register* and *The Times* (from 1800, with a few issues missing). Apart from the *Journals* of New Brunswick (1898–1910) and the *Canadian Gazette* (1867–1939), Parliamentary records of Commonwealth countries have not been acquired. There is some census material, for instance of New Zealand and Ceylon. The file of *South Australia Statistical Register* is almost complete. Examples of Colonial blue-books earlier than 1939 are kept, together with current issues of official yearbooks of Commonwealth countries.

Printed material on Asia is confined to writings in western languages on relations of the West with eastern countries, such as *East India Company Court Minutes*, and the various series of Fort St. George and other factory papers. There are good runs of the *East India Register* and the *Bombay Register*. The special collection on Military and Naval History is strong in *Army Lists* and *Navy Lists*, official campaign histories, bibliographies and guides.

Bibliographical material on all aspects of history is a salient feature of the Institute; catalogues of libraries and manuscript collections in Britain and abroad are numerous.

Information concerning the recording of migrations of manuscripts in the Institute's *Bulletin* is given at p. 14.

Works of reference in the library include long runs of the *Court and City Register*, the *British Almanack and Companion*, the *Royal Calendar*, the *Statesman's Year Book*, and the various series of *Colonial Office, Foreign Office* and *India Office Lists*. There are also examples of early Colonial directories and almanacs.

The Library is open from 9 a.m. to 9 p.m. from Mondays to Fridays, and from 9 a.m. to 5 p.m. on Saturdays. It is intended primarily for postgraduate students of history preparing for higher degrees or pursuing other approved courses of study, university teachers of history and other historians engaged in research. Permission to consult works difficult of access elsewhere is occasionally given to other applicants. Forms of application for admission may be obtained from the Secretary and Librarian. Books may not, in any circumstances, be borrowed.

Institute of Navigation
1 Kensington Gore, S.W.7

The Institute possesses a small library of approximately 500 volumes of technical works, not readily accessible elsewhere, devoted to sea and air navigation. Accredited research workers are admitted between the hours of 9.30 a.m. and 5 p.m., Monday to Friday.

Institute of Transport
80 Portland Place, W.1

The Institute's library contains some 10,000 volumes and pamphlets and 160 current periodicals devoted to the economics and administration of transport by land, sea and air, including much material relating to the British Commonwealth. Accredited research workers are admitted between 10 a.m. and 5 p.m., Monday to Friday, and 10 a.m. and 12 noon on Saturdays.

Institution of Mechanical Engineers
1 Birdcage Walk, S.W.1

The Institution's Library contains some 60,000 volumes and 400 periodicals devoted mainly to the science of mechanical engineering, but it does, however, contain material of Commonwealth interest—shipping, marine engineering and Imperial communications (land, sea, air and radio). The Library is intended only for the use of members of the Institution, but in exceptional cases accredited students from Commonwealth countries may, on application, be given permission to make temporary use of the Library.

The Library is open from 9.30 a.m. to 5.30 p.m., Monday to Friday, and from 9.30 a.m. to 12.30 p.m. on Saturdays, except Saturdays preceding Bank Holidays.

Institution of Mining and Metallurgy
44 Portland Place, W.1

The Institution's library contains some 30,000 volumes and 500 journals and serials devoted to economic geology, mining, mineral dressing and metallurgy throughout the Commonwealth and foreign countries. There is also available an extensive collection of reports from Government mining and geological departments throughout the world. Research workers are admitted, on application to the Librarian, between 10 a.m. and 5 p.m., Monday to Friday.

The Institution also houses the Secretariat of the Commonwealth Council of Mining and Metallurgical Institutions.

International African Institute
St. Dunstan's Chambers, 10–11 Fetter Lane, E.C.4

The library of the Institute contains some 3,100 volumes, mainly on the ethnography, sociology and philology of Africa, and 142 current periodicals including those in the French, German, Spanish, Italian, Portuguese and Dutch languages. It is open to accredited research workers from 9.30 a.m. to 6 p.m., Monday to Friday.

The Institute publishes *Africa*, which includes a bibliography of current publications, and *African Abstracts*, a quarterly review of studies appearing in current periodicals. It also maintains a bibliographical card-index of books, reports and articles relating to a wide range of African studies, mainly south of the Sahara.

International Missionary Council
2 Eaton Gate, S.W.1

The Council possesses a small miscellaneous library but it has available a good collection of Annual Reports of Missionary Societies throughout the Commonwealth and foreign countries. Its archives, consisting mainly of minute books and letters from about 1920, are available for consultation by appointment only and on suitable recommendation.

International Sugar Council
28 Haymarket, S.W.1

The Council possesses a collection of works on the industrial, economic and commercial aspects of sugar, sugar beet and sugar cane, official reports issued by the Governments of sugar producing countries, sugar year-books published in the Commonwealth and all British, Commonwealth and foreign periodicals on the subject, some from the year 1931 onwards, including the *Australian Sugar Journal*, the *South African Sugar Journal* and *Indian Sugar*. It also maintains a collection of articles, notes and press-cuttings on sugar, arranged in files by countries, since 1931.

The collection is available for consultation between the hours of 9.30 a.m. and 5.30 p.m., Monday to Friday.

International Wool Secretariat
Dorland House, 18–20 Regent Street, S.W.1

The Secretariat, which is non-governmental and non-profit making, was established in 1937 for the promotion of wool and is financed by statutory levies imposed on wool sold in Australia, New Zealand and South Africa.

The library contains some 3,000 books and papers together with about 220 periodicals, relating to the economics, history, science and technology of wool, Official publications (and particularly statistical bulletins) are received regularly from Australia, New Zealand, South Africa and Canada, in addition to other material relating to wool producing and manufacturing industries of those countries and the United Kingdom. The library also contains some material of a similar character dealing with India and Pakistan.

Research workers are admitted on application to the Librarian. The library is open from 9.30 a.m. until 5.30 p.m., Monday to Friday.

Iron and Steel Institute and Institute of Metals
Joint Library, 4 Grosvenor Gardens, S.W.1

The joint library of the two Institutes contains some 30,000 volumes and 850 current periodicals devoted to the production of iron and steel and the properties and treatment of both ferrous and non-ferrous metals and kindred subjects. It is open to research workers, on application to the Librarian, between 10 a.m. and 5 p.m., Monday to Friday.

King's College
(University of London)
Strand, W.C.2

The libraries of the College contain some 186,000 volumes, of which approximately 50,000 are in the general library. In addition to the general library the College has twenty-three departmental libraries, including those on history, Imperial history, laws and geography. The collection of material on Imperial history is particularly valuable; it contains some 3,500 books, including the Laughton Collection of naval history, and is kept regularly up to date. Other collections of special interest are the Marsden Library, which includes early works of description and travel, and the Portuguese Library, which is rich in material on colonial history.

Parliamentary papers are not acquired as a whole, only individual papers are obtained as needed. The library does, however possess sets of the Journals of both Houses of Parliament, Parliamentary debates (with some gaps after 1909) and the Calendars of State Papers.

Some 300 periodicals ranging over the College's field of study are taken and bound for permanent reference.

Students who are not members of the College may be granted permission to use the library—normally only during the vacations—and applications should be submitted to the Librarian. Books are available for loan only through the National Central Library and may not be borrowed by non-members individually.

The Library is open in term from 9.30 a.m. to 6.45 p.m., Monday to Friday; Saturday from 9.30 a.m. to 1 p.m.; in vacation from 10 a.m. to 4.30 p.m., Monday to Friday; Saturdays from 10 a.m. to 12 noon.

Information concerning the use of the libraries is to be found in the current *Calendar* of the College; particulars of special collections, e.g. the Marsden Library, are to be found in the *Calendar* for 1939–40.

London Missionary Society
43 Broadway, Westminster, S.W.1

The Society's archives date back to 1795 and consist of letters, reports and journals covering the Society's work in many parts of the world. Its first endeavours were concentrated in the South seas and South Africa and papers relating to those areas are comprehensive; they include journals and letters from 1796, Committee minutes from 1827 (with some gaps due to war loss) and outgoing letters from 1820. There are also letters and journals dealing with Papua from the 1870's on-

wards. South Africa and Matabeleland letters date from 1797 and journals from 1798, including a good collection of Livingstone letters, both
in original and copy, from 1834 to 1872. Letters and journals relating
to Central Africa, Madagascar and Mauritius and to India cover the
whole of the nineteenth century. West Indian material is extensive.
Other papers include letters and journals from South, North and
Central China and Malaya, general reports covering all fields and a full
set of outgoing letter-books from 1823 onwards (a few tissue-paper
copies of letters in the period 1823 to 1831 are, unfortunately, illegible).
The Society's activities also extended to Canada and Newfoundland
and it possesses small quantities of early nineteenth-century correspondence relating thereto. The archives, many of which have been
calendared, are open for inspection by research workers up to the year
1905; the use of some material is restricted and can be seen only with
special permission. (A list of the Society's archives is also available in the
Institute of Commonwealth Studies.)

The Library contains some 10,000 volumes of a general and historical
nature, with a good collection of works of exploration, description and
travel. The South seas and Africa are particularly well represented—
there is a good collection of pamphlets on South African affairs covering
the period 1800–60. Linguistic material, including works in the vernacular, relates to the Pacific, China, India, Madagascar and parts of
Africa.

Parliamentary papers and official publications on subjects related to
the Society's work, with emphasis on the South seas, are available. The
collection of periodicals is not extensive but mention should be made of
a set of the *Indian Mail* from 1837–57 and of the *Asiatic Journal* from
1817.

The library is open from 9.30 a.m. until 5.30 p.m., Monday to Fridays, and research workers are admitted on suitable recommendation.

London School of Economics and Political Science
(University of London)
Houghton Street, Aldwych, W.C.2

The British Library of Political and Economic Science of the London
School of Economics, in spite of its special interest in the field of the
social sciences, should be regarded as one of the larger general libraries.
Founded in 1896, it now numbers over 370,000 bound volumes, some
400,000 controversial and other pamphlets and leaflets, many thousands
of government and official publications and over 6,000 periodicals. It
has a good working collection of treatises and periodicals on general

and political history of the British Commonwealth. It is particularly strong in the fields of government, constitutional law and history, public administration and law (Commonwealth and international); the sociological and anthropological collection is one of the best in London; geography is well covered; the economic aspect of agriculture, forestry and fisheries is adequately represented. In general the collection of material on the social and economic sciences is unsurpassed in the country. Mention should be made of one speciality in particular, namely its collection of statistical material. It is a depository library for United States Government publications and the publications of the United Nations. It also possesses an almost complete collection of League of Nations documents and publications of the International Labour Office.

The Library's collection of manuscripts includes the following of Commonwealth interest:

Account book of a Trinidad Sugar planter, 1793–1819 (Coll. Misc. 266).

Courtney Collection (S.R. 1003). Contains 234 letters, a draft manifesto and a speech about the Boer war to or by Leonard and Kate Courtney.

Ciffen Collection. Contains a section on Imperial organization; statement and letters, mostly by or on behalf of Sir Frederick Pollock. 1904–5.

Letters written by men of mark in New Zealand to the Hon. W. P. Reeves (Agent-General for New Zealand) MS. and typescript, *c.* 1895–1908 in 1 vol. (Misc. 198).

E. D. Morel Papers. His chief interest was the Congo. He was also proprietor of the *West African Mail* (a file of which is available) and there is some correspondence relating to West Africa generally.

Notes on the trade of New South Wales, *c.* 1835–40 (Coll. Misc. 262).

Passfield Trust Papers. (i) Beatrice Webb's Diaries—relevant sections deal with the Webbs' tour of Australia and New Zealand in 1898 and with Sidney Webb's Colonial Office period in 1929–31. (ii) Letters, ditto. VII.2.xv: *Our Pilgrimage* (includes an account of the 1898 tour).

Sidney Webb Papers. East African papers (typescript and manuscript), 6 vols., 1929–31. (Colonial Secretary's private (unregistered) papers, including papers relating to the Joint Select Committee) (Coll. Misc. 156).

Two printed collections are worthy of special mention—Alberta social credit, pamphlets, reports, etc., 89 parts in 6 vols., 1934–8 (Misc. 90); and the Anti-Slavery Society, reports, petitions, etc., 23 parts in 1 vol., *c.* 1815–1900 (Misc. 101).

Parliamentary Papers and official publications include the following:

UNITED KINGDOM

Parliamentary Papers: House of Commons almost complete from 1801 to date (in addition to the reprint edition of papers from 1715 to 1801 in 15 vols.); House of Lords complete from the beginning, except for those duplicated in the Commons collection.

Parliamentary Debates (Hansard): Almost complete from 1803 to date, together with other historical material containing debates before 1803.

Journals: House of Lords complete from 1509 to date; House of Commons complete from 1547 to date.

London Gazette, 1693–4 with gaps, 1927 to date.

Calendars of State Papers complete to date.

British and Foreign State Papers 1818 to date.

Treaty Series, 1892 to date; *League of Nations* and *United Nations* Treaty Series complete to date.

Diplomatic and Consular Reports from 1855, both the series issued as parliamentary papers and those issued since 1915 by the Department of Overseas Trade and subsequently by the Board of Trade.

COMMONWEALTH

AUSTRALIA

New South Wales. Parliamentary debates, 1879/80 to date; Journals of the Legislative Council, 1872/3–1905, with gaps, 1930/32 onwards; Votes and proceedings of the Legislative Council, 1852–4; Votes and proceedings of the Legislative Assembly, 1852 onwards (incomplete); Joint volumes of papers of the Legislative Assembly and Legislative Council, 1904 onwards (incomplete).

Queensland. Parliamentary debates, 1909–13, 1916–17; Parliamentary journals, 1922–4.

South Australia. Parliamentary proceedings [and papers], 1851–8 (incomplete), 1859 onwards; Parliamentary debates, 1857/8 onwards, except 1863/4; House of Assembly debates, 1896–1913 (incomplete); Legislative Council debates, 1896–1913.

Tasmania. Parliamentary journals and printed papers, 1855/6 onwards (incomplete).

Victoria. Parliamentary debates, 1856/7 onwards; Papers presented to both Houses of Parliament, 1862–81 (incomplete); Votes, proceedings and papers of the Legislative Assembly, 1853/4 onwards; Proceedings of the Legislative Council, 1853/4 onwards.

Western Australia. Minutes and votes and proceedings, 1891/2 to date (incomplete); Parliamentary debates, 1890/91 to date.

Commonwealth. Parliamentary debates, 1901/2 to date; Parliamentary papers, 1901/2 to date (incomplete).

CANADA

British Columbia. Journals of the Legislative Assembly, 1875–1931 (incomplete); Sessional papers of the Legislative Assembly, 1879–1918 except 1883.

Manitoba. Legislative Assembly journals and Sessional papers, 1880–1917 (incomplete).

New Brunswick. Journals of the House of Assembly, 1856–92 (incomplete); Journals of the Legislative Council, January/April 1847; Journals of the Legislative Assembly, 1893–1920; Proceedings of the Legislative Assembly, 1893–7.

Newfoundland. House of Assembly journals, 1907, 1908.

Nova Scotia. House of Assembly journals and proceedings, 1851/2–1905 (incomplete); Legislative Council journals and proceedings, 1844–1911 (incomplete).

Ontario. Journals of the Legislative Assembly, 1891 to date.

Prince Edward Island. Legislative Assembly journals, 1898, 1904, 1914, 1927, 1935.

Quebec. Journals of the Legislative Assembly, 1869–1919 (incomplete); Journals of the Legislative Council, 1894/5–1902 (incomplete); Sessional papers, 1894–1920.

North West Territories. Legislative Assembly journals (and sessional papers), 1900, 1901.

Dominion. House of Commons debates, 1875–1937 (incomplete), 1950 to date; Senate debates, 1876–1935 (incomplete); House of Commons journals, 1883 to date (some gaps before 1923); Senate journals, 1891 to date (incomplete); Sessional papers, 1864–1925 (incomplete).

NEW ZEALAND

Parliamentary debates, 1891–7, 1922–4, 1932, 1947 to date; House of Representatives journals, 1858, 1922–4; Legislative Council journals, 1922–4; Legislative Council votes and proceedings, 1858.

SOUTH AFRICA

Cape of Good Hope. Minutes of the Legislative Council and votes and proceedings of the House of Assembly, 1883, 1905, 1907–10; House of Assembly debates, 1887–1902 (incomplete); Government gazette, 1882–98 (incomplete).

Natal. Legislative Assembly votes and proceedings, 1893–5; Legislative Council votes and proceedings, 1867–1909/10 (incomplete).

Transvaal. Legislative Assembly votes and proceedings, 1907; Legislative Council minutes, 1903/4, 1907–9; Legislative Council votes and proceedings, 1903–6 (incomplete); Provincial Council votes and proceedings, 1911.

Orange River Colony. Legislative Council debates, 1903–4.

Transvaal and *Orange River Colony.* Inter-Colonial Council debates, 1906; Inter-Colonial Council minutes, 1906, 1907.

Union. House of Assembly debates, 1931–3; House of Assembly votes and proceedings, with printed annexes, 1929 to date (incomplete) (annexes from 1911); Senate debates, 1931–2; Minutes and annexes of the South African National Convention, 1909; Government gazette, 1910–41 (incomplete).

Colonial official publications (including some legislative debates and official gazettes) have been regularly received from 1931, but before that date (with some exceptions) only miscellaneous items are available.

Official Year Books, Blue books, Statistical Registers, Statistical Abstracts and similar material include the following:

AUSTRALIA

New South Wales. Official year book, 1904/5 to date; Blue book, 1874–94 (incomplete); Statistical register, 1858 to date (incomplete); Year-book, 1900–3; The Wealth and Progress of New South Wales, 1886/7–1900/01.

Queensland. Year book, 1937 onwards; Blue book, 1887–1916 (incomplete); Statistics of the State of Queensland, 1878–1933/4 (incomplete); ABC of Queensland statistics, 1905–36 (incomplete).

South Australia. Blue book (in Parliamentary proceedings [and papers]); Statistical register (in Parliamentary proceedings [and papers]); Statistics of 1867.

Tasmania. Statistics of the State of Tasmania, 1854 to date (in Parliamentary journals and printed papers); Official handbook, 1892.
Victoria. Year book, 1873 to date (with gaps before 1926/7).
Western Australia. Blue book, 1872–95 (incomplete); Statistical register, 1898 to date (except 1942/3); year-book, 1890–1904 (incomplete).
Commonwealth. Official year book, 1901/08 to date.

CANADA

British Columbia. Year book, 1911 (with Addenda, 1914).
New Brunswick. Year book, 1910, 1919.
Newfoundland. Year book, 1924, 1926, 1930.
Quebec. Statistical year book, 1914 to date.
Dominion. Canada: the Official handbook, 1930–3, 1936, 1937, 1939 to date; Year book, 1896 to date.

NEW ZEALAND

Official year-book, 1892 to date; Statistics of the Dominion, 1853/1856, 1857–92, 1894–1920.

SOUTH AFRICA

Cape of Good Hope. Blue book, 1881, 1884; Statistical register, 1886–91, 1893–1909.
Natal. Blue book, 1861–92/3; Statistical year book, 1893/4–1909.
Transvaal. Statistics of the Transvaal Colony, 1902/7, 1903/8, 1904/9.
Union. Half yearly (later quarterly) abstract of Union statistics, 1919–23; Year book, 1917 to date; Statistical year book, 1912/13, 1913/14, 1914/15.

Colonies: Many Colonial statistical Blue Books, etc., are available, but not all the Colonies are represented in the collection neither are sets complete for those which are represented. It is, however, a good miscellaneous collection.

The Library provides a wide range of periodicals, British Commonwealth and foreign, in the fields of economics, sociology, politics, law and history—the collection amounts to over 6,000 series. Newspapers, with a few minor exceptions, are not available. A file of *The Times* is, however, maintained from 1813.

All standard bibliographies are secured and much bibliographical material has been assembled over the years. A large collection of maps of the world is available in the Geography Department of the School, but for the Commonwealth it is not as good as those of the British Museum and the Royal Geographical Society.

The collection of current works of reference of the United Kingdom and the Commonwealth is excellent, and includes the following:

Annual Register from 1758 (with gaps 1915, 1931 and 1939); *British Imperial Calendar*, 1810 to date (with gaps); *Colonial Office (and Dominions Office) Lists*, 1867–1939 (incomplete); *Colonial Office List*, 1946 to date; *Commonwealth Relations Office List*, 1951 to date; *Foreign Office List*, 1865 to date (incomplete);

K

India Office and Burma Office List, 1947; *Statesman's Year Book* from 1864 (except 1924); *Whitaker's Almanack* from 1869 (incomplete); *Who was Who* and *Who's Who* from 1897.

A subject catalogue has been published entitled a *London Bibliography of the Social Sciences*. It includes not only material in the British Library of Political and Economic Science but also that in other libraries as follows:

Vols. I–V

Holdings up to 1931 of the British Library of Political and Economic Science, Edward Fry Library of International Law, Goldsmiths' Library of Economic Literature (University of London), National Institute of Industrial Psychology, Royal Anthropological Institute, Royal Institute of International Affairs and Royal Statistical Society.

Special collections in the libraries of The Reform Club (political and historical pamphlets), University College, London (the Hume, Ricardo and other economic and political collections) and the University of London (works on economics and related subjects).

Vol. VI

Additions from 1931 to 1936 to the British Library of Political and Economic Science, Edward Fry Library of International Law and Goldsmiths' Library of Economic Literature.

Vols. VII–IX

Additions from 1936 to 1950, other than works in the Russian language, to the British Library of Political and Economic Science and Edward Fry Library of International Law.

Vols. X–XI: Additions 1950–5. In the press.

An alphabetical list of the periodicals in the Library in 1929 is given in Volume IV; supplementary lists up to 1936 are given in Volumes V and VI, after which they have been discontinued. It is hoped to produce a separate catalogue of periodicals. Author indexes are given in Volumes IV (for Volumes I–III), V, and VI, but not in Volumes VII–IX.

A *Reader's Guide* to the library was published in 1937, part of which has been revised and re-issued as a *Guide to the Collections* (1948) and the rest as *Notes for Readers* (latest edition 1955). It contains sections on general reference books and government publications, followed by chapters on specific subjects. Apart from its usefulness as a guide to the library it is a handy 'source' book of material. Further information is available in *The Libraries of London* (ed. Irwin), 1949, ch. xi (The British Library of Political and Economic Science, by G. Woledge).

The library is open daily from 10 a.m. until 9.20 p.m., Saturdays until 5.50 p.m. It is closed six days at Christmas, Good Friday and the four weekdays following, Whit Monday, August Bank Holiday and all Saturdays in July and August. Admission is confined to members of the School, persons to whom permits have been issued and day visitors (at the discretion of the Librarian). Permits may be issued to persons engaged in research which cannot be pursued elsewhere; professors and lecturers of any recognized University; persons engaged in any branch of public administration; and such other persons as the Director may allow.

Applications for Library permits must be made on the prescribed forms and should be addressed to the Librarian. They should be supported either by a member of the school staff or by a letter of recommendation from a person of position. Permits are not transferable. Fees are normally remitted for persons engaged on academic research.

London School of Hygiene and Tropical Medicine
(University of London)
Keppel Street, W.C.1

The School library contains about 37,000 volumes, some 550 current periodicals and serials, as well as many thousands of pamphlets devoted mainly to hygiene and tropical medicine and allied subjects. Its particular value for studies of the Commonwealth lies in its collection of material dealing with anthropology in tropical areas, entomology, parasitology, trypanosomiasis and human nutrition throughout the British Commonwealth and territories of other Colonial powers. It also possesses official reports and other publications issued by governments of tropical territories on medicine, public health, hygiene, sanitation, vital statistics and veterinary medicine, many dating from the nineteenth century. A collection of maps of tropical areas showing the distribution of diseases is also available.

The library is open to accredited research workers between the hours of 9.30 a.m. and 5 p.m., Monday to Friday, and from 9.30 a.m. to 12 noon on Saturdays.

The School incorporates the Ross Institute of Tropical Hygiene and houses the Bureau of Hygiene and Tropical Diseases.

Malta Government Office
39 St. James's Street, S.W.1

A small library is maintained, mainly for staff use, containing a few general works on the history, archaeology and economics of Malta. A set of the Laws of Malta, the Official Gazette (containing Government departmental reports) from 1946, the Statistical Abstract from 1946, Shipping and Trade Reports from 1945, Census material from 1948 and the Year-book from 1954 are available. An Index to the Laws in Force is maintained up to date.

The library is open to research workers from 10 a.m. to 5 p.m., Monday to Friday, and from 10 a.m. to 11.30 a.m. on Saturdays.

Methodist Missionary Society
25 Marylebone Road, N.W.1

The archives and library of the Society (founded in 1786) are housed in its headquarters. The former consist of letters and journals of missionaries in the following territories and countries—Gibraltar from 1804; Malta from 1815; West Indies from 1803; Ceylon from 1814; India from 1817; Burma from 1886; Sierra Leone from 1812; the Gambia from 1821; Gold Coast from 1855; Nigeria from c. 1842; Australia, 1812–76; Tasmania, 1823–76; New Zealand, 1819–76; Friendly Islands, 1822–59; Fiji, 1835–60; Canada (including Newfoundland, New Brunswick and Nova Scotia), 1802–70; South Africa from 1807; and Rhodesia from 1891. Synod Minutes for these areas are also available from the early nineteenth century. In addition the Society has the Minutes of its General Committee from 1804, printed Annual Reports from 1789, and a Magazine (giving, in the nineteenth century, very full extracts from letters) from 1816. The Women's Organization, which sent out women missionaries independently, has Minutes and printed Annual Reports from 1858.

Records of the missionary activities of the former branches of the Methodist Church (prior to the Union of 1932) exist as follows—the Methodist New Connexion (Canada, Australia and New Zealand) from 1844; the Bible Christians (Canada, Australia and New Zealand) from 1869; the United Methodist Free Church (Jamaica, Tasmania, Australia, Sierra Leone, Kenya and New Zealand) from 1869—these three branches formed the United Methodist Church in 1907. The archives are for the most part Minutes of Committees only. For the Primitive Methodist Church (Nigeria with Fernando Po, South Africa and Rhodesia) Minutes date from 1863 and correspondence from c. 1890. Printed annual reports and magazines are also available.

The reference library contains some 4,000 volumes, mainly historical and sociological background material relating to the countries in which the Society has operated. There are collections of translations in some seventy languages and of published works by missionaries or on missionary activities. A collection of prints, drawings and photographs is being built up, together with microfilms of material in other hands.

Research workers, with written recommendations, are permitted to use the archives and reference library on application to the Archivist. Hours of opening are from 9.45 a.m. until 4.45 p.m., Monday to Friday.

Ministry of Agriculture, Fisheries and Food
3 Whitehall Place, S.W.1
Food Section: Great Westminster House, Horseferry Road, S.W.1

The joint libraries total approximately 120,000 volumes and nearly 2,000 current periodicals and serials. Material in the Whitehall Place library relating to the Commonwealth is confined to those countries which have a system of agriculture similar to that of the United Kingdom, principally Canada, Australia and New Zealand. The library also contains some Commonwealth material on forestry and timber and on soil science. Works on specific commodities—coffee, cocoa, tea, rice, sugar, etc.—are in the Food Section library. Two selective indexes to current periodicals are maintained, one in each library and appropriate to its subject matter.

The libraries are open to research workers from 9 a.m. to 5 p.m., Monday to Friday.

National Institute of Economic and Social Research
2 Dean Trench Street, Smith Square, S.W.1

The library of the Institute contains some 12,000 volumes mainly in the field of economics; the subjects covered include economic theory, income and wealth, industrial and agricultural economics, finance and demography. Statistical material is particularly well represented; it includes United Kingdom censuses and censuses of production as well as a set of the *Guide to Current Official Statistics*, 1922 to 1938. Official publications of the United Kingdom and some Commonwealth countries within the Institute's field of interest are acquired selectively. Special efforts are made to secure reports issued by the various research institutions since 1945.

Approved research workers may use the library on application to the Librarian. It is open from 10 a.m. until 5.30 p.m., Monday to Friday (it is closed on Saturdays).

The Institute's publications include the *Register of Research in the Social Sciences, Economic and Social Studies, Occasional Papers*, and (with the University of Cambridge Department of Applied Economics) *Studies in the National Income and Expenditure of the United Kingdom*.

New South Wales
Office of the Agent-General
56 Strand, W.C.2

The Office of the Agent-General possesses a small library consisting mainly of official publications together with some historical works and general works of reference. Included in the official publications are a complete set of Public and Private Statutes of New South Wales from 1824, the Official Year-books since 1904, the Statistical Year-books since 1939 and departmental annual reports since 1939.

The library is open Monday to Friday, from 9.30 a.m. until 5 p.m.; a limited service is available on Saturdays between 9.30 a.m. until 11 a.m. Admission is unrestricted.

New Zealand
Office of the High Commissioner
New Zealand House, 415 Strand, W.C.2

The New Zealand Government Library contains some 14,000 volumes consisting of material on history, description and constitution of New Zealand and official publications. Of the latter there is a particularly fine collection including Journals and Appendices of the House of Representatives from 1854, Journals of the Legislative Council, 1850–1950, the New Zealand Gazette from 1857, Parliamentary Debates from 1867 (with a few gaps), Statutes from 1854, Statutory Regulations from 1936/37, Law Reports from 1883, New Zealand Statistics, 1853–1856 and from 1858 and Monthly Abstracts of Statistics from 1914/15.

Reference material includes a complete set of the Official Year-book and issues of Who's Who. The library is particularly strong in New Zealand bibliographical material. Approximately eighty periodicals are taken and the Index to New Zealand Periodicals from 1947 is available.

Research workers are admitted to the library, which is open from 9 a.m. to 5 p.m., Monday to Friday, on application to the Information Officer, preferably by letter in advance.

Nigeria
Office of the Commissioner
5 Buckingham Gate, S.W.1

The Office has a small general library consisting mainly of Government publications from 1946, Debates of the Legislative Council from 1950, the Official Gazette from 1951 and current laws and law reports. Books may be borrowed from the library which is open from 9.30 a.m. until 5.30 p.m., Monday to Friday.

Northern Rhodesia
Office of the Commissioner in London
57 Haymarket, S.W.1

Northern Rhodesia House keeps a small library for official publications. It includes the Government Gazette from 1948, with supplements only from 1929, the Laws of Northern Rhodesia, the Blue Book 1924–37, 1943, 1945–8, Debates of the Legislative Council from 1931, Departmental Annual Reports since 1947, and the proceedings of the African Representative Council.

Copies of the Northern Rhodesia newspapers and the *Rhodesia Herald* are received by airmail and are kept for six months. Cuttings from the British Press relating to the territory are also filed.

The library is available for reference purposes during normal office hours, Monday to Friday and on Saturday mornings.

Ontario
Office of the Agent-General
13 Charles II Street, S.W.1

The library contains approximately 800 volumes mainly on history and the constitution but with some devoted to economics, sociology and geography. It also possesses current Official Reports of the Province together with a set of Statutes. Canadian works of reference are well represented. Some current newspapers are available for two or three weeks but press cuttings are retained for longer periods. The library is open from 9 a.m. to 5 p.m., Monday to Friday, and from 9 a.m. to 12 noon on Saturdays. Books may be borrowed.

Patent Office
(Board of Trade)
25 Southampton Buildings, Chancery Lane, W.C.2

The Library of the Patent Office contains approximately 350,000 volumes of books and periodicals, covering the fields of industrial property, applied science and technology, physics and chemistry. The industrial property collection includes the patent specifications and official patent, trade mark and copyright journals of British Commonwealth countries as well as those of the United Kingdom and many foreign countries. There is also an up-to-date collection of legal textbooks covering the industrial property laws of all countries. The 12,000 scientific and technical periodicals, of which 4,000 are current, include many from Commonwealth countries.

The library, which is for reference only, is open to the public from 10 a.m. to 9 p.m., Monday to Friday, and from 10 a.m. to 5 p.m. on Saturdays. There is open access to most of the stock, but some older volumes are in store.

Further information may be obtained from *The Libraries of London* (ed. Irwin), 1949, ch. vi (The Patent Office Library, by F. W. Gravell).

Public Record Office
Chancery Lane, W.C.2

The Public Record Office, established in 1838 by Act of Parliament, is the repository of the national historical records and archives of government. There is a branch depository at Ashridge Park to which direct access is not permitted except in very exceptional cases; material is brought to Chancery Lane for consultation as required.

Government departments have transferred their records to the Public Record Office for preservation, including the Colonial Office (to the year 1938) and the Commonwealth Relations Office (to the year 1935). For further information see pp. 7, 8.

Material other than official records is also available. Various collections of private papers have been deposited but are too numerous to list here. Information concerning them is to be found in the catalogues and indexes maintained in the Public Record Office; some are noted in Giuseppi's *Guide*, vol. i (1923), at pp. 348–51. The following, however, may be mentioned as examples—Cornwallis Papers (relating to the affairs of the American Plantations and of the East Indies, 1741–1819), the Ellenborough Papers (Earl of Ellenborough as Governor-General of India, 1841–4), the Manchester Papers (Virginia Plantations and the Bermudas, James I and Charles I), the Rodney Papers and the Shaftesbury Papers (documents relating to Jamaica, Barbados and Bahamas).

Two Search Rooms are provided for public use, the Literary (or Round) Search Room and the Legal Search Room. Except in the case of certain legal records no fees are chargeable. Admission is by ticket for which application should be made on the appropriate form signed by some responsible person who knows the applicant personally or who can vouch for his *bona fides*. A set of Rules and Regulations made by the Master of the Rolls respecting the public use of the Records can be obtained on application.

The Search Rooms are open on every day except Sunday, Good Friday, Saturday before Easter, Easter Monday, Saturday before Whit Sunday, Whit Monday, August Bank Holiday, Christmas Day, Boxing Day and any other day which may be appointed a public holiday. The hours of admission are—for literary searches, from 9.30 a.m. to 5 p.m., except on Saturdays, when they are from 9.30 a.m. to 1 p.m.; for searches subject to the payment of fees, from 9.30 a.m. to 4.30 p.m. on Mondays to Fridays only.

For particulars of lists, indexes, etc., of public archives and guides to the Public Record Office, see pp. 9, 10.

Quebec House
Westerham, Kent

Quebec House, the home of James Wolfe, contains a small library of approximately 170 volumes relating to the life and times of Wolfe and the early history of Quebec and of Canada generally, together with a collection of portraits, prints and relics. A list of the books available appears in a printed guide book and catalogue *Quebec House, Westerham* (National Trust, n.d.).

The library is open for reference between 10 a.m. and 1 p.m. and between 2 p.m. and 5 p.m. on Tuesdays, Thursdays and Saturdays (except in the months of January and February).

Queensland
Office of the Agent-General
409 Strand, W.C.2

The Office of the Agent-General possesses a small library of some 300 volumes of a general character, including historical works on Queensland, biographies, voyages and expeditions. It also contains a good agricultural and botanical section on Queensland and New Guinea, including a collection of agricultural pamphlets, together with works dealing historically with the sugar trade. Queensland labour laws since 1922 and Queensland Statistics since 1888 are also available together with the official Almanac and Directory since 1909. Some periodicals are retained for permanent reference, including the Geographical Society of Australia, Queensland Branch, *Transactions*, 1885–9; the Royal Society of Queensland *Transactions*, vols. i–xxxvi; the Queensland Government *Mining Journal* from 1900; the Queensland *Agricultural Journal* since 1914 (vol. ii onwards); the Queensland *Industrial Gazette* since 1916 and the *Queensland Magazine* since 1922.

Rhodesia and Nyasaland Federation
Office of the High-Commissioner
429 Strand, W.C.2

The Office of the High Commissioner contains a small Reference Library of general works on Northern Rhodesia, Southern Rhodesia and Nyasaland, numbering some 500 volumes. It also contains official publications such as Parliamentary debates, departmental annual reports and Government Gazettes. It also possesses official year-books and statistical information. Most Rhodesian and Nyasaland newspapers are available; copies are usually retained for six months.

The library is open daily from 9.30 a.m. to 5 p.m., and admission is unrestricted. Books are not allowed out on loan.

Royal Anthropological Institute
21 Bedford Square, W.C.1

The Institute's library contains 35,000 volumes devoted mainly to anthropology, physical and cultural, together with material on economics, agriculture and geography within the anthropological sphere. It also contains works on native and customary law and a collection of material on race relations. The Sir Richard Burton library consisting of approximately 2,000 books and pamphlets, mainly on Africa and India, has recently been acquired.

In addition to more than 320 current periodicals the library possesses a fine collection of anthropological journals from all parts of the world. The Institute has prepared for publication a *Survey of Anthropological Journals and monograph series in the United Kingdom* which lists locations and holdings of many libraries.

Admission to the library is normally confined to Fellows, Associate Members and readers from affiliated institutions but permission to use it may be granted to research workers on suitable recommendation and application should be made by letter addressed to the Librarian. The library is open from 9.30 a.m. to 6 p.m., Monday to Friday, and from 9.30 a.m. to 1 p.m. on Saturdays.

Royal Asiatic Society
56 Queen Anne Street, W.1

The Society is open to members only on payment of an annual subscription of three guineas or an Associate's fee of 30s. per annum which carries with it use of the library.

The library possesses some 60,000 volumes devoted to history, art and literature of India, Pakistan, Ceylon, the Middle East, South East Asia generally and the Far East. It also contains more than 100 current periodicals. It possesses some manuscript material—Sanskrit, Malay, Burmese and Singhalese.

Royal Central Asian Society
2 Hinde Street, Manchester Square, W.1

The Society possesses a library of approximately 8,000 volumes, pamphlets and periodicals concerning Central Asia, the Middle and Far East. Its use is restricted to subscribers. Applications should be addressed to the Secretary.

Royal Empire Society
Northumberland Avenue, W.C.2

The library of the Royal Empire Society is probably the largest collection of material on the British Empire and Commonwealth in the United Kingdom, numbering over 320,000 items. It is safe to say that every part of the Commonwealth is represented on the shelves. Emphasis is on historical and descriptive material and on works of discovery, voyages and travel. In dealing with such a comprehensive collection it is difficult to single out any individual section of the library for particular mention. Special reference should, however, be made to certain types of material.

Official Publications. One of the most valuable features is the collection of official publications of the United Kingdom and countries and territories of the Commonwealth. Of the British official publications relating to the Commonwealth there is a small number prior to 1845, those from 1845 to 1867 are complete and bound in sessional volumes, and from 1867 they are arranged according to territories and bound in appropriate groups. There are very extensive, although not complete, collections of Parliamentary papers, sessional papers and other official publications (including census material) of the Commonwealth from the earliest times to date. The Indian material, however, consists mainly of Council and Parliamentary proceedings and debates. Australian, Canadian and South African material is extremely good. Of Southern Rhodesia the set of legislative debates is one of the few complete sets available. Some early official Gazettes are in the library but from about the year 1900 they are nearly complete. The collection of blue-books deserves special mention, many of the early issues are in manuscript and are extremely rare. Good sets of official year-books are in the library—federal issues being complete but sets of state and provincial issues are broken. Official publications of the Commonwealth include the following:

AUSTRALIA

Commonwealth. Journals of the Senate, Journals of the House of Representatives, Votes and Proceedings, and Parliamentary papers, 1901 to date.

New South Wales. Legislative Council Minutes, 1824–31; Votes and Proceedings, 1832–54 (with some gaps); Journals of the Legislative Council, 1856 in progress (including parliamentary papers up to 1904); Legislative Assembly Votes and Proceedings, 1856 in progress (including parliamentary papers up to 1904); Joint volumes of papers, Legislative Council and Assembly, 1904 in progress.

Queensland. Legislative Assembly Votes and Proceedings, with documents 1860–1901 (with some gaps); Legislative Council Journals, with papers, 1860–

1901 (with some gaps); Journals of Parliament, 1902 in progress; Parliamentary Papers, 1902 in progress.

South Australia. Proceedings of Parliament, with copies of Papers, 1851 in progress.

Tasmania. Legislative Council Journals, 1852–83; House of Assembly Journals, 1856–83; Journals and Printed Papers, 1884 in progress.

Victoria. Legislative Assembly Votes and Proceedings, with documents, 1856 in progress; Legislative Council Votes and Proceedings and Minutes, with documents, 1852 in progress; Papers presented to both Houses of Parliament, 1856 in progress.

Western Australia. Legislative Council Parliamentary Debates, 1876–89; Parliamentary Debates, 1890–1913, 1923 in progress; Minutes and votes and proceedings of Parliament, 1870–1907, 1923 in progress.

CANADA

Dominion. Legislative Assembly Journals, 1859–66; Legislative Assembly Sessional Papers, 1859–66; Parliament, Sessional Papers, 1867–1925, departmental reports, 1928 in progress; House of Commons Journals, 1867 in progress; House of Commons Debates, 1870 in progress; Senate Journals 1867 in progress (with a few gaps); Senate Debates 1876 in progress (with some gaps); Canada Gazette, 1869 in progress.

Alberta. Legislative Assembly Journals, 1906 in progress; Sessional papers, 1925 in progress.

British Columbia. Legislative Council Journals, 1864–8; Legislative Assembly Journals, 1872 in progress; Sessional papers, 1873 in progress.

Manitoba. Legislative Assembly Journals and Sessional Papers, 1884–1920.

N.W. Territories. Council Journals, 1877–1903; Legislative Assembly Journals, 1889–1903.

New Brunswick. Legislative Assembly Journals, 1837–1920, with reports and papers; Legislative Council Journals, 1836–92.

Newfoundland. House of Assembly Journals and sessional papers, 1851–1908 (with some gaps); Legislative Council Journals, 1869–1908 (with some gaps); Proceedings of the House of Assembly and Legislative Council, 1912–24; Gazette, 1910 in progress.

Nova Scotia. House of Assembly Debates and Proceedings, 1876–1916 (with some gaps); House of Assembly Journals and Proceedings, 1857 in progress; Legislative Council Journal and Proceedings, 1858–1927 (with appendices of papers and reports), (with some gaps); Debates and proceedings of the Legislative Council, 1877–1922.

Ontario. Legislative Assembly Journals and appendices, 1867 in progress; Sessional Papers, 1868 in progress.

Prince Edward Island. Legislative Assembly Journal and appendices, 1856 in progress (with some gaps).

Quebec. Legislative Assembly Journals, 1875–1922; Legislative Council Journals, 1875–1922; Parliament, Sessional Papers, 1875–1922.

Saskatchewan. Legislative Assembly Journal, 1906 in progress; Sessional Papers, 1920 in progress.

CEYLON

Government Gazette, 1892 in progress; Legislative Council Debates, 1870/1 in progress; Papers laid before the Legislative Council, 1860 in progress; Proceedings of the Legislative Council, 1864 in progress.

INDIA

Abstract of proceedings of the Council, 1883–1920; Debates of the Council of State, 1921–44; Debates of the Legislative Assembly, 1921–47; Constituent Assembly Debate, 1948–9, Legislative series, 1947–9; Parliamentary Debates, 1950 in progress; Government Departmental reports, a wide selection.

NEW ZEALAND

Legislative Council Journals and appendices, 1854 in progress; House of Representatives Journals, 1863 in progress; Parliamentary Debates, 1854–8, 1861–3, 1867 in progress; Gazette, 1889 in progress.

PAKISTAN

Constituent Assembly Debates, 1947–54, Legislative series, 1948–54.

SOUTH AFRICA

Union. House of Assembly Debates, 1910–15, 1924 in progress; Votes and proceedings, 1910 in progress; Senate Debates, 1910–15; Senate Minutes, 1911 in progress; Gazette, 1910 in progress.

Cape. House of Assembly Debates, 1892–1909; Votes and Proceedings of the Legislative Council and of the House of Assembly, 1859–1910; Provincial Council Minutes, 1911 in progress; Gazette, 1887 in progress.

Natal. Legislative Assembly Debates, 1893–1910; Sessional Papers, 1893–1910; Votes and Proceedings, 1893–1910; Legislative Council Debates, 1879–93; Sessional Papers, 1872–93; Votes and proceedings, 1857–93; Provincial Council Minutes, 1911 in progress.

Orange. Legislative Council Minutes, 1903–7; Debates, 1903–7; Provincial Council Votes and proceedings and annexures, 1911 in progress; Gazette, 1900 in progress.

Transvaal. Legislative Assembly Reports and papers, 1908–10; Votes and proceedings, 1908–10; Legislative Council Reports of Committees, 1903–6; Votes and proceedings, 1903–6; Provincial Council Votes and proceedings, 1911 in progress; Gazette, 1900 in progress.

Books. Although, as has been mentioned, the whole library contains works on every part of the Commonwealth attention should be drawn to the collections on Australia (which includes some early Australiana), Canada, East Africa and Cyprus (the Cobham Collection). Much material on colonization, including colonization by foreign powers, is available. Another valuable section of the library is that devoted to slavery and the slave trade (books, pamphlets and official reports).

The collection of printed archival material is good and includes publications of Canada, South Africa, the East India Company and the Historical Records of New South Wales and Australia. Complete sets of historical societies publications include the Champlain, Van Riebeck, Hudson's Bay, Hakluyt, Linschoten and the Navy Record societies. Proceedings of other learned societies and publications of museums throughout the Commonwealth are available.

There are also some reports and journals of Chambers of Commerce, banks and trading organizations and annual reports of municipalities.

Much of the legal section was destroyed during the Second World War but a smaller collection of laws and ordinances and works on social and administrative law has since been built up.

A good collection of Commonwealth bibliographies and works of reference (almanacs, calendars, directories, etc.) is also available.

Periodicals and Newspapers. The library has a wide range of periodicals; over 2,000 current and non-current titles are permanently retained and a number of Government newspapers and some ephemeral items are kept for short periods. The collection is particularly rich in Commonwealth historical journals. It also possesses a number of historical journals published in the United States, relating to states bordering Canada or those which originated as British Colonies. There are numerous agricultural and economic periodicals and a representative collection on literature and the arts.

Until 1939 all important periodical articles were indexed and included in the library's printed and card catalogues. The service was suspended during the war but it has now been resumed and it is hoped eventually to close the gap.

The newspaper room has a representative collection of papers from Commonwealth countries and territories numbering about 100; none, however, is filed for permanent reference.

Manuscripts. Collections of private papers are few but those of value include the Burney Papers (1820–30) on Burma and Siam, the Sir George Arthur papers on British Honduras (1814–22), the Childers Papers and Correspondence on general Imperial questions (1870–80) and a small collection of the papers of the North West Company of Canada (late eighteenth and early nineteenth centuries). A list of manuscripts in the library to the year 1925 appears in the *Bulletin* of the Institute of Historical Research, 2: pp. 80–2. The library is building up a collection of micro-film copies of documents and papers of Commonwealth interest located outside the United Kingdom.

Photographs. A large and varied collection of photographs of Commonwealth interest, the majority of which were taken during the period from the 1870's to 1910, is in the library.

A *Subject Catalogue of the Library* has been printed and published in four volumes (1930–7). It forms a fairly comprehensive bibliography of Commonwealth literature except that official material issued before 1910 (other than Canadian) has not been included. The card catalogue in the library is kept up to date. Monthly accession lists are issued in duplicated form; they have recently been extended to include lists of important holdings, e.g. Colonial blue-books and Canadian historical periodicals and other serial publications.

The Library is primarily for the use of Fellows of the Society but research workers are admitted on a Fellow's introduction or on other suitable recommendation. Application for admission should be made in writing to the Librarian.

The Library is open normally from 10 a.m. until 7 p.m., Monday to Friday, and until 6 p.m. on Saturdays; it is closed earlier in the evenings and on Saturdays during certain periods of the year. Books are not available on loan to non-members.

Royal Geographical Society
1 Kensington Gore, S.W.7

The Society's library contains approximately 100,000 books mainly on geography and the geographical sciences, travel and exploration but material on economics, sociology, anthropology, agriculture and demography in so far as it impinges on the geographical field is also available. Parliamentary and official publications include the more important British blue books since 1850.

The map collection numbers about 500,000 maps, atlases and gazetteers including the most important Commonwealth material, both current and historical. Maps regularly acquired include those issued by the Australian Department of National Development and Department of the Interior, the Canadian Department of Mines and Technical Surveys, the New Zealand Lands and Survey Department, the South African Department of Mines and Geological Survey, the Directorate of Colonial Surveys and the Survey Departments of Oversea Territories.

The library acquires some 700 current periodicals and serials; a list of geographical serials in the library, current as well as those which have ceased publication, was compiled and issued in duplicated form in 1953. The more important periodical articles are catalogued and included in the library's card catalogue. A bibliography of geographical bibliographies is maintained on cards. A classified Catalogue of the Library was published in 1871 and a revised general catalogue in 1895. The

Society regularly issues *New Geographical literature and Maps*, a six monthly accession list.

Admission to the library is granted to non-members, on suitable recommendation, on application to the Librarian. The map room is open to the public for reference.

The library and map room are open from 9.30 a.m. until 5.30 p.m., Monday to Friday, and until 1 p.m. on Saturdays.

Royal Institute of International Affairs
Chatham House, 10 St. James's Square, S.W.1

The library of Chatham House is the principal library on international affairs generally. It also includes material on the Commonwealth in international affairs and on inter-Commonwealth relations. The total collection numbers some 35,000 volumes, 55,000 pamphlets and 600 current periodicals, many of which are retained for permanent reference.

Complete sets of publications of the League of Nations and the United Nations are available. Commonwealth material includes a number of Government publications as well as complete sets of current treaty series of Australia, Canada, Ceylon, New Zealand and Pakistan.

The Press Library consists of a collection of press cuttings in English, French, German and Italian taken from a wide variety of English, foreign and some Commonwealth papers since 1924. All aspects of international and inter-Commonwealth relations are covered. The clippings are classified in very great detail under geographical and subject heads, and records of speeches entered in a speaker's index. Admission is normally restricted to members, but readers' tickets are issued to research workers on application to the Press Librarian and upon payment of a fee of 10s. per week or £2 for three months.

Admission to the library is normally restricted to members but readers' tickets may be issued to other persons on the recommendation of a member or of some responsible body. Accommodation is strictly limited and tickets, application for which should be submitted in writing to the Librarian, are only granted for access to material which is neither available in the British Museum nor through the National Central Library.

The library is open from 10 a.m. until 6 p.m. on Mondays, Tuesdays, Wednesdays and Fridays, from 10 a.m. until 8 p.m. on Thursdays and from 10 a.m. until 5 p.m. on Saturdays except in July and September when it closes at 1 p.m. on Saturdays. It is closed entirely during the month of August.

The Department of Racial Studies also has a small library of books, periodicals and pamphlets on racial questions. Press cuttings are also available. (See also p. 200.)

Royal Institute of Public Administration
76A New Cavendish Street, W.1

The library contains approximately 6,000 volumes and 7,000 pamphlets dealing mainly with all aspects of public administration, including material relating to the Commonwealth. Some 130 current periodicals are available which are regularly indexed and included in the library's card catalogue.

Accredited research workers are admitted to the library between the hours of 10 a.m. and 5 p.m., Monday to Friday.

The Institute issues an annual *Survey of Research in Progress* in the Universities.

Royal Statistical Society
21 Bentinck Street, W.1

The library contains approximately 80,000 volumes consisting mainly of statistical material and works of statistical method, as well as some devoted to economics, agriculture and demography, of the United Kingdom, the British Commonwealth and many foreign countries. Current periodicals available number some 400. The collection of official and other statistical publications is outstanding, particularly with regard to early material of the nineteenth century—for the United Kingdom there is fairly good coverage; for Australia and New Zealand the coverage is remarkably good; for Canada, South Africa and India and the West Indies and other important territories the coverage is extensive. Statistical material includes statistical registers, censuses, vital statistics and statistics of trade and agriculture. Some of the material relating to the Australian colonies dates from 1804 (Tasmania), 1849 (New South Wales), 1861 (South Australia, Victoria and Western Australia) and 1871 (Queensland). The New Zealand statistics commence in 1853. Complete sets of federal Official Year-books as well as some of the state and provincial issues are available.

Accredited persons may use the library for reference by permission and applications should be submitted to the Librarian. The library is open from 10 a.m. to 5 p.m., Monday to Friday, and from 10 a.m. to 12 noon on Saturdays.

A printed *Catalogue* was issued in 1884 (with Index, 2 vols.); it is very comprehensive and still valuable as a bibliography. A modified *Catalogue* (which excludes U.K. official publications) was published in 1921.

L

Royal United Service Institution
Whitehall, S.W.1

The Institution exists for the promotion and advancement of science
and literature of the three Services, including Commonwealth countries, in all aspects as well as Imperial and Colonial relations of Great
Britain and European powers. Its library possesses 30,000 volumes,
7,000 maps and 52,000 charts. It is open to non-members by special
permission between 10 a.m. and 5 p.m. (Saturdays 10 a.m. and 4.30
p.m.).

Saskatchewan
Office of the Agent-General in London
28 Chester Street, Belgrave Square, S.W.1

Saskatchewan House maintains a small library devoted mainly to works
on history and government, with some material on economics, agriculture and forestry, geography and statistics. It has good collections of
material on wheat, the development of Canada and the Canadian
West and North, water resources and power development. Official
publications of the Province are well represented—the Saskatchewan
Gazette, annual Departmental reports, reports of Royal Commissions
and Crown Corporations, material on the natural resources of Saskatchewan and miscellaneous publications on social welfare, education
and trade and industry. It also possesses some works of reference,
including the Provincial telephone directories, and Saskatchewan newspapers.

The collection is available for reference by accredited research workers between the hours of 9.30 a.m. and 5.30 p.m., Monday to Friday.

School of Oriental and African Studies
(University of London)
W.C.1

The School's library contains some 200,000 books and pamphlets and
over 1,500 manuscripts in the field of Oriental and African studies.
Collections of material relating to India, Pakistan, Ceylon and Malaya
are particularly good whilst that on Africa is one of the most outstanding. A speciality of the library is its collection of material on
languages and literatures in its particular field which contains books in
or about some 2,500 languages and dialects. The library also possesses a
large collection of books and pamphlets (formerly belonging to the late
Sidney H. Ray) relating to the languages and ethnology of the peoples
of the Pacific Ocean. In addition to historical works, material is available

on government, constitutional development, economics, sociology, anthropology, geography and law. Indian law is particularly well represented.

Some 600 periodicals are taken. A comprehensive index has been compiled of periodical literature relating to the Far East and South East Asia from 1920 to date. It is maintained on cards and kept up to date; from 1954 additions have been cumulated into annual volumes and published. The work of compilation involved the search through more than 500 periodicals in the School and other libraries.

The manuscripts relate mainly to the Orient but the library possesses some material on Commonwealth territories notably the Sir William Mackinnon papers relating to the Imperial British East Africa Company (Mackinnon was the Company's first President). Information on the location of manuscripts in other libraries and private collections relating to India and other Asian countries and to Africa is being assembled.

Some information relating to the Library is published in the annual Calendar of the School. The library is open from Monday to Friday from 9.30 a.m. until 6 p.m. in term and until 5 p.m. out of term. On Saturdays it opens at 10 a.m. and closes at 12.30 p.m. The School and library are closed over the usual public holidays.

The Librarian may admit persons not being members of the University staff or students of the University on production of satisfactory references. Application may be made in person or by letter. Books may be borrowed by such persons on payment of a deposit of £2 and on production of references.

The School adjoins the University Senate House and may be approached from Malet Street or Woburn Square.

Science Museum Library
South Kensington, S.W.7

The Science Library ranks as one of the great national libraries—it is maintained as a department of the Science Museum, South Kensington. Its stock numbers some 400,000 books and pamphlets and over 8,000 current periodicals. In view of its nature, pure and applied science, it would seem at first sight to be outside the scope of this *Guide* but the Commonwealth research worker in the field of the social and economic sciences will find there specialized collections of works on agriculture, mineralogy, geology, mining and economic geology and metallurgy. Every purely scientific subject such as genetics or statistical theory has been pursued over its borders into sociology and economics. There is some anthropology and ethnology, much on biometrics, demography and on the more social and sanitary aspects of medicine, on the border-line between neurology, psychology and sociology (e.g. industrial psychology, operational research, etc.), animal sociology, the more scientific aspects of geography and, of course, the history of science and technology and their social background. A systematic effort has been made to cover such borderline subjects. There has been no effort, of course, to confine these to the Commonwealth field. Material on individual commodities is also available, including works on cocoa, coffee, cotton, rice, rubber, sugar, tea, timber, tin, etc.

The library is open to the public and application for tickets of admission may be made in writing to the Keeper of the Library who is also available, by appointment, to give advice and assistance to visiting scholars. It is open daily from 10 a.m. until 6 p.m.

Further information may be obtained from *The Libraries of London* (ed. Irwin), 1949, ch. iii (Science Museum Library, by D. J. Urquhart).

Society for Promoting Christian Knowledge
Holy Trinity Church, Marylebone Road, N.W.1

Although the Society does not possess a library it has a fine collection of its archives from the year 1699 which will be available for consultation by appointment and on suitable recommendation. They consist of minute books, abstract letter books, original letters and miscellaneous papers, to which there is an index. It also possesses the papers of Henry Newman (Secretary from .1708 to 1743) dealing with the Society's affairs including draft letters and minutes.

It is anticipated that the Society will settle in at its new premises, Marylebone Road, during the year 1957 after which the archives will be available.

Society for the Oversea Settlement of British Women
43/44 Parliament Street, S.W.1

In 1919 all existing women's emigration societies were amalgamated, under Government auspices, into one organization, the Society for the Oversea Settlement of British Women, which was recognized as the Women's Branch of the Oversea Settlement Department of the Colonial Office. As the work of the Society mainly concerns independent countries of the Commonwealth the Society's liaison is now with the Commonwealth Relations Office rather than with the Colonial Office. Unfortunately, most of the early records of the former societies are missing but the present society does possess some archives from the second half of the nineteenth century to date, consisting mainly of minute books, reports and incoming and outgoing letters. Not all of the papers are available but those which are accessible may be consulted by research workers on application to the General Secretary.

An account of women's Empire migration from earliest times and of the early societies devoted thereto is to be found in *S.O.S.B.W.: a survey of voluntary effort in Women's Empire Migration*, by G. F. Plant, London (The Society), 1950.

The Society has published an annual report since 1920.

Society for the Propagation of the Gospel
15 Tufton Street, S.W.1

The Society possesses a fine collection of archives from its foundation in 1701 to date. They have been well maintained and are in excellent condition. The collection includes the Journal of the Proceedings of the Society from 1701, the Journal of the Society, 1701 to 1860, and Committee Minutes from 1702. Original letters, numbering many thousands, from all parts of the world are available from 1702. They include letters from the American colonies, the West Indies, Canada, Newfoundland, India, Australia, New Zealand and Africa. Missionaries' reports date from 1854 and continue to the present day. A collection of Fulham Papers consists of letters from abroad to the Bishop of London in 4 vols., including letters from the East Indies, India, Africa, Australia and North America, 1813 to 1827, and the West Indies, 1803 to 1826. Much of the material has been classified and bound but the process of sorting and arranging continues. A small leaflet, by J. W. Lydekker, descriptive of the archives, was published in 1931 but it is now somewhat out of date. Current lists and indexes are available in the Society and a list of Commonwealth material is in the Institute of Commonwealth Studies.

A most valuable record of the Society and its work *Two Hundred Years of the S.P.G., an historical account, 1701–1900*, by C. F. Pascoe, was published in 1901. It also forms a descriptive guide to the Society's archives.

The library contains some 23,000 volumes on missionary work and the Church overseas as well as history, travel, biography, anthropology and race relations and a miscellaneous collection numbering about 2,000 of unbound, but catalogued, pamphlets on topical matters, many of Commonwealth interest. It also possesses grammars and dictionaries of most oriental and African languages and a good collection of nineteenth-century diocesan magazines from many parts of the world, dealing with historical and political events. The library is open daily,

Monday to Friday, from 10 a.m. until 5.30 p.m. Lending library facilities are available to non-subscribers on payment of a fee.

Research workers are permitted to refer to the archives on suitable recommendation. Application for admission to the library may be made in person or by letter to the Librarian.

The archives and library are situated in the Society's headquarters, Westminster.

South Australia
Office of the Agent-General
499 Oxford Street, W.1

South Australia House contains a small library, including some early historical works. Its main attraction, however, is the collection of official material—Proceedings of Parliament and Papers, 1852 to 1953; Debates, from 1873; Statutes, from 1837; Government Gazettes, from 1846; Education Gazettes, from 1940. It also possesses *Mining Reviews*, Nos. 30 to 98 (1920 to 1953), the *Geological Survey of South Australia*, Nos. 1 to 33 (1912 to 1954) and the *Department of Agriculture Journal* from 1938. Some current reference works and newspapers are also available.

The library is open from 9.30 a.m. to 5 p.m., Monday to Friday, and from 9.30 a.m. to 12 noon on Saturdays. Applications for admission should be addressed to the Librarian.

Tasmania
Office of the Agent-General
457 Strand, W.C.2

A small general library is available, consisting mainly of historical material and official publications, including Journals and printed papers of Parliament and Government Gazettes from 1950, Statistics from 1930/31 and Public General Acts of Tasmania. Reference works include Pocket Year-books from 1948, Australian Who's Who and Walch's Tasmanian Almanac from 1948. State Survey maps and the Regional Planning Atlas are also available. Copies of three daily newspapers are retained for three months.

Admission is granted to accredited research workers and applications should be addressed to the Official Secretary. The Library is open from 9.30 a.m. to 5 p.m., Monday to Friday.

Tea Bureau
22 Regent Street, S.W.1

The Bureau maintains a reference library of some 200 books on the history of tea, the tea industry (production and manufacture, commerce and promotion) and on allied subjects, including tea research Institutes' publications. It subscribes to six current periodicals on the subject. A catalogue has been printed and published.

The library is open to the public on Mondays to Fridays from 9 a.m. until 5 p.m. (Saturdays by special arrangement only). Prior written applications are not required.

Timber Development Association
21 College Hill, E.C.4

The Library of the Association contains some 2,000 volumes, together with several thousand pamphlets and cuttings, on forestry and timber, mainly of a technical character although there are some devoted to the economic aspect of the industry. A little Commonwealth material on botany and forest pathology and on description, structure and identification of timbers is included.

The Library is open to research workers from 9.30 a.m. until 5 p.m., Monday to Friday.

The latest edition (4th) of the *Library Catalogue* was printed and published in 1953.

Tin Research Institute
Fraser Road, Greenford, Middlesex

The Library of the Institute contains more than 1,000 volumes, 15,000 pamphlets and many thousands of cuttings devoted to metallurgy and the economics, history and technology of tin. Over 150 current periodicals are available.

Research workers are admitted on application to the Librarian. It is open from 9 a.m. until 5.30 p.m., Monday to Friday.

Union of South Africa
Office of the High Commissioner in London
South Africa House, Trafalgar Square, W.C.2

South Africa House library contains some 2,000 volumes devoted mainly to history, government, constitutional history and law of South Africa. In addition, an excellent collection of official publications complete from 1910 onwards is available, including government reports and papers, Senate and House of Assembly debates and journals and Statutes. A set of the Official Gazette is also available to which an index is maintained on cards. Other official material includes Statutes of the Cape of Good Hope, 1652–1906, of Natal, 1845–1906, of Transvaal, 1839–1910 and of South West Africa from 1915; censuses from 1904 and education statistics from 1922. Reference works include sets of the Official Year-book and the South African Who's Who, both from 1910 and a collection of City Guides. Current leading periodicals are taken but retained only for two to three weeks, with the exception of the *South African Journal of Economics*, available from 1933. Current issues of South African newspapers are kept for short periods.

The Library is open to the public, on application to the Librarian, between 9.30 a.m. and 12.30 and 2 p.m. and 4 p.m., Monday to Friday.

Universities' Mission to Central Africa
35 Great Peter Street, S.W.1

The library of the Universities' Mission contains some 500 books and pamphlets mainly devoted to the history and geography of Africa and to the work and history of the Mission. It also includes material on biography, missions and missionaries and sociology.

Research workers are admitted to the library on application to the Librarian, between the hours of 9.30 a.m. and 5 p.m., Monday to Friday.

Books are available on loan on payment of a small fee. A *Lending Library Catalogue* was issued in 1952.

The Mission was established in 1859 and its records are available for consultation on application to the General Secretary. They are in the process of being catalogued.

University College
(University of London)
Gower Street, W.C.1

The College library contains some 630,000 books and pamphlets on all the subjects taught in the College, namely, in the five faculties of arts, laws, science, engineering and the medical sciences. The general library, the law library, the arts libraries and bibliographical and reference works are in the main building. Three sectional libraries, too large to be accommodated in the main library (one of which is the history collection) are in houses in Gordon Square. Amongst the smaller departmental libraries housed within the departments are those of statistics and anthropology.

The history library includes all the College books on political economy, British history, European history, Latin-American history and American history of which the material dealing with the American colonial period is particularly good. It also contains the Hume Tracts consisting of some 5,000 tracts published between 1810 and 1850, amongst which are to be found a number dealing with colonial matters, in particular Africa, Canada and the West Indies, and slavery and the slave trade. The Lansdowne collection consists of about 2,400 tracts on political problems, published in the seventeenth and eighteenth centuries. The Library also contains complete sets of *Parliamentary Debates* (*Hansard* and earlier material containing debates), *Journals* of both Houses of Parliament, the *Calendars of State Papers* and the *Annual Register*. Parliamentary papers are, however, limited to the periods 1783 to 1800, a very scarce and valuable collection, and 1801 to 1850.

There is a good library of law and international relations (including Roman-Dutch and South African law).

Material on the Commonwealth is not especially acquired.

Current periodicals number over 3,000 with a bias, perhaps, towards the scientific. Bibliographies are particularly well represented and a good collection of reference works is available.

Among the manuscripts available are those of Jeremy Bentham consisting of papers and correspondence on social reform and political theory (of which a printed Catalogue was issued in 1937) and over 50,000 letters addressed to Lord Brougham dealing with every aspect of his varied interests. Although there are many more letters in this collection of the later part of Brougham's life than of the earlier years there are some interesting bundles of letters entirely devoted to his anti-slavery activities and his interests in colonization.

Further information on the library is to be found in the current *Calendar* of the College, in Rye's and Harrod's Guides and in Bellot's centenary history, *University College London, 1826-1926*.

The library is open on weekdays from 9.30 a.m. until 9 p.m. (5 p.m. in vacation) and from 9.30 a.m. until 12.30 p.m. on Saturdays. It closes for one week at Christmas and Easter and on the usual public holidays.

Application for admission should be made to the Librarian who may admit non-members of the College on the receipt of satisfactory references and recommendations.

University of London Library
Senate House, W.C.1

The Library of the University now contains some 650,000 volumes and pamphlets. The collection is general in character but it also includes several well-equipped specialist libraries for the promotion of research of which the Goldsmiths' Company's Library of Economic Literature is the best example and the one of special interest to the overseas research worker.

History, both general and political, is particularly well represented. Sets of *Hansard* (and earlier material containing debates), *Journals* of both Houses of Parliament, *Calendars of State Papers* and the *Annual Register* are complete. Some *Consular and Diplomatic Reports* are also available. There is also a collection of House of Commons papers although not complete—it contains the early reprint in fifteen folio volumes, an incomplete run of papers from 1801-54, a better run from 1854/5 to 1929/30, and a complete set from 1940. The set of House of Lords Papers dates only from 1940 although individual papers of earlier date are in the Library, especially in the Goldsmiths' collection.

The Goldsmiths' library of material on economic history is probably unsurpassed, for British and Commonwealth material of the period before 1850, by any library other than the British Museum and the Bodleian. More recent material is available, but it is not so comprehensive although still a very fine collection. Fields covered include the following—early history of English trade, companies and colonies, mercantile and colonial policy, navigation laws, the rise of the East Indian and American trades, emigration and population movements, growth and change of foreign trade, international monetary policy and the history and theory of statistics. It also contains a large collection of books and pamphlets and rare material on slavery and the slave trade.

The Library, being of comparatively recent foundation, has not been able to build up a large collection of manuscripts and 'papers'. A few of value, however, are available in the Goldsmiths' library dealing with colonial affairs, in particular the East India Company, the Hudson's Bay Company, the Royal Africa Company and a few others. In addition it possesses a fine collection of pamphlets on the East India Company.

Material relating to Commonwealth countries is not extensive. Official publications as such are not taken. There are, however, some Indian papers covering the period 1850-1936 approximately, consisting of debates and proceedings of legislative councils, reports on the administration of particular provinces and reports on special subjects (including trade), and some census material (1881, 1901, 1911, 1921, 1931 and 1941). The Library possesses some publications of unofficial bodies and societies (mainly scientific, however) and a large set of the *Imperial Gazetteer of India* and various district Gazetteers. It also has a few annuals and Who's Who of India and Pakistan from 1940.

There is a fairly large collection (the Biggar Collection) of pamphlets of the nineteenth and twentieth centuries on Canadian history; the

Canada Year Book is complete from 1909, and there are some volumes of the Canadian Censuses of 1911 and 1931.

A useful collection of Australian annuals include the Official Year Book from 1901, the New South Wales Year Book from 1904 (with some gaps), the Queensland Year Book from 1937 and Bulletin of the Government Statistician from 1938, the South Australian Statesman's pocket year book from 1951, Walch's Tasmanian Almanac from 1894 (with some gaps) and some Western Australian statistical volumes from 1947/8 onwards. The New Zealand Year Book is available from 1896 and that of South Africa from 1910.

There are complete collections of Calendars of State Papers, the British and Foreign State Papers, the official Treaty Series and the League of Nations and United Nations Treaty Series. Other League and United Nations publications are available but the collection is very selective. The International Labour Office studies and reports are well represented.

A fine range of some 3,400 current periodicals is available in the Library and particular efforts are made to acquire all Union lists of periodicals and printed indexes to periodical literature. A *List of Periodicals*, including other serials, was printed and published in 1956. Newspapers, other than *The Times* (from 1830, with some miscellaneous years prior to that date), are not taken. The collection of bibliographies and other bibliographic material is one of the best in London.

The rapidly growing collection of maps (now numbering about 20,000) includes most of the smaller scale maps issued by the Commonwealth Surveys, with specimens of the larger scale series, and of those published by the Directorate of Colonial Surveys. It also possesses a good collection of modern atlases.

There is a very wide coverage of general works of reference—Almanacs, Calendars, Year-books, Guides, Who's Who, etc.—British, foreign and Commonwealth, including the following: The Colonial Office and Dominions and Commonwealth Relations Offices *Lists* from 1927, the India Office *List* (with some gaps), the *British Imperial Calendar* from 1947 (with a few earlier issues), the *Statesman's Year Book* from 1907 to date and complete sets of *Whitaker's Almanack* and *Who Was Who* and *Who's Who*.

Theses and dissertations presented by successful candidates for the higher degrees of the University are deposited in the Library and are available for public reference. The Library has, for many years, been building up a collection of foreign University theses (mainly from the continent of Europe but with some American), particularly in Arts subjects. An arrangement has recently been made to receive a complete set of printed theses of all French Universities in Arts subjects, including law—they are available from the beginning of 1953.

A photographic department is maintained and copying of material can be undertaken for Readers for which a charge is made. Micro-readers are available in the Library.

The latest edition of the *Readers' Guide to the University Library* was published in 1939. It is somewhat out of date but copies are available for reference purposes. A new, but modest, *Guide to the use of the Library* is, however, available for distribution. Printed lists of classified accessions have been published since 1906, at first quarterly and later annually. Since 1953 they have been issued six times a year. Further information is available in Rye's *Guide* and in *The Libraries of London* (ed. Irwin), 1949, ch. x (The University of London Library and some other Libraries in the University, by J. H. P. Pafford).

Applications for admission by persons not specifically referred to in the 'Rules and Regulations for the University Library' should be made in writing and addressed to the Goldsmiths' Librarian, University of London, W.C.1.

The Library is open on weekdays during term and the Easter vacation from 9.30 a.m. to 9 p.m.; Saturdays from 9.30 a.m. to 6 p.m. In the Christmas and Summer vacations it closes at 6 p.m. each evening.

Victoria
Office of the Agent-General in London
Victoria House, Melbourne Place, Strand, W.C.2

A small general reference library is maintained chiefly of official publications, including sets of the Victoria Statutes, Debates and Government Gazette, which are available from 1890 to date and the Victoria Year-book from 1900. Current departmental reports and papers are also available but are retained only for a period of ten years. Other material in the library includes censuses and vital statistics. The Melbourne newspapers are taken but are kept for two to three weeks only.

Works of reference may be perused in the Library or borrowed on short loan upon application either by personal call or letter.

War Office
Whitehall, S.W.1

The Library of the War Office contains over 150,000 volumes, devoted mainly to military science and history. The collection does include, however, material of particular interest to the Commonwealth. It contains an almost complete collection of Regimental (and other Unit) Histories of every country and territory in the Commonwealth. It also contains histories of Colonial campaigns, as well as biographies of Colonial soldiers. Early War Office papers and documents are in the custody of the Public Record Office and are available for reference up to the year 1902. Papers not in the Record Office include Military Intelligence reports on Colonial territories; those issued before the year 1914 are available in the Library.

Accredited research workers are admitted to the Library on application to the Librarian.

The Library is open from 9 a.m. to 5.30 p.m., Monday to Friday, and from 9 a.m. to 12 noon on Saturdays.

West India Committee
40 Norfolk Street, Strand, W.C.2

The Committee was established about 1750. It is an association of British subjects and firms whose object is, by united action, to promote the interests of the agricultural and manufacturing industries and the trade of the British West Indies, British Guiana and British Honduras, and thus increase the general welfare of those colonies.

A valuable reference library is available containing some 4,000 books on West Indian history, industry and commodities—citrus, cocoa, coffee, cotton, sugar, tea and tobacco—as well as on agriculture, colonization, economics, government and administration and labour. It is particularly rich in material on slavery and emancipation and on the sugar industry. Some official publications are also available, including a good collection of Blue-books.

Files of the principal West Indian newspapers are kept for about three months.

A Catalogue of the Library was printed and published in 1941.

The Committee's own monthly journal and other publications are also in the Library as well as its Reports and Accounts and Reports of *ad hoc* committees. The Minute Books are also accessible from 1769, with the exception of those for the last few years.

Admission to the Library and reading rooms is granted to students and research workers on suitable recommendation and applications should be made in writing addressed to the Secretary. They are open daily from 10 a.m. to 5 p.m., Saturdays from 10 a.m. to 12 noon.

Western Australia
Office of the Agent-General in London
115 Strand, W.C.2

A small general reference library is maintained containing some 300 volumes on Western Australia. Official publications are well represented and include Western Australia Statutes from 1832, Government Gazettes from 1870, Votes and Proceedings (including Parliamentary papers) from 1880, and Debates from 1890, together with Blue Books and Statistical registers from 1874. It also possesses a bibliography of United Kingdom Parliamentary papers on Western Australian affairs from 1829 to 1890. The library is open to the public from 9.15 a.m. to 5.15 p.m., Monday to Friday.

Westminster Public Library
Central Reference Library
St. Martin's Street, W.C.2

The Westminster Central Reference Library is one of the most important public libraries of the Metropolis; it contains some 100,000 volumes. For the advanced research worker in the field of Commonwealth studies its chief value lies in the collection of works of reference. It also possesses good general collections in the fields of history, economics and anthropology.

Government publications and Parliamentary papers are well represented—House of Commons Papers, House of Lords Papers, Command Papers as well as other publications issued by H.M. Stationery Office not in numbered series are almost complete from 1920. Of the period 1800 to 1919 there is a considerable collection. It also possesses complete sets of the Journals of the House of Commons and House of Lords and *Calendars of State Papers*. There are also available a large collection of League of Nations publications and complete sets of the publications of the United Nations and its Specialist Agencies, issued in the United Kingdom, and of the International Labour Office.

One of the Library's specialities is a fine collection of general statistical material—abstracts, yearbooks and handbooks—of Great Britain and the Commonwealth. Official Year-Books (Federal, state and provincial) of Australia, Canada, New Zealand and South Africa are retained from 1946 as well as annual Colonial administrative Reports, which are bound and kept for permanent reference.

The reference material includes a most valuable collection of general, commercial and specialist Directories, Guides, Handbooks, etc., and telephone directories of the Commonwealth and many foreign countries, as well as dictionaries (vernacular and technical), encyclopaedias, dictionaries of biography and Who's Whos and good sets of *Whitaker's Almanack*, the *Statesman's Year-Book*, the *Colonial Office List* and the *Foreign Office List*.

There is a world coverage of maps, which number some 12,000 (but not those issued by the Colonial Survey) and a representative collection of Gazetteers.

Some 500 general, historical and economic periodicals are bound and retained; indexes to periodical literature include the International Index, the Readers' Guide, the Arts Index and the Biographical Index (of which there are complete sets) and the Public Affairs Information Service, the Engineering Index and the Industrial Arts Index. *The Times* newspaper from 1785 (mostly on microfilm), together with its Index, from 1860 is also available.

The Library is open daily (Monday to Saturday inclusive) from 10 a.m. until 8 p.m., except bank holidays. There are no restrictions as to admission. Books may be borrowed under certain circumstances in consultation with the Librarian. Lists of accessions have been issued quarterly and yearly since 1950; five yearly cumulations will be published at intervals.

Zinc Development Association
34 Berkeley Square, W.1

The Association's library contains some 600 volumes, 10,000 pamphlets and 200 current periodicals devoted to metallurgy generally and to the use of zinc as well as statistical material on non-ferrous metal production and consumption. Research workers may be admitted to the library, on application to the Librarian, between 9.30 a.m. and 12.45 p.m., and between 2 p.m. and 5.30 p.m., Monday to Friday.

II. COLLECTIONS IN OXFORD

The Bodleian

The Bodleian is one of the world's great libraries and, in England, ranks second only to the British Museum in size—it contains approximately two million books. It has been a depository library since 1610, first by agreement with the Stationers' Company and now under the provisions of the Copyright Acts by which it may demand copies of all books and papers published in the United Kingdom. Unlike the British Museum its acquisitions under the Acts are selective and not automatic. In dealing with such a vast collection it is imposssible here to describe concisely its nature or content. The *Handbook to the University* states 'in a great and ancient depository like this there is hardly any field of human knowledge which is not represented by some greater or smaller body of raw material for research; but, needless to say, the Bodleian is stronger in some than in others. It does not offer special attractions to the student of contemporary or very recent economic and political affairs. It has not the resources for forming very ambitious collections of the official publications of foreign governments, and even in the ordinary literature of modern studies it is not as strong as might be wished. Even here, however, it has occasionally something to offer: it is strong in continental academic dissertations, and now and again will be found to have something of this sort which is not available elsewhere in England. Its greatest strength, however, lies in earlier centuries.' The student of Commonwealth history, economics or politics will be best served by two of the Bodleian's three dependent libraries, namely, those of Rhodes House (history of the British Commonwealth and the United States of America) and the Indian Institute (Indian and Pakistani studies) both of which are described below. These two libraries house the Bodleian collections of material within their appropriate fields, other than the earliest printed works. The Bodleian consists of the Old Library (including the famous Duke Humphrey's library) and the New Library in Parks Road, opened in 1946, containing bookstacks, reading rooms and administrative offices; the buildings are connected by an underground mechanical conveyor. The general research library is in Duke Humphrey. Modern parliamentary papers and official documents are kept in the philosophy, politics and economics reading room in the New Library.

The manuscript collection numbers some 50,000 volumes and there are, in addition, many thousands of rolls and charters. Duke Humphrey's library is used mainly as the reading room for the manuscript collection where are also to be found the catalogues of manuscripts. A leaflet of *Instructions to Readers* has been prepared and may be obtained free of charge from the Department of Western Manuscripts. Additions to the collection are noted in the *Bodleian Library Record* and the *Annual Reports* and in the *Bulletin* of the Institute of Historical Research (University of London). Commonwealth 'papers' are, however, scanty and are mainly of Indian interest, namely, the papers of Sir Charles and Mr. Charles Russell, 1803–43, letter-books of John Palmer (Merchant), 1808–35 and the Scattergood Papers (East India Company), 1681–1723. Other collections of papers of Commonwealth interest are to be found in Rhodes House.

The main attraction of the Bodleian for the Commonwealth scholar is its 'basic' United Kingdom material, namely, Parliamentary Papers (House of Commons papers and Papers by Command, complete; House of Lords papers incomplete); Parliamentary debates (Hansard), complete; Journals of both Houses, complete; London Gazette, complete (some early volumes, however, are imperfect); Calendars of State Papers; British and Foreign State Papers and the Treaty Series. It also possesses complete runs of the *Annual Register*, the *Colonial Office List*, the *Dominions Office and Commonwealth Relations Office Lists*, *Foreign Office List*, *Imperial Service Calendar*, the *India Office List*, *Statesman's Year Book*, *Whitaker's Almanack* and *Who was Who* and *Who's Who*. Its collection of periodicals, British, Foreign and Commonwealth, is very extensive. Details of Commonwealth periodicals available are to be found in the list of *Current Foreign and Commonwealth Periodicals in the Bodleian Library and in other Oxford Libraries* (revised 1953, Supplement, 1951–4, 1957).

A large collection of maps and survey material is available, but the collection of historical maps is not particularly good.

Theses are deposited in the Library but those of Commonwealth interest have been passed to Rhodes House (D.Phil. complete, B.Litt. complete from 1953, before that date only a selection has been made).

The Bodleian is a depository library for United Nations documents.

There is no 'handy' guide to the Bodleian. A chapter on 'Libraries' in the *Handbook to the University of Oxford* (current edition 1955) will be found useful by the intending reader who will learn something of library facilities available in Oxford (both the Bodleian and the 'special' libraries). Two major works from which much information may be

M

obtained are Macray's *Annals of the Bodleian Library* (2nd edn, 1890) and Craster's *History of the Bodleian Library, 1845–1945* (1952).

Application for admission to the Bodleian and its dependent libraries by those not belonging to the University must be submitted to Bodley's Librarian on a specially printed form which must be completed by a 'recommender' and signed by the applicant. A 'recommender' 'must be someone in a responsible position whose credentials can be readily verified'. Admission may be granted to *all* reading rooms or may be restricted to the Radcliffe Camera, the New Library and the dependent libraries.

The Old Library is open from 9.30 a.m. until 7 p.m. (Saturdays 9.30 a.m. until 1 p.m.) and the New Library from 9 a.m. until 1 p.m. and from 2 p.m. until 10 p.m. in term (in vacation it closes at 7 p.m. either side of term and at 5 p.m. in the middle of vacation), (Saturdays 9 a.m. until 1 p.m.). The Old Library is closed on January 1st, Good Friday, Easter eve, Easter Monday, the first Wednesday in the long vacation, the week beginning the first Monday in August, December 24th to 31st and on Sundays. The New Library is closed on the five weekdays next before Easter Sunday, Easter Monday, the first Wednesday in the long vacation, the week beginning the first Monday in August, December 22nd to 28th and on Sundays.

Agricultural Economics Research Institute
Parks Road

The Institute library contains approximately 6,000 volumes, 2,000 pamphlets and 320 current periodicals devoted to agricultural economics and allied subjects of the United Kingdom, the Commonwealth and under-developed territories. Other subjects covered are rural sociology, marketing, labour and international trade. Official publications of the United Kingdom and Commonwealth appropriate to the field (departmental reports, bulletins, etc.) are taken as well as all those of the Food and Agricultural Organization and some of the United Nations (statistical and economic). Sets of Commonwealth official Year-books from the 1920's are also in the library. Statistics are particularly well represented—agricultural statistics, national income, censuses and demographic. Theses presented since 1945 by students of the Institute for the degrees of B.Litt. and D.Phil. may be consulted in the library by permission of the authors.

Accredited research workers may be admitted on application to the Librarian. Books may be borrowed.

The library is open from 9 a.m. until 5.30 p.m., Monday to Friday; Saturdays from 9 a.m. until 1 p.m.

Department of Agriculture
Parks Road

The library contains some 7,000 volumes on agriculture and its basic sciences, including plant physiology, soil sciences, etc., of which 3,000 are textbooks and the remainder periodicals. Of the latter, 300 titles are held, of which about two-thirds are current, covering a wide range of British, Commonwealth and foreign publications.

A good collection of Colonial material is also held including Departmental Reports, Bulletins and other official publications.

A *List* of Periodicals, Annual Reports, Bulletins, etc., held in the library is issued and revised annually.

Accredited research workers may be admitted on application to the Librarian. The library is normally open from 9.30 a.m. until 1 p.m. and from 2 p.m. until 5 p.m. (Saturdays 9.30 a.m. until 1 p.m.). During the University terms the hours are extended.

Imperial Forestry Institute
Department of Forestry
South Parks Road

The Imperial Forestry Institute possesses an outstanding library of some 10,000 volumes of material on forestry and ancillary subjects in the United Kingdom, the Commonwealth and foreign countries. Although mainly scientific and technical it includes much on the economic aspects of forestry, and on agriculture in so far as it impinges on the same field. It also includes a good collection of statistical material and parliamentary papers and official publications of the Commonwealth appropriate to its field. The official publications include departmental reports, bulletins and occasional papers. Current periodicals number some 280—a *List of Periodicals and Serial Publications* in the library was published by the Department in 1949.

The library also holds University theses on the subject of forestry (to which there is a separate catalogue) and about 400 special maps (vegetation, geology, irrigation, mineral, etc.) many of which are listed in *Special Maps in Oxford Libraries* (School of Geography), 1956.

A comprehensive card-index of world forestry literature from the year 1934 onwards is maintained, from which entries for the quarterly *Forestry Abstracts* are selected. Additions to the index at present number about 24,000 cards annually. Pre-1934 literature was and still is fully indexed, in typed foolscap folders kept in box-files.

The library, primarily for departmental use, is open to accredited research workers between the hours of 9 a.m. and 7 p.m. in term, and 9 a.m. and 5 p.m. in vacation; Saturdays between 9 a.m. and 1 p.m. Application for admission should be made to the Librarian. Books may be borrowed.

The Institute houses the Commonwealth Forestry Bureau (see further p. 195).

Indian Institute
(The Bodleian)
Catte Street

The Indian Institute is a centre for studies connected with India and Pakistan—its interests, however, also extend to Burma, Nepal, Siam, Tibet and Afghanistan. The library houses all the Bodleian books on those studies, it being one of the dependent libraries. Indian manuscripts and older printed books on India, however, remain in the Bodleian so that the library does not form a separate unit to the same extent as Rhodes House. It is, however, within its sphere, second only to the India Office Library in London. It contains some 80,000 volumes covering many fields including history, economics, politics, law (statutes and reports, with some text-books), languages, religion, art and archaeology. It possesses a fine collection of Sanskrit material. Works in the vernaculars, although not so strongly represented as Sanskrit, nevertheless number over 5,000 and new books are still being added.

A selection of parliamentary papers and official publications issued about, or in, the areas with which they are concerned is available— United Kingdom, from earliest times; India, a selection including legislative debates, from 1921 onwards (with some imperfections), the Gazette of India from 1930, and most of the provincial gazettes.

About eighty current periodicals are taken and kept for permanent reference and some twenty earlier non-current sets have been retained. An index of periodical literature from 1950 is maintained; it will be extended backwards in time as and when assistance becomes available. Three of the more important newspapers are filed permanently—*The Statesman* (Calcutta), *Dawn* (Karachi) and *The Hindu* (Madras), all from the year 1950 onwards.

A few reference books are purchased, including two Indian annuals, and a set of the *India Office List* is retained. A small selection of maps is held but the major collection is in the Bodleian itself.

Non-members of the University may be admitted to the library on formal recommendation submitted to Bodley's Librarian on the Bodleian Library application form. The library is open in term from 9.30 a.m. to 1 p.m. and from 2 p.m. to 5 p.m. except on Saturdays when it closes at 1 p.m. Out of term the periods of admission are slightly shorter. It is closed on the usual holidays and for the month of August.

Institute of Commonwealth Studies
(formerly Institute of Colonial Studies)
10 Keble Road

The Institute is a centre for Colonial studies in the fields of government, economics and recent history. It has a small selective library of books, reports, periodicals and press cuttings.

Its emphasis is on the contemporary problems of dependent territories, both British and foreign, and of those which have recently acquired independent status. It has a good collection on the French Union, including 'journaux officiels' of some oversea territories (West Africa, the Cameroons, Equatorial Africa and Madagascar) generally since 1950, as well as some other publications not available elsewhere in the country.

Admission to the library is given to 'accredited readers' and application should be made to the Librarian. It is open daily in term from 9 a.m. to 1 p.m. and from 2 p.m. to 7 p.m., Saturdays from 9 a.m. to 1 p.m. Out of term the library closes at 5 p.m. It is also closed over the usual holiday periods.

Institute of Social Anthropology
11 Keble Road

The purpose of the Institute library is to provide teaching and research facilities for students working for the diploma and for research degrees in anthropology. It contains some 4,700 volumes, 1,500 pamphlets and offprints and fifty current periodicals. There is a strong African and Indian section as well as one devoted to Arabic-speaking and Moslem communities. The library also possesses the Skeat Collection of works on Indonesia and Melanesia.

Non-members of the University may use the library by permission and applications should be addressed to the Librarian. Books are not, as a general rule, lent outside the University. The library is open during term from 9.30 a.m. to 5.30 p.m. (except Saturday afternoon) and at restricted hours during vacations.

Institute of Statistics
(housed temporarily in St. Cross Road)

This Institute was established in 1947 under the general supervision of the Faculty of Social Studies. Its work includes the study of the theory of statistics and of the method of statistical analysis and the application of statistical methods to economic and social problems. A library is being built up and at present contains some 12,000 books and pamphlets within its field of interest. It is not, however, confined to British material and a useful collection of statistics and statistical works relating to Commonwealth countries and some colonies from about the year 1930 is being assembled. Some earlier material is available but the collection is not yet comprehensive. Persons not being members of the University are admitted on application to the Librarian. The library is open on weekdays from 10 a.m. to 1 p.m. and from 2.15 p.m. to 6 p.m.

Nuffield College

Nuffield College, established to encourage research especially, but not exclusively, in the field of social studies, has an attraction for Commonwealth scholars by reason of the facilities it offers and the research it fosters. It maintains a good library of British, Commonwealth and foreign material, now numbering some 20,000 volumes and includes the G. D. H. Cole collection of social history. Current periodicals, especially economic and political, are a speciality—including Commonwealth and American and some other foreign serials—mainly from 1947 onwards, although back sets are being acquired. It contains all the publications of the International Labour Office since 1947 and a selection of those of the United Nations.

The library is available to graduate research workers and such other persons as may be admitted by the Warden. Applications should be submitted to the Librarian and, in the case of persons in the latter category, should be supported by a Fellow of the College or by letters of recommendation from two persons of position. Books may not be borrowed. The library is open from 9.30 a.m. to 1 p.m. and from 2 p.m. to 6 p.m., Saturdays 9.30 a.m. to 1 p.m. It is closed over the normal holiday periods.

Rhodes House Library
(The Bodleian)
South Parks Road

Rhodes House is a centre for advanced study of the political, social and economic history and development, past and present, of the British

Commonwealth (excluding India and Pakistan) and the United States of America. The library is a dependent library of the Bodleian from which all books within the fields mentioned have been transferred, except works published before 1760. New British publications on those subjects are also transferred as they are received. In addition the Rhodes Trustees purchase material to complete gaps in the Bodleian collection and books and periodicals published in the Commonwealth and the United States. The Trustees also deposit in the library books, documents, manuscripts and similar material belonging to them. The Governments of Commonwealth countries and the United States supply an extensive selection of their official publications (departmental reports, Parliamentary papers and proceedings, etc.). Similar material from the Colonies is available from about the year 1920; earlier material is still being acquired. The library also contains a collection of the publications of the League of Nations and the United Nations, which includes material on the former mandatory system and on the present trust and non-self-governing territories, together with all important unofficial material in this field.

The Scicluna collection devoted to Malta is reputed to be one of the finest in the world.

The collection of private papers is a valuable one. As would be expected such of the Rhodes papers as are available in this country are deposited in the Library (1890 to 1903), although not all of them may be consulted without special permission obtained from the Secretary to the Rhodes Trustees. The collection consists of twenty-eight bound folio volumes, with an index. In addition, there is a number of bound volumes of copies of Rhodes' telegrams. (Other papers are housed in the Central African Archives, Salisbury, Southern Rhodesia; about one-third of all Rhodes' papers, being the later material, were tragically lost during air-raids on London during the late war.)

Papers to which special reference should be made are:

The Cawston papers (British South Africa Co., Reports and miscellaneous papers and correspondence, 1888–1911); the Scarbrough papers relating to the Royal Niger Company, 1884–1930 as well as some Lugard correspondence, 1901–19; Sir R. Burke's correspondence and letter books relating to his administration of the Cape, 1825–8; the Codrington diaries, letters, etc., relating to missionary work in Melanesia, 1867–87; the F. G. Hall letters, papers and diaries (British East Africa), 1880–1901; Lord Lugard's Uganda diaries and West African diaries and a letter-book, 1890–4; Lord Macartney's letter-books, etc., 1797–8 (Cape); Sir J. C. Molteno's papers (1857–85) and letter-books (1837–58) (Cape and South Africa); Sir G. H. Portal's letter-books, diaries and correspondence, 1881–95 (Egypt and East Africa); E. J. H. Russell's diaries (1895–1900) (British East Africa Co.); the Thornton papers on East Africa, 1858–62; the Waller papers (Africa), including material relating to Livingstone (1862–72) and Gordon (1874–84); Diaries, travel notes and letters of Basil Williams, 1900–46; Journals, letters and maps of C. Sturt's three expeditions of discovery in South and Central Australia, 1828–1846; Sir R. Coupland's travel diaries and albums, 1913–36; Correspondence relating to the Young Estates in the West Indies, 1768–1835; Agreements, wills, plantation accounts, inventories of slaves, etc., concerning the Greg Estates in the West Indies, 1765–1834.

There are also some miscellaneous papers on Australia, Canada and the West Indies. A list of manuscripts available is to be found in the account of the library by L. B. Frewer, mentioned at the end of this entry.

The archives of the Anti-Slavery Society are also available in the Library having been purchased by the Rhodes Trustees. They cover the period 1820 to 1941 and consist of letters of the British and Foreign Anti-Slavery Society and the Aborigines Protection Society, letter books, files of 'out' letters, Minute books, ledgers and account books, etc. The collection will be added to once every decade when the Society will deposit its files for the previous ten years. This vast collection, although sorted, is at present mostly unbound.

Microfilm copies have also been made of several series of nineteenth-century documents in American archives dealing with the suppression of the slave trade, the African Squadron and negro colonization.

Parliamentary Papers and Official publications available include the following:

AUSTRALIA

New South Wales. Legislative Assembly Votes and Proceedings, 1856–1904 (imperfect); Legislative Council Votes and Proceedings, 1835–41, 1846, Journals, 1857–88 (imperfect); Parliamentary debates from 1879 to date (with some gaps); Government Gazettes, a miscellaneous collection from 1834 to 1845, 1861 to 1883, and from 1886 onwards; various Departmental reports; Statistical material, miscellaneous and imperfect from 1860 onwards (including Blue books 1863–6, 1868, 1878 and 1881); Year books 1904–40, 1945–6.

Queensland. Legislative Assembly Votes and Proceedings, 1870–89 (some gaps), Journals, 1878–9; Legislative Council Journals, 1876–98; Parliamentary Debates, 1865, 1867–71, 1880, 1892, 1897–1901, 1904, 1905, 1916/17; official Gazette from 1947 onwards; miscellaneous Departmental Reports; Statistical material from 1872 to date (with some gaps) (including Blue books, 1873, 1876, 1878–1916); Year books, 1903–7, 1937–41, 1945 onwards.

South Australia. Parliamentary Proceedings and Papers, from 1852 to date; Parliamentary Debates, 1857–8 to date (with a few minor gaps); official Gazette, 1840–1930, 1932 to date; miscellaneous Departmental Reports; Statistical Register, 1885, 1886, 1898, 1900–7, 1925/26, 1931/32 to date.

Tasmania. Legislative Assembly Journals, 1857–83 (some gaps); Legislative Council Journals and Papers, 1858–83 (some gaps); Parliamentary Journals and Papers, 1884 to date; official Gazette, 1938 onwards (also the earlier Hobart

Town Gazette, 1827, 1830–2, 1836–45, 1847–9, 1852, 1868, 1869, 1880–3);
miscellaneous Departmental Reports; miscellaneous Statistical material 1895,
1899, 1904/5, 1918/19, 1933/34 onwards.

Victoria. Legislative Assembly Votes, Proceedings and Papers, 1856–7 onwards;
Legislative Council Votes and Proceedings, 1851/2 to 1859/60, 1861/2, 1862/3,
1867, 1880, 1885, 1886, Minutes 1892/3 onwards (some gaps); Parliamentary
Debates, 1856/7, 1867/8, 1866 onwards; official Gazette, 1851–1933, 1937
onwards; miscellaneous Departmental Reports; Statistical Register 1858–9,
1861, 1867–98, 1900–13; Year books, 1873–1895/8, 1902–1917/18, 1920/21
onwards.

Western Australia. Legislative Council Votes and Proceedings 1883, 1884, 1886,
1887, 1887/8; Parliamentary Debates from beginning to date, with some gaps;
Parliamentary Minutes, Votes and Proceedings from 1890 to date; official
Gazette from 1946; miscellaneous Departmental Reports; Statistical material,
including Blue books from 1874 to 1900 (with some gaps), Statistical Abstract,
1905–17 and the Statistical Register from 1896 to date (with some minor gaps);
Year books (some 'Pocket' edns) 1892/93 to 1902/04, 1931 to date.

Commonwealth. Parliamentary Debates, 1901 onwards; Senate Journals, 1901 onwards; official Gazette, 1901 onwards; Departmental Reports, various and miscellaneous from 1901 onwards; Census material from 1901; Year books, covering the year 1901 to date. (There are also some miscellaneous volumes of Federal
Council debates, journals and papers, 1886, 1888, 1889, 1891, 1893, 1895 and
1897.)

CANADA

Alberta, British Columbia and *Manitoba.* Good collections of Departmental Reports,
although the Alberta material is far from complete.

New Brunswick. House of Assembly Journals, 1836–1920; Legislative Council
Journals, 1859–66, 1868, 1869; good collection of Departmental Reports.

Newfoundland. Official Gazette, 1946 onwards; miscellaneous Departmental
Reports.

Nova Scotia. House of Assembly Journals, 1851–9, 1863–8, 1882–4, 1886–94;
Legislative Council Journals, 1839–41, 1844–74, 1881, 1882, 1884, 1886–90,
1891–4; a good miscellaneous collection of Departmental Reports.

Ontario. House of Assembly Journals, with Appendices, 1792–4, 1798–1808, 1810–
1812, 1814, 1816–24, 1832/3, 1835–40; Legislative Assembly Journals 1868 onwards; Legislative Council Journals, 1792–4, 1798–1808, 1810–12, 1814, 1819
1821–4; a good collection of Departmental Reports; Upper Canada Gazette,
1793–1845.

Prince Edward Island. House of Assembly Journals, 1827, 1838, 1840–52, 1854,
1856–7, 1859, 1861–70; Legislative Assembly Journals, 1930 onwards.

Quebec. Legislative Assembly Sessional Papers, 1869–90; Legislative Assembly
Journals, 1867 onwards (with some minor gaps); Legislative Council Debates,
1887–90, 1892–5; Legislative Council Journals, 1819–21, 1823–35, 1867–71,
1873–8, 1880–90, 1892, 1893, 1895 onwards; House of Assembly Journals,
1793–8, 1801, 1810–14, 1816, 1818, 1819, 1823–36; a good collection of
Departmental Reports; Statistical Year books, 1914 onwards.

Saskatchewan. Legislative Assembly Journals and Sessional Papers, 1906, 1908,
1909, 1913–20, 1922, 1924 onwards; some Departmental Reports.

Dominion. Legislative Assembly Journals, 1842–66; Legislative Council Journals,

1841–66 (with some gaps); House of Commons Journals, 1868 onwards; Senate Journals, 1868 onwards; Parliamentary Debates, 1846, 1854–64/5, 1866–70, 1873–4 (on microfilm); House of Commons Debates, 1875 onwards; Senate Debates, 1870 onwards; Sessional Papers, 1867–1925, an excellent collection of Departmental Reports; official Gazette, 1867 onwards; Miscellaneous Census and Statistical material; Year books, 1864, 1867–79, 1896, 1905 onwards.

• NEW ZEALAND

House of Representative Journals (with appendices containing Departmental annual reports), 1855 onwards; Parliamentary Debates, 1854 onwards; Legislative Council Journals (with appendices), 1862 onwards; official Gazette 1930 onwards; Census material, 1896 onwards (some gaps); Statistical Reports, 1853 onwards (some gaps in earlier years); Year books, 1885–6, 1886–7, 1893 onwards.

SOUTH AFRICA

Cape. Parliamentary Votes and Proceedings, 1846–1883 (incomplete); official Gazette, 1898–1911; Blue books, 1859–62, 1878–85; Statistical Register, 1886–1909.
Natal. Legislative Council Votes and Proceedings, 1859–61, 1863–72, 1874–6, 1878–82; Blue books, 1861–91, 1894/5, 1897–9, 1907, 1908.
Orange. Government Gazette, 1903–11.
Territories. Official publications, a selection.
Union. House of Assembly Debates, 1924 onwards; Senate Debates, 1924 onwards; Government Gazette, 1945 onwards; Year books, 1910 onwards.

COLONIES

Departmental reports, legislative debates and journals, legislation, official gazettes, blue books and other official publications of the Colonies are available from the year 1920 but earlier material is still being acquired.

All current Commonwealth periodicals of importance in the fields of history, politics and the social and economic sciences are taken in the library, and the major articles therein are indexed and included in the library catalogue.

A selection of Commonwealth newspapers is available together with long runs on microfilm of early South African newspapers (*Natal Mercury*, 1852–1904; the *Standard and Diggers' News*, 1889–1900; the *Friend of the Free State*, 1850–90; *Cape Mercantile Advertiser*, 1852–89; the *South African Commercial Advertiser*, 1824–47; and the *Eastern Province Herald*, 1845–1910) and early Canadian (Federal and Provincial) newspapers (including *La Gazette de Québec*, 1764–1817; the *Upper Canada Gazette*, 1793–1845; the *British Colonist*, 1858–71; the *Manitoban*, 1870–4; the *Nova Scotian*, 1824–39; the *New Brunswick Courier*, 1833–1865; *La Minerve*, 1826–54). A run on microfilm of the *Debates o Parliament* between 1846 and 1874 is also available. Sets of current newspapers include the *Sydney Morning Herald*, from 1840, the *Montreal Gazette*, from 1930, the *Cape Times*, from 1905 (with some gaps), the *East African Standard*, from 1929, the *New Zealand Herald*, from 1945, and the *Ceylon Daily News*, from 1954.

Current issues of the *New York Times* and the *New York Herald Tribune* are held together with microfilm copies of the earliest years of the former paper and some others.

In the matter of works of reference all available material published throughout the Commonwealth is purchased and retained for permanent reference. Sets or good runs of the *Colonial Office List*, the *Dominions Office and Commonwealth Relations Office Lists*, the *Statesman's Year Book* and *Whitaker's Almanack* are also available. The library possesses some early Colonial maps and atlases but modern material is to be found only in the Bodleian itself.

Theses of Commonwealth interest submitted for the Oxford degrees of Doctor of Philosophy and Bachelor of Letters are deposited at Rhodes House (D.Phil. complete, B.Litt. complete from 1953, before which time only a selection has been made). They may be consulted by permission of the authors, where appropriate.

Non-members of the University may be admitted to the Library on formal recommendation submitted to the Superintendent of the Library on Bodleian application forms. The Library is open in term from 9 a.m. to 1 p.m. and from 2 p.m. to 7 p.m. on weekdays, out of term the library closes at 4.30 p.m. It is open on every Saturday from 9 a.m. to 1 p.m. It is closed from Good Friday to Easter Monday inclusive, the first week in August, and from the 24th until the 31st December. A lending library of Commonwealth literature is maintained from which non-members may borrow books.

Further information may be obtained from Frewer's *Rhodes House Library, its function and resources* (*Bodleian Library Record*, vol. v, No. 6, October 1956) which includes a list of manuscripts in the library. Another interesting and useful guide is *Cecil Rhodes and Rhodes House* (8th edn, 1952). A publication still of some value, although it is now somewhat out of date, is *Research at Rhodes House, Oxford*, a pamphlet published in 1931.

School of Geography
Mansfield Road

The library, which contains some 20,000 volumes, is devoted mainly to geography and allied subjects (historical, political, social, economic and physical geography) of the United Kingdom, the Commonwealth and foreign countries. It includes much material on history, economics (including the location of industry), sociology, the geographical aspects of race relations and human geography, particularly the problems of colonization and settlement. Current periodicals number about seventy-two, together with about fifty sets of earlier series. The library also possesses a collection of some 6,000 pamphlets and reprints, many of Commonwealth interest. There is a collection of maps and atlases of the world, including Colonial Survey maps and large selections of Australian and Canadian material. World gazetteers are available, including some of the Commonwealth particularly of India of which there is a fine set. The library issued in 1956 a valuable union list: *Special Maps in Oxford Libraries* (geological, climatic, economic, population and other non-topographic maps published after 1940).

Some official publications within the library's field of interest are available, as well as Colonial Blue-books from the 1930's, good runs of Official Year-books and some official statistics.

Accredited research workers are admitted on application to the Librarian. The library is open from 9 a.m. to 1 p.m. and 2.30 p.m. to 7 p.m., Monday to Friday, and from 9 a.m. to 1 p.m. on Saturdays. During vacations it closes at 5 p.m.

Queen Elizabeth House
21 St. Giles

The House was founded in 1954 as the result of a benefaction by Sir Ernest Oppenheimer and a Government grant. A Royal Charter was granted in the same year. The purposes of the House are, briefly: (1) to facilitate and encourage Commonwealth studies, (2) to provide a centre in Oxford to which people, especially of 'authority or influence', may come for the study of Commonwealth problems and the exchange of information relating thereto, and (3) to establish and maintain contacts between such people and the relevant academic agencies in the United Kingdom.

Black Hall, in St. Giles, has been made available as headquarters and the task of conversion is proceeding. The House commenced to function modestly in October, 1956. A library is to be built up.

Further information may be obtained from the Warden.

Almost every college, institution, school and department of the University maintains a library. College libraries are mainly for the use of their individual members and, generally do not attract the overseas research worker, although the Milner papers are housed in the Library of New College and the Salisbury papers in Christ Church. Admission is more easily gained by non-members of the University to the libraries of Institutions and Departments which will be found of particular value, each in its own sphere. Mention should be made of the History Faculty Library, the library of University College (early Americana), the Codrington Library of All Souls College (history, political economy and law, although the only section of particular interest to the Commonwealth student is the South African) and the Barnett House Library of economics, sociology and related subjects. Further information about these, and other, libraries, is available in the *Handbook to the University* and in the pamphlet on *Facilities for Advanced Study and Research*, issued by the University's Committee for Advanced Studies (latest edition 1952) or from the individual Librarians, to whom applications for admissions should be made.

III. COLLECTIONS IN CAMBRIDGE

University Library

The Library of the University of Cambridge is one of the great national libraries and has enjoyed the right, since 1662, of receiving under the Copyright Acts a copy of all books, etc., published in the United Kingdom. It is not, however, bound to accept copies of every work published as is the British Museum and its acquisitions have, therefore, been selected. It now contains well over two million volumes and thousands of manuscripts and maps and it would be impossible here to attempt an analysis of so vast a collection. Printed historical source material—Calendars of State Papers, Parliamentary and official publications, Parliamentary Debates, Journals of both Houses of Parliament, etc.—is to be found in the Library together with works on all subjects.

PARLIAMENTARY AND OFFICIAL PUBLICATIONS

The holdings of Parliamentary and official publications of the United Kingdom are as follows:

Parliamentary Papers. House of Commons, complete from 1801 to date (in addition to the fifteen-volume collection of reports from 1715–1801); House of Lords, from 1835 to date, but with some imperfections; Abbot collection on microprint, 1731–1800 (but imperfect in parts).

Non-Parliamentary Papers. Probably complete.

Parliamentary Debates (Hansard). Complete from 1803 to date.

Journals. House of Commons complete from 1547 to date; House of Lords complete from 1509 to date.

London Gazette. 1665–1724, 1742–6, 1755 to date.

Calendars of State Papers. Complete to date.

British and Foreign State Papers. Complete to date.

Treaty Series. Complete to date.

Diplomatic and Consular Reports (issued from 1855 to 1915 as parliamentary papers and later as reports of the Board of Trade or Department of Overseas Trade, as non-parliamentary papers): complete.

COLLECTIONS OF PAPERS

The Library has recently acquired the letters and papers of Lord Hardinge of Penshurst (1858–1944); forty-two volumes cover his period of service in the diplomatic field and thirty-three the period of his viceroyalty of India (1910–16). The collection is regarded as one of outstanding importance. For the time being it will be subject to the same conditions as govern access to official archives of H.M. Government.

The Jardine Matheson Archive, consisting of the nineteenth-century records of the Jardine Matheson Company of China, is housed in the Library. It contains (i) correspondence (original in-coming letters from various parts of the world, including China, Africa, Australasia, India, Ceylon, the East Indies, Siam, Malaya and Hong Kong); (ii) Accounts, etc.; (iii) Prices current and market reports; and (iv) miscellaneous material (bills of lading, reports, memoranda, documents, etc.). There is a calendar and index covering part of the correspondence but the work of compilation is still in progress. The Archive may be consulted with the permission of Matheson & Co., Ltd., 3 Lombard Street, London, E.C.3, and of the University Librarian.

Other manuscript material includes the Badger papers (Zanzibar), the Raffles papers (Java, Prince of Wales Island, the Straits Settlements, etc.) and the Cowell papers (India).

COMMONWEALTH MATERIAL

Material relating to the Commonwealth published in the United Kingdom has been selected and demanded under the Copyright Acts. Material published overseas has been purchased in the ordinary course. Such acquisitions have been moderate over the years. Indeed it can be said that Cambridge is not 'rich' in Commonwealth material, either official or unofficial. Dominion and Colonial official series, with some exceptions, commence in the 1930's. The Asian countries of the Commonwealth are fairly well represented. In 1948 a review of Commonwealth official publications was conducted; it is recorded that 'when the official publications files were examined after the war for items not yet received it was noticed how unequal were the Library's collections. While the Library possesses practically complete files for Great Britain and India and, since 1932, for the Colonies, it has only a fragmentary collection of Dominion and foreign official publications . . .; the increasing interest taken in Dominion affairs has led to requests for material which is not to be found in Cambridge, and it seems advisable that the Library should try to acquire a representative collection of the publications of these governments.' With the exception of India and Pakistan, Commonwealth countries now send copies of their important official publications; supplies are also received regularly from most of the Colonial governments. Efforts are still being made to improve the collection and the present position may be summarized as follows:

AUSTRALIA

Commonwealth. Parliamentary Debates, 1901 onwards; Parliamentary Papers, 1946 onwards; Senate Journals and House of Representative Votes and proceedings, 1950 onwards; Census reports, from 1911; Trade and statistical publications, 1944/45 to date; Year books, 1901 to date; Miscellaneous departmental reports; Historical Records of Australia, Series 1, 3 and 4.

New South Wales. Statistical material, miscellaneous and imperfect, from 1878. Year books, 1904/5–35 (some gaps), 1948/49 to date. Miscellaneous departmental reports.

Queensland. Statistical material from 1872 (with some gaps), including Blue books, 1873–1916. Census reports, 1876–1901. Year books, 1937 to date. Miscellaneous departmental reports.

South Australia. Statistical register, 1950/1 to date. Miscellaneous departmental reports.

Tasmania. Statistics of the State, 1925/6 to date.

Victoria. Parliamentary Debates, 1875–83, 1885–91. Government Gazette, 1854–1928 (with some gaps). Statistical register, 1858, 1867–1914. Census reports, 1871 and 1881. Year books, 1873 to date (with some gaps). Miscellaneous departmental reports.

Western Australia. Parliamentary Minutes, Votes and Proceedings, 1890–1914 (with some gaps). Statistical register, 1949 to date. Census reports, 1901. Year books, 1896–1902/4.

CANADA

Dominion. Senate Debates, 1876 to date (imperfect), Commons Debates, 1910/11–1928 (imperfect), 1953/4 to date (efforts are being made to complete the gap); House of Commons Journals, 1894–1915 (imperfect), 1949 to date;

Senate Journals, 1894–1915 (imperfect), 1949 to date; Parliamentary Sessional papers, 1867 to 1925; Year Books, 1890, 1905 to date; Census reports 1901 to date; Technical publications and reports (mines, geological surveys, etc.), reasonably good sets.

Provinces. Very little material apart from Archives of British Columbia, Memoirs, 2–4, 6 onwards; Reports of Department of Public Records and Archives, Ontario, 1903–33; Prince Edward Island Legislative Assembly Journals, 1917–1920, 1922 to date.

CEYLON

Sessional papers, complete since 1932; Debates, complete since 1922; Official Gazettes, complete since 1934; Official Year Books, 1948 to date; Blue books, 1912, 1922–38; and a good set of 'record' publications.

INDIA

Departmental reports and statistical material, Central and state governments, fairly complete from about 1880 to 1940, since when the collection is sketchy; Legislative and parliamentary debates, 1921–47, 1948 to date.

NEW ZEALAND

House of Representatives Votes and proceedings, 1854–6 (on microfilm); House of Representatives Journals, 1871 to date; Appendix to the Journals (departmental reports, etc.), 1858 to date; Parliamentary Debates, 1854 to date; Year books, 1885–6, 1886–7 and from 1921/2 to date; Census reports from 1921; Various statistical publications, some complete from 1921 to date, others complete from 1936 to date.

PAKISTAN

Constituent Assembly debates from 1948; Statistical bulletins and Year Books (miscellaneous).

SOUTH AFRICA

Cape. Minutes of the Legislative Council and Votes and proceedings of the House of Assembly (with appendices), 1880–1910/11.

South African Republic. Volksraad Notulen der Verrichtingen, 1892–8 (slightly imperfect).

Transvaal. Legislative Council Debates, 1903/4, 1909; Legislative Assembly Debates, 1907–9; Debates of both Houses, 1909–10. Annexures to the Legislative Assembly Votes and proceedings, 1907–09 (imperfect).

Union. Parliamentary Papers, very little before 1953; House of Assembly Debates, 1924 to date; Senate Debates, 1910/11, 1913–15, 1924–40 (imperfect), 1946/7 to date; Year books, 1918 to date.

COLONIES

Apart from a few miscellaneous items the collection of official publications, including legislative debates and journals and official gazettes, commences in 1932 and therefrom appears to be complete to date. There is, however, a good set of Fijian publications dating from 1878 and a run of the rare British Central Africa Gazette (later Nyasaland Government Gazette) from 1894–1914. The Library also possesses sets (some imperfect) of statistical Blue books—Fiji from 1898; the

Gambia from 1904; the Gold Coast from 1901; Nigeria from 1914; and Sierra Leone from 1899.

PERIODICALS AND NEWSPAPERS

Periodicals in the Library are considerable in number, with a bias, per haps, towards the scientific. There is a representative collection of Commonwealth journals but it is not extensive. A list of *Current periodicals available in the University Library and in other libraries connected with University*, 1955, has been published; no subject index has as yet been issued.

No special efforts have been made in the past to acquire newspapers and only the British national papers have been retained. *The Times* is complete; Palmer's Index from 1841 and the Official Index from 1906 are available. Very few Commonwealth papers are filed (those available have been noted in the Institute of Commonwealth Studies' Union List).

MAPS

The University Library possesses a magnificent collection of maps (up wards of 390,000) and atlases of all periods, including, of course, those of the Commonwealth published both in the United Kingdom and overseas.

REFERENCE BOOKS

Standard works of reference available include:

Annual Register, complete.
British Imperial Calendar, 1847–55, 1857–1916, 1918, 1919, 1925–41, 1946 to date.
Colonial Office List, complete to date.
Dominions and Commonwealth Relations Offices List, complete to date.
Foreign Office List, complete to date.
India Office List, complete to 1947.
Statesman's Year Book, complete to date.
Whitaker's Almanack, 1869, 1871, 1877 to date.
Who's Who and *Who was Who*.

The Library is open during term and long vacation residence from 9.30 a.m. to 6.30 p.m., but after 4.30 p.m. in the Michaelmas and Lent terms the bookstacks are closed, only the catalogue room, Anderson room, the periodicals room and the main reading room remain open. Out of term the Library opens at 9.30 a.m. but the whole building closes at 4.30 p.m. It is open on Saturdays from 9 a.m. until 1 p.m. both during and out of term. (The map room closes daily between 1 p.m. and 2.15 p.m.) The Library is closed on Sundays, on usual Holidays and for two days following the quarter days March 31, June 30 and Decem ber 31. It also closes from the 1st until the 15th September.

N

Admission is granted to accredited research workers of other Universities but application in writing should first be made to the Librarian.

A *Readers' Guide to the Library* has been printed and is revised from time to time. (Copies are on sale at the Library, 3*d*. each.) It contains brief notes on the *use* of the Library, the classification, special collections, catalogues available, etc., together with a plan of the building.

Marshall Library
Downing Street

The Marshall Library contains several thousand volumes dealing mainly with economics and allied subjects. It has a fairly extensive collection of periodicals in this field, British, Commonwealth and foreign. British parliamentary papers on economic questions have been collected and bound together in subjects. It contains complete, or nearly complete, files of the *Economist*, the *Economic History Review*, the *Canadian Journal of Economics and Political Science*, the *South African Journal of Economics* and other similar periodicals. Books are on open access and readily available.

Admission is granted to accredited research workers and application should be made to the Librarian.

Squire Law Library
Old Schools, Cambridge

With the exception of International law, Roman law, Jurisprudence, Legal History and Constitutional law, the University Library's current law collection is housed in the Squire Law Library which contains treatises, statutes, digests, law reports and legal periodicals of Great Britain and the Commonwealth. Only the current collections of statutes, laws, ordinances and codes are to be found in the Squire, earlier editions and collections are returned to the University Library. The Commonwealth collection of law reports and statutes is extensive and all the major series are available. The statutes of the Provinces of Canada and South Africa are complete, but not those of the Australian States. Sets of the law reports of Manitoba and Saskatchewan and the Provinces of South Africa are available as well as the more modern series of Ontario, New South Wales and South Australia. Holdings are noted in the University's list of *Current Periodicals*, and in the *Survey of Legal Periodicals . . . in British Libraries* (1957) and *Union List of Commonwealth Law Literature in Oxford, Cambridge and London* (1952), (both published by the University of London Institute of Advanced Legal

Studies) except that the latter does not include material on India and Pakistan.

Admission is granted to accredited research workers and application should be made in writing to the Librarian.

The Library is open from 9 a.m. to 1 p.m. and 2 p.m. to 7 p.m., Monday to Friday, and from 9 a.m. to 1 p.m. on Saturdays, in full term; from 9.30 a.m. to 1 p.m. and 2.30 p.m. to 5 p.m., Monday to Friday, and from 9.30 a.m. to 1 p.m. on Saturdays, in vacation.

Other Libraries

The Seeley Historical Library (Downing Street) consists of works on history, political science and international law. It is intended primarily for students reading for the historical tripos and research workers are not normally attracted.

The University School of Agriculture (Downing Street) has a library of approximately 20,000 books and many thousands of pamphlets.

The Library of the Department of Geography (Downing Street) contains some 5,000 volumes devoted to geography and allied subjects.

Each College of the University has its own library which, at one time, contained only older works collected over several centuries, the majority being of antiquarian interest rather than of practical value. In recent years, however, modern books have been added to the libraries. Admission is usually restricted to members of the College concerned but other persons are admitted under special circumstances. In each case application for admission must be made to the College Librarian.

The *Student's Handbook to the University and Colleges of Cambridge* contains brief notes on the University and libraries of Cambridge and much useful information is to be found in an article on the *Departmental Libraries of the University of Cambridge*, by D. W. Butcher, in the *Jo. of Documentation*, vol. vii, pp. 221–43 (December 1951).

Part III

I. UNIVERSITIES IN THE UNITED KINGDOM OFFERING FACILITIES FOR COMMONWEALTH STUDIES

Universities and Colleges in the United Kingdom provide facilities for study of Commonwealth aspects of many subjects, particularly Agriculture and Forestry, Anthropology, Economics, Geography, History, Politics and Government, Law, Medicine, Tropical Medicine and Veterinary Science. Full information can be obtained from the Calendars, Prospectuses and Regulations issued by individual Universities and Colleges (noted under each entry below), and from the *Year Book of the Universities of the Commonwealth*, issued annually, which contains 'entries for all Commonwealth University institutions of good standing, including general information and a full staff directory for each University, and appendices dealing with special academic topics'. One appendix is devoted to 'Commonwealth studies in United Kingdom Universities'. Other appendices relate to Postgraduate Awards (fellowships, scholarships, grants, etc.) for advanced study and research tenable both in the United Kingdom and outside; they are also issued separately in pamphlet form. Reference may also be made to *Higher Education in the United Kingdom—a handbook for students from overseas* (issued for the British Council and the Association of Universities of the British Commonwealth).

The following is a brief survey of facilities for study and research in Commonwealth problems, with particulars of Colleges offering courses in, and of Chairs and other academic appointments appropriate to, Commonwealth studies.

University of Aberdeen

A lectureship in History (to which is assigned British Imperial, Colonial and Dominion History) is established in the University. Two institutes are of particular interest to overseas students—the Rowett Research Institute for Animal Nutrition and the Macaulay Institute for Soil Science. A *Calendar* is published annually.

University of Bristol

There is established in the University a Chair of Imperial History, a

Lectureship in Colonial History and Administration and a Readership in Far Eastern history.

The University publishes annually a *Calendar, Handbook and Directory* and faculty *Prospectuses*.

University of Cambridge

There are no Colleges or Institutions particularly associated with Commonwealth studies. There is, however, a Colonial Studies Committee as well as an Institute of Oriental Studies; lectures and courses of instruction are regularly held in the University. Research generally is under the direction of the Board of Research Studies.

Faculties appropriate to Commonwealth studies:

> Economics and Politics.
> History.
> Law.
> Geography and Geology.
> Agriculture.
> Archaeology and Anthropology.

Higher degrees and diplomas:

> LL.M., M.Litt., M.Sc., Ph.D.
> Diplomas in Agricultural Science, Agriculture, Anthropology, Economics and Oriental Languages.

Chairs, Readership and Lectureship:

> Vere Harmsworth Chair of Imperial and Naval History.
> Smuts Chair of the History of the British Commonwealth.
> Smuts Readership for the further advancement of Commonwealth Studies.
> Lectureship in Colonial Studies.

Further information is available in the various publications of the University, namely, the *Annual Register, Statutes and Ordinances, Students' Handbook* and *Facilities for Study and Research*.

University of Durham
(Durham Division)

There is a School of Oriental Studies in the Faculty of Arts (sub-faculty of Oriental Studies). Attached to the School are, *inter alia*, the following lectureships—Lectureship in Modern Near Eastern History and the Spalding Lectureship in Indian Philosophy and Religion.

The oriental section of the Library contains some 35,000 volumes. The collection is housed at Elvet Hill.

The University publishes annually a *Calendar* (in two parts) and the Durham Division a *Handlist*.

University of Edinburgh

Lectureships at the University include those in Imperial and American History, Colonial Agriculture and Diseases of Tropical Climates. A *Calendar* is published annually.

University of Glasgow

There is a Lectureship in African Studies. The University publishes annually a *Calendar* and *Handbook for Overseas Students and Graduates*.

University of London

Colleges, Schools and Institutes offering courses, lectures and seminars:

Birkbeck College.
Institute of Commonwealth Studies.
Institute of Education.
Institute of Historical Research.
King's College.
London School of Economics and Political Science.
Royal Holloway College.
School of Oriental and African Studies.
University College.
Westfield College.
Wye College.

Faculties in the University appropriate to Commonwealth Studies:

Arts (Anthropology, Education, Geography, History, Oriental and African Languages and Literatures).
Laws.
Economics and Political Science (Anthropology, Economic History, Economics, Geography, Law, Public Administration, Social Administration, Sociology, Statistics).
Medicine.

Higher degrees and diplomas:

M.A., LL.M., M.Sc., M.Sc.(Econ.), Ph.D.
Academic Postgraduate Diplomas in Anthropology, Applied Parasitology and Entomology, Tropical Medicine and Hygiene, and Colonial Studies; Academic and External Diplomas in Geography, Education and Public Administration; External Diploma in Social Studies; Academic Postgraduate Certificates in Applied Parasitology and Entomology and in Tropical Medicine and Hygiene.

Chairs and Readerships associated with Commonwealth Studies include:

Chair of Bantu Languages.
Chair of Commonwealth Affairs.
Chair of East African Languages.

Chair of Education with special reference to Education in Tropical Areas.
Chair of Oriental History.
Chair of Tropical Hygiene.
Rhodes Chair of Imperial History.
Wellcome Chair of Clinical Tropical Medicine.
Readership in Applied Anthropology.
Readership in Economics (with special reference to economics of under-
    developed countries).
Readership in Imperial History.
Readership in the History of India.
Readership in West African Languages.

Subjects of special interest are to be found in many courses of study
and further information is to be found in the *University of London
Calendar*; *Regulations for Internal Students* and *Regulations for External
Students*, all published annually. Regulations applicable to individual
degrees and diplomas contained in the last two publications are also
printed and issued separately.

BIRKBECK COLLEGE
Malet Street, W.C.1

Evening lectures on Colonial History are provided as part of the course
for the B.A. Honours degree in History. Post-graduate students,
whether full-time or part-time, are also admitted. Further information
may be obtained from the College *Prospectus* and *Calendar*, both issued
annually. Intending students are advised to consult the Registrar.

INSTITUTE OF COMMONWEALTH STUDIES
27 Russell Square, W.C.1

Seminars on the history of the Commonwealth and on its political,
social and economic problems are regularly held at the Institute.
Admission to the Institute and seminars is by recommendation of
Supervisors of Studies or by permission of the Director. There are no
fees. Further information may be obtained on application to the
Secretary/Librarian.

INSTITUTE OF EDUCATION
Malet Street, W.C.1

The Department of Education in Tropical Areas provides courses for
graduate students, with or without teaching experience oversea, who
desire to read for the Postgraduate Certificate in Education and the
Academic Diploma in Education, the former including students preparing for the educational services of the colonies. Courses are also
available for experienced graduate teachers reading for the M.A. and
Ph.D. in Education. A course for non-graduate teachers who have had

experience oversea is available, leading to the Professional Certificate of the Institute. A course leading to the Associateship of the Institute is available for experienced trained teachers both graduate and non-graduate. Courses are also provided in Community Development and Adult Education. There is a Chair of Education with special reference to Education in Tropical Areas attached to the Institute, in addition the Department has two Senior Lecturers and eight Lecturers. There is an Adviser to Oversea Students at the Institute.

Further information may be obtained from the Institute's *Handbook*, published annually.

INSTITUTE OF HISTORICAL RESEARCH
Senate House, W.C.1

The Institute provides postgraduate courses and seminars in history (including the British Commonwealth) for students and postgraduates reading for the higher degrees of the University. Admission is also open to others, duly qualified, paying the fees and engaged upon specific lines of research. It issues annually a publication entitled *School of History and Institute of Historical Research—Instruction Courses* which lists all courses and seminars in the historical field offered by the various Colleges, Schools and Institutes throughout the University, many of which are given in the Institute.

Further information may be obtained from the Secretary/Librarian.

KING'S COLLEGE
Strand, W.C.2

The departments of history and geography both have courses relevant to Commonwealth studies. The Rhodes Professor of Imperial History is a member of the former department. Postgraduate research seminars in history are held in the College and in the Institute of Historical Research. Geography is taught in the Joint School of Geography at the College and the London School of Economics. A separate *Syllabus* is issued for each faculty and further information may be obtained from the College *Calendar* published annually.

LONDON SCHOOL OF ECONOMICS
Houghton Street, Aldwych, W.C.2

The School is a School of the University in the faculties of Arts, Laws and Economic and Political Science (including Commerce and Industry) and the subjects taught include economics, geography, history, law, political studies (international relations, politics and public administration), social studies (anthropology, demography, social science and administration and sociology) and statistics. Departments appropriate to Commonwealth studies include anthropology, demography, economics, geography, history (economic and political), international history, international relations, law, money, banking and public finance, politics and public administration, social science and administration, sociology and statistics.

The Readerships in Economics (with special reference to the economics of under-developed countries) and Applied Anthropology are attached to the School.

The range of lectures and seminars provided is exceedingly wide and for details the annual *Calendar* of the School must be consulted. A pamphlet on *Postgraduate Studies* is also published.

ROYAL HOLLOWAY COLLEGE
Englefield Green, Surrey

Lectures on Colonial and Commonwealth history are given weekly during term. Full information may be obtained from the pamphlet *Courses* of the School of History and the Institute of Historical Research. The College also publishes annually a *Calendar*.

SCHOOL OF ORIENTAL AND AFRICAN STUDIES
The University, W.C.1

Departments of the School include Languages and Cultures of India, Pakistan and Ceylon; Languages and Cultures of S.E. Asia and the Islands; Languages and Cultures of the Far East; Languages and Cultures of the Near and Middle East: Languages and Cultures of Africa; History; Law; and Cultural Anthropology. Teaching and training is provided in Oriental and African languages, culture and history, law and linguistics. There is a wide range of lectures and seminars, particulars of which may be found in the School's annual *Calendar*.

UNIVERSITY COLLEGE
Gower Street, W.C.1

The departments appropriate to Commonwealth studies are Anthropology, Geography, History and Political Economy, all in the faculty of Arts. Postgraduate and research students may be admitted to the College on recommendation of Professors and Heads of Departments in which they desire to work. Anthropological students should consult the Head of the Department concerning arrangements for supervision and seminars. Facilities for research in geography are available and include advice and supervision of work by appropriate members of the staff. Postgraduate courses in history are held at the Institute of Historical Research. A postgraduate seminar on Political Economy is held.

The College publishes a *Calendar* annually and the various faculties and departments issue *Prospectuses*.

WESTFIELD COLLEGE
Kidderpore Avenue, Hampstead, N.W.3

The Readership in Imperial History is attached to the College and lectures on Colonial and Commonwealth history are regularly given. The College issues an annual *Prospectus*.

WYE COLLEGE
Near Ashford, Kent

Courses are provided for students taking the degrees of B.Sc. (Agriculture) with Honours, B.Sc. (Agriculture) and B.Sc. (Horticulture) of London as well as higher degrees and the College Postgraduate Certificate in Horticulture. Research is carried on in all departments of the College. A *Prospectus* is available on application to the Registrar.

University of Oxford

Colleges and institutions particularly associated with Commonwealth Studies:

Agricultural Economics Research Institute.
Indian Institute.
Institute of Commonwealth Studies.
Institute of Social Anthropology.
Institute of Statistics.
Imperial Forestry Institute (University Department of Forestry).
Nuffield College.
Rhodes House.
St. Antony's College.

Faculties in the University appropriate to Commonwealth Studies:

Modern History.
Law.
Oriental Studies.
Social Studies (sub-faculties of politics and economics).
Agriculture and Forestry.
Anthropology and Geography.

Higher degrees and diplomas:

B.Litt., B.Phil., B.Sc., B.C.L., D.Phil.
Diplomas in Agricultural Economics, Anthropology, Economic and Political

Science, Education, Forestry, Public and Social Administration, Social Training and Statistics.

Chairs, Readerships and Lectureships:

Beit Chair of History of the British Commonwealth.
Chair of Commonwealth Economic Affairs.
Rhodes Chair of Race Relations.
Readership in Commonwealth Government.
Readership in Indian History.
Beit Lectureship in the History of the British Commonwealth.
Lectureships in African Sociology, Economics of Underdeveloped Territories, African Geography, Colonial History, Commonwealth Government, Economics of Tropical Agriculture, Indian Sociology, Luganda, Social Anthropology, Swahili, Tropical Agriculture.

There is also a Committee for Commonwealth Studies.

Further information is to be found in the various publications of the University—*Calendar, Handbook,* collections of *Statutes, Responsions Regulations, General Information* (concerning admission, residence, etc.) and *Facilities for Advanced Study and Research.*

AGRICULTURAL ECONOMICS RESEARCH INSTITUTE
Parks Road, Oxford

The work of the Institute consists mainly of research in the fields of farm organization and management, organization of marketing, land economics and rural social organization. Instruction and lectures in agricultural economics are provided, as well as supervision of students for research degrees and assistance to postgraduates of other universities at home and overseas.

INDIAN INSTITUTE
Broad Street, Oxford

The Institute is the centre for studies connected with India and Pakistan. All the regular courses of instruction in Indian languages and history are given here as well as occasional public lectures by distinguished Orientalists and administrators. Its library is one of the Bodleian group.

INSTITUTE OF COMMONWEALTH STUDIES
(formerly Institute of Colonial Studies)
10 Keble Road, Oxford

The Institute was established in 1945 as a centre for colonial studies in the fields of government, economics and recent history. One of its functions is the organization of courses for the Oversea Civil Service. It has two or three Research Officers and, in addition, has attached to it the following University Lectureships: Economics of Under-developed Territories, Economics of Tropical Agriculture, Tropical Agriculture, Colonial History, Social Anthropology, Luganda and Swahili.

INSTITUTE OF SOCIAL ANTHROPOLOGY
11 Keble Road, Oxford

The Institute provides teaching and research facilities for students working for the diploma and for research degrees in anthropology.

INSTITUTE OF STATISTICS
St. Cross Road, Oxford

The work of the Institute includes the study of the theory of statistics and of the methods of statistical analysis and the application of statistical methods to economic and social problems. The Institute sponsors research and provides seminars.

IMPERIAL FORESTRY INSTITUTE
(Department of Forestry)
South Parks Road, Oxford

The Department of Forestry, with which the Institute is merged, provides higher education in forestry in all its branches. It also provides specialized and advanced training for graduates and forestry officers deputed by their governments. The Commonwealth Forestry Bureau, a separate organization (one of the Commonwealth Agricultural Bureaux), is housed with the Department and Institute. (See also p. 195.)

NUFFIELD COLLEGE

The college was founded 'to encourage research especially but not exclusively in the field of social studies, and especially by making easier the co-operation of academic and non-academic persons'.

The college may appoint not more than forty graduate students who are required to work for a higher degree in Oxford or otherwise engage in approved research. The official fellowships of the College include the Nuffield Fellowship in Imperial Government; the Chair of Commonwealth Economic Affairs is attached to the College.

RHODES HOUSE
South Parks Road, Oxford

Rhodes House is a memorial to Cecil Rhodes. It houses a magnificent library (see p. 166) of British Commonwealth and American history (a section of the Bodleian) and provides halls and public rooms for university and other purposes and serves as the centre for the adminis-tration of the Rhodes Scholarships.

ST. ANTONY'S COLLEGE

Woodstock Road, Oxford

A college for men working for higher degrees, with a special reference to modern subjects, particularly history and international relations. The Rhodes Professorship of Race Relations is attached to the College.

University of Wales

There is a Lectureship in Colonial History tenable at the University College of Aberystwyth. The University issues a *Calendar* and each of the colleges a *Prospectus*.

Tropical Medicine, Entomology and Parasitology and Veterinary Science

Tropical Medicine is taught in the Universities of London (King's College Hospital Medical School, the London School of Hygiene and Tropical Medicine and the Middlesex Hospital Medical School), Liverpool (Incorporated Liverpool School of Tropical Medicine), Oxford and Edinburgh.

Entomology and parasitology are taught at Birmingham, Bristol, Cambridge, Durham, Liverpool (Incorporated Liverpool School of Tropical Medicine), London (Imperial College of Science and Tech-nology, London School of Hygiene and Tropical Medicine, East Malling Research Station and Rothamsted Experimental Station), Oxford, Wales (University College of Cardiff), Aberdeen and Edin-burgh.

Veterinary science is taught in London (Royal Veterinary College), Bristol, Cambridge and Edinburgh.

Further information may be obtained from the *Calendars* of the respective Universities and Colleges.

II. RESEARCH AND ADVISORY ORGANIZATIONS

Comprehensive lists of research institutions and organizations through-out the Commonwealth are to be found in the following publications:

Europa Publications (London):
The British Commonwealth, 1956.
The World of Learning, 7th edn, 1957.
The Middle East, 4th edn, 1957.
Orbis, loose-leaf, kept regularly up to date.

International Institute of Differing Civilizations:
International guide to study centers on civilizations and their publications (Brussels), 1955.

National Institute of Economic and Social Research:
Register of Research in the Social Sciences . . . and Directory of Research Institutions (London), annually.

Scientific Council for Africa South of the Sahara:
Directory of scientific institutions, organizations and services in Africa south of the Sahara (London Secretariat) 1954.
List of scientific societies in Africa south of the Sahara (Provisional), (London Secretariat), 1955.

Unesco, Reports and Papers in the Social Sciences:
No. 3, 1955. *International Organizations in the Social Sciences.*
No. 5, 1955. *Research Councils in the Social Sciences.*

Union of International Associations:
Yearbook of International Organizations (Brussels), 1955–6.

COLONIAL OFFICE

Various Research Committees and Advisory Councils and Committees have been set up by the Colonial Office to advise the Secretary of State on specific matters. A list of these bodies giving particulars as to membership, terms of reference and the name of the Secretary, is to be found in the current issue of the Colonial Office *List*. It includes the following:

Advisory Committee on Colonial Colleges of Arts, Science and Technology.
Advisory Committee on Colonial Geology and Mineral Resources.
Advisory Committee on Co-operation in the Colonies.
Advisory Committee on Education in the Colonies.
Advisory Committee on Social Development in the Colonies.
Colonial Advisory Council of Agriculture, Animal Health and Forestry.
Colonial Advisory Medical Committee.
Colonial Agricultural Machinery Advisory Committee.
Colonial Economic Research Committee.
Colonial Fisheries Advisory Committee.

O

Colonial Pesticides Research Committee.
Colonial Labour Advisory Committee.
Colonial Medical Research Committee.
Colonial Native Law Advisory Panel.
Colonial Products Council.
Colonial Research Council.
Colonial Social Science Research Council.
Committee for Colonial Agricultural, Animal Health and Forestry Research.
Tsetse Fly and Trypanosomiasis Committee.

COMMONWEALTH AGRICULTURAL BUREAUX
Farnham House, Farnham Royal, Bucks.

The Bureaux act as effective clearing houses for the interchange of information of value to research workers in the agricultural sciences and forestry throughout the various parts of the Commonwealth. They can provide opportunities for advanced research within their field of activity though naturally such opportunities would usually be bibliographical; the Directors can advise on such facilities even when they cannot themselves provide them. Each Bureau is primarily a centre of information. As such its main function is the publication of abstract journals, technical communications and other monographs on particular subjects. Information is also supplied on request to Commonwealth and other countries.

The Executive Council, composed of one representative of each of the participating governments, is the central agency which co-ordinates the work of the Institutes and Bureaux. Member countries are Australia, Canada, Ceylon, Colonial Territories (represented by the Colonial Office), India, New Zealand, Pakistan, Southern Rhodesia, Union of South Africa. Associate members are the Republic of Ireland and the Sudan.

Formal letters have been exchanged with the Food and Agriculture Organization concerning reciprocal representation at conferences and technical meetings and relations are maintained with UNESCO and the Organization for European Economic Co-operation in Paris.

The Institutes and Bureaux which make up the organization are as follow:

Commonwealth Bureau of Agricultural Parasitology (Helminthology), St. Peters Street, St. Albans, Herts. The library contains 500 volumes, 150 current periodicals; open from 10 a.m. to 5 p.m., Monday to Friday, 10 a.m. to 12 noon on Saturdays.

Commonwealth Bureau of Animal Breeding and Genetics, Institute of Animal Genetics, University of Edinburgh, Kings Buildings, West Mains Road, Edinburgh 9. The library contains 2,000 volumes and 200 current periodicals;

open from 10 a.m. to 5 p.m., Monday to Friday, 10 a.m. to 12 noon on Saturdays.

Commonwealth Bureau of Animal Health, Ministry of Agriculture and Fisheries Veterinary Laboratory, New Haw, Weybridge, Surrey. Joint library with the Veterinary Laboratory which contains 4,000 volumes, 24,000 pamphlets, 140 current periodicals; open 9 a.m. to 5 p.m., Monday to Friday, 9 a.m. to 12.30 p.m. on Saturdays.

Commonwealth Bureau of Animal Nutrition, Rowett Research Institute, Bucksburn, Aberdeenshire. Joint library with the Rowett Institute, which contains 1,000 volumes, 10,000 pamphlets, 300 current periodicals; open 9.30 a.m. to 5.30 p.m., Monday to Friday, 9.30 a.m. to 12.30 p.m. on Saturdays.

Commonwealth Bureau of Dairy Science, National Institute for Research in Dairying, Shinfield, Reading, Berks. Joint library with the National Institute which contains 11,000 volumes, 24,000 pamphlets and 500 current periodicals; open from 9.30 a.m. to 5.30 p.m., Monday to Friday, 9.30 a.m. to 12 noon on Saturdays.

Commonwealth Bureau of Horticulture and Plantation Crops, East Malling Research Station, East Malling, Maidstone, Kent. Joint library with the Research Station which contains over 8,000 volumes, 48,000 pamphlets, 650 current periodicals.

Commonwealth Bureau of Pastures and Field Crops, Grassland Research Station, Hurley, Maidenhead, Berks. Joint Library with the Research Station which contains 3,200 volumes, 22,000 pamphlets, 750 current periodicals; open from 8.45 a.m. to 5 p.m., Monday to Friday, 8.45 a.m. to 11.45 p.m. on Saturdays.

Commonwealth Bureau of Plant Breeding and Genetics, University of Cambridge School of Agriculture, Downing Street, Cambridge. No separate library facilities. The School of Agriculture possesses an extensive library.

Commonwealth Bureau of Soil Science, Rothamsted Experimental Station, Harpenden, Herts. No separate library facilities. The Rothamsted library is available at the discretion of the Librarian; it is open from 9 a.m. to 5.30 p.m., Monday to Friday, and from 9 a.m. to 12 noon on Saturdays. It contains some 55,000 volumes and pamphlets and about 1,650 current serials. A *Catalogue of Serial Publications in the Library* at Rothamsted was re-issued in 1953; it contains more than 4,700 entries.

Commonwealth Forestry Bureau, Imperial Forestry Institute (University of Oxford Department of Forestry), South Parks Road, Oxford. No separate library facilities. (For information concerning the Imperial Forestry Institute library, see p. 163.) The Bureau is open from 9 a.m. to 5 p.m., Monday to Friday, 9 a.m. to 1 p.m. on Saturdays. It operates a *Centralized Title Service.*

Commonwealth Institute of Biological Control, Science Building, Carling Avenue, Ottawa, Canada.

Commonwealth Institute of Entomology, c/o British Museum (Natural History), Cromwell Road, S.W.7. The library is situated at 56 Queen's Gate, S.W.7. It contains approximately 13,750 volumes, 42,500 pamphlets and 670 current periodicals; open from 10 a.m. to 5 p.m., Monday to Friday, 10 a.m. to 1 p.m. on Saturdays.

Commonwealth Mycological Institute, Ferry Lane, Kew, Surrey. The library contains 7,000 volumes, 45,000 pamphlets and reprints, 300 current periodicals; open from 10 a.m. to 5 p.m., Monday to Friday, 10 a.m. to 1 p.m. on Saturdays.

Publications of the Institutes and Bureaux include Bulletin of Entomological Research (Q.), Review of Applied Entomology (Series A: Agricultural; Series B: Medical and Veterinary) (both M.), Zoological Record (part Insecta), Distribution Maps of Insect Pests, Review of Applied Mycology (M.), Review of Medical and Veterinary Mycology, Index of Fungi, Distribution Maps of Plant Diseases, Bibliography of Systematic Mycology, Mycological Papers, Commonwealth Phytopathological News, Helminthological Abstracts (six issues p.a.), Animal Breeding Abstracts (Q.), Index Veterinarium (Q.), Veterinary Bulletin (M.), Veterinary Reviews and Annotations (half yearly), Nutrition Abstracts and Reviews (Q.), Dairy Science Abstracts (M.), Forestry Abstracts (Q.), Horticultural Abstracts (Q.), Herbage Abstracts (Q.), Field Crop Abstracts (Q.), Plant Breeding Abstracts (Q.), Soils and Fertilizers (six issues p.a.), Bibliography of Soil Science Fertilizers and General Agronomy, in addition to numerous special monographs (Technical Communications).

The Commonwealth Agricultural Bureaux (originally known as the Imperial Agricultural Bureaux) were founded in 1928 as a result of the recommendations of the Imperial Agricultural Research Conference of 1927. The Executive Council came into being on April 1, 1929, and eight bureaux started working that year. Following the Ottawa Conference of 1932, the Imperial Committee on Economic Consultation and Co-operation was formed. The Committee approved the organization of the bureaux and extended their work so that, from October 1, 1935, the Council was entrusted with the supervision and administration of the Imperial Institute of Entomology and of the Imperial Mycological Institute (later renamed 'Commonwealth'). As a result of recommendations by the British Commonwealth Scientific Conference of 1936 two more bureaux were established, Dairy Science and Forestry. In 1940 the Imperial Parasite Service, originally a branch of the Imperial Institute of Entomology, moved to Canada and later became the Commonwealth Institute of Biological Control.

ACTON SOCIETY TRUST [Current social and economic problems]
39 Welbeck Street, W.1.

AGRICULTURAL RESEARCH ASSOCIATION
Cunard Building, 15 Regent Street, W.1.

AGRICULTURAL RESEARCH COUNCIL
Cunard Building, 15 Regent Street, S.W.1.

ANTI-LOCUST RESEARCH CENTRE
c/o British Museum (Natural History), Cromwell Road, S.W.7.

BRITISH BUREAU OF NON-FERROUS METAL STATISTICS
132 Hagley Road, Birmingham, 16.
The Bureau collects and publishes comprehensive statistics relating to non-ferrous metals and manufacturers of the United Kingdom, the Commonwealth and foreign countries. Accommodation is limited so that the office is not available for the use of research workers but the Bureau is willing to offer assistance to researchers wishing to use its material for research purposes.

BRITISH COMMONWEALTH FORESTRY CONFERENCE (and Standing Committee on British Commonwealth Forestry)
1 Princes Gate, S.W.7.

BRITISH COMMONWEALTH SCIENTIFIC CONFERENCE (and Standing Committee)
Africa House, Kingsway, W.C.2.

BRITISH COTTON INDUSTRY RESEARCH ASSOCIATION
Shirley Institute, Didsbury, Manchester 20.

BRITISH IRON AND STEEL RESEARCH ASSOCIATION
11 Park Lane, W.1.

BRITISH NON-FERROUS METALS RESEARCH ASSOCIATION
81 Euston Road, N.W.1

BUREAU OF HYGIENE AND TROPICAL DISEASES
c/o London School of Hygiene, Keppel Street, W.C.1.

CANADIAN NATIONAL RAILWAYS (RESEARCH AND DEVELOPMENT DEPT.)
17–19 Cockspur Street, S.W.1.

COLONIAL BUILDING LIAISON SECTION
Building Research Station, Garston, Watford, Herts.

COPPER DEVELOPMENT ASSOCIATION
Kendals Hall, Radlett, Herts.
The Association's library contains about 1,500 books, 8,000 pamphlets (scientific papers and reports), 2,500 British and American trade catalogues and 130 current periodicals on the mining, processing and economics of copper. It maintains a selective classified catalogue of over 68,000 entries including some information on the British Commonwealth. Research workers are admitted

to the library but applications should be submitted to the Librarian in advance.

DEPARTMENT OF SCIENTIFIC AND INDUSTRIAL RESEARCH
Headquarters: Charles House, 5–11 Regent Street, S.W.1.
Overseas Liaison Division: Africa House, Kingsway, W.C.2.
Building Research: Building Research Station, Bucknalls Lane, Garston, Watford, Herts.
Chemical Research Laboratory: Teddington, Middlesex.
Fire Research Organization: Fire Research Station, Boreham Wood, Herts.
Food Investigation: 20A Regent Street, Cambridge.
Forest Products Research: Forest Products Research Laboratory, Princes Risborough, Aylesbury, Bucks.
Fuel Research: Fuel Research Station, River Way, East Greenwich, S.E.10.
Geological Survey of Great Britain and Museum of Practical Geology: Exhibition Road, South Kensington, S.W.7; and Branches.
Hydraulics Research: Hydraulics Research Station, Howbery Park, Wallingford, Berks.
Mechanical Engineering Research: Mechanical Engineering Research Laboratory, East Kilbride, Glasgow.
National Physical Laboratory: Teddington, Middlesex.
Pest Infestation: Pest Infestation Laboratory, London Road, Slough, Bucks.
Radio Research: Radio Research Station, Ditton Park, Slough, Bucks.
Road Research: Road Research Laboratory, Harmondsworth, West Drayton, Middlesex.
Water Pollution Research: Water Pollution Research Laboratory, Elder Way, Stevenage, Herts.

ECONOMIC RESEARCH COUNCIL
18 South Street, W.1.

EMPIRE COTTON GROWING CORPORATION
12 Chantry House, Eccleston Street, S.W.1.

FABIAN SOCIETY
11 Dartmouth Street, S.W.1.

HOUBLON-NORMAN FUND [Research into applied economics]
c/o Bank of England, E.C.2.

INTERNATIONAL AFRICAN INSTITUTE
 10–11 Fetter Lane, E.C.4.

INTERNATIONAL ASSOCIATION FOR RESEARCH IN INCOME AND WEALTH
 c/o National Institute of Economic and Social Research, 2 Dean
 Trench Street, Smith Square, S.W.1.

INTERNATIONAL SCIENTIFIC COMMITTEE FOR TRYPANOSOMIASIS RESEARCH
 c/o Colonial Office, Church House, S.W.1.

MEDICAL RESEARCH COUNCIL
 38 Old Queen Street, S.W.1.

NATIONAL INSTITUTE FOR MEDICAL RESEARCH
 The Ridgeway, Mill Hill, N.W.7.

NATIONAL INSTITUTE OF ECONOMIC AND SOCIAL RESEARCH
 2 Dean Trench Street, Smith Square, S.W.1.

NATIONAL INSTITUTE FOR RESEARCH IN DAIRYING (University of Reading)
 Shinfield, near Reading, Berks.

NEWCOMEN SOCIETY FOR THE STUDY OF ENGINEERING AND TECHNOLOGY
 c/o Science Museum, South Kensington, S.W.7.

RESEARCH ASSOCIATION OF BRITISH RUBBER MANUFACTURERS
 Shawbury, Shrewsbury, Salop.
    The Library of the Association contains some 77,000 books and
 pamphlets and 370 current periodicals ranging over the whole field
 of rubber literature including material relating to planting and the
 use of rubber throughout the Commonwealth. The library exists
 mainly to serve the needs of industry but accredited research
 workers are admitted between the hours of 9 a.m. and 5.30 p.m.,
 Monday to Friday.

ROSS INSTITUTE OF TROPICAL HYGIENE
 London School of Hygiene, Keppel Street, W.C.1.

ROTHAMSTED EXPERIMENTAL STATION [Soil and Plant Growth]
 Harpenden, Herts.

ROYAL INSTITUTE OF INTERNATIONAL AFFAIRS
 Chatham House, 10 St. James' Square, S.W.1.
    The Institute exists to facilitate study of international relations,
 and to conduct research into international politics, economics and
 jurisprudence, including Commonwealth affairs. In addition to the
 Director-General, who is also Director of Studies, the staff includes
 a Director of Studies in Race Relations, the Abe Bailey Research
 Professor of British Commonwealth Relations, and the Sir Henry
 Price Professor of International Economics.

The Department of Racial Studies produces two monthly summaries of press news and comment; the first deals with racial questions in Central and South Africa and Kenya, the second with Coloured People in Great Britain. The Department also has a small library of material on racial questions.

ROYAL INSTITUTE OF PUBLIC ADMINISTRATION
76A New Cavendish Street, W.1.

SOCIAL SURVEY
Montague Mansions (Block 1), Crawford Street, W.1.

TAVISTOCK INSTITUTE OF HUMAN RELATIONS
2 Beaumont Street, W.1.

TIN RESEARCH ASSOCIATION
Fraser Road, Greenford, Middlesex.

WOOL INDUSTRIES RESEARCH ASSOCIATION
Torridon, Headingley, Leeds 6.

III. ADDITIONAL LIST OF INSTITUTIONS AND ORGANIZATIONS (OFFICIAL AND UNOFFICIAL)
Concerned with Various Aspects of Commonwealth Affairs

Association of British Malaya, 18 Northumberland Avenue, W.C.2. [Concerned with matters of public interest affecting Malaya, Singapore, Sarawak and North Borneo.]

Association of Universities of the British Commonwealth, 36 Gordon Square, W.C.1. [To provide liaison between Universities of the British Commonwealth.]

British Academy Archaeological and Historical Advisory Committee for the Colonial Territories, British Academy, Burlington Gardens, W.1. [A consultative committee to advise the Secretary of State in matters relating to archaeology and history of the Colonial Territories.]

British Commonwealth League, 27 de Walden Street, W.1.

British Commonwealth of Nations Scientific Liaison Offices, Africa House, Kingsway, W.C.2. [To keep in touch with scientific developments, to deal with inquiries, to act as advisers to High Commissioners and Governments.]

British Commonwealth Producers' Organization, 25 Victoria Street, S.W.1.

British Council, 65 Davies Street, W.1. [To promote wider knowledge of the United Kingdom abroad and to develop closer cultural relations between the

United Kingdom and other countries for purpose of benefiting the British Commonwealth.]

Bureau of Hygiene and Tropical Diseases, at the London School of Hygiene and Tropical Medicine, Keppel Street, W.C.1.

Colonial Development Corporation, 33 Hill Street, W.1.

Colonial (Geodetic and Topographic) Surveys, Kingston Road, Tolworth, Surbiton, Surrey.

Colonial Geological Surveys, Imperial Institute Building, Exhibition Road, S.W.7.

Colonial Income Tax Office, 26 Grosvenor Gardens, S.W.1.

Colonial Office Consultative Committee on the Welfare of Colonial Students in the United Kingdom, Colonial Office, S.W.1. [To advise the Secretary of State on problems of welfare of Colonial students.]

Colonial Products Laboratory, Imperial Institute Building, Exhibition Road, S.W.7.

Commonwealth Agricultural Bureaux. See pp. 194–6.

Commonwealth Air Transport Council, Berkeley Square House, Berkeley Square, W.1. [To keep under review progress and development of Commonwealth civil air communications, to act as a medium for exchange of views and information between Commonwealth countries, and to consider and advise on matters referred by Commonwealth countries. Affiliated bodies are the Southern Africa Air Transport Council, Cape Town, and the South Pacific Air Transport Council, Melbourne.]

Commonwealth Economic Committee. See p. 106.

Commonwealth Parliamentary Association, Houses of Parliament, S.W.1. [Maintenance of permanent machinery to facilitate exchange of visits and information between those engaged in parliamentary government in the Commonwealth.]

Commonwealth Press Union, 154 Fleet Street, E.C.4. [To promote welfare of Commonwealth newspapers, to give effect to opinions of its members on matters of the press and to promote conferences.]

Commonwealth Shipping Committee, Berkeley Square House, Berkeley Square, W.1. [Functions are, *inter alia*, to inquire into complaints with regard to freights, facilities and conditions in inter-Commonwealth trade and to survey facilities for maritime transport.]

Commonwealth Telecommunciations Board, 28 Pall Mall, S.W.1. [To advise partner Governments on matters relating to external telecommunications systems.]

Dominions Fellowship Trust, 23A Cadogan Gardens, S.W.3. [To welcome and befriend Rhodes Scholars and other scholars of the Commonwealth.]

East India Association (India, Pakistan and Burma), 3 Victoria Street, S.W.1. [Affairs of the three countries are discussed at meetings; it fosters friendly contact between their nationals.]

English Speaking Union of the Commonwealth, 37 Charles Street, W.1. [Exists to draw together in the bond of comradeship the English speaking peoples of the world.]

Federation of the Chambers of Commerce of the British Empire, 69 Cannon Street, E.C.4.

Imperial College of Tropical Agriculture (Trinidad), London Office, 40 Norfolk Street, W.C.2.

Imperial Institute, Exhibition Road, S.W.7. [Devoted to educational activities concentrated mainly on spreading knowledge of the Commonwealth.]

Inter-University Council for Higher Education Overseas, 1 Gordon Square, W.C.1. [To strengthen co-operation between Universities in the United Kingdom and overseas territories, foster development of higher colleges overseas and to take action to develop higher and especially University education overseas.]

International Committee on Christian Literature for Africa, 2 Eaton Gate, S.W.1.

London and Cambridge Economic Service, c/o The Times, Printing House Square, E.C.4. [Devoted to study of current economic developments.]

London House, Guilford Street, W.C.1. [A residential and social collegiate centre for men students of the Commonwealth.]

Over-Seas League, St. James's, S.W.1. [Promotion of friendship and understanding between peoples of the Commonwealth.]

Pakistan Society, 70 Victoria Street, S.W.1. [To foster mutual understanding between Pakistan, the United Kingdom and other members of the Commonwealth and to provide facilities for study of Pakistan history and affairs.]

Ross Institute of Tropical Hygiene, London School of Hygiene and Tropical Medicine, Keppel Street, W.C.1.

Royal African Society, 18 Northumberland Avenue, W.C.2. [To foster and encourage interest in Africa, particularly in territories of the Commonwealth and for the study of African affairs.]

Royal India, Pakistan and Ceylon Association, 3 Victoria Street, S.W.1. [To promote better understanding and appreciation of the cultures of the sub-continent.]

Royal Society of Tropical Medicine, 26 Portland Place, W.1.

Society for the Overseas Settlement of British Women, 43 Parliament Street, S.W.1. [Advises on conditions in Commonwealth countries, supplies skilled and professional women with information about overseas employment and assists women settlers with immigration information, etc.]

Victoria League, 38 Chesham Place, S.W.1. [To further friendship between all peoples of the Commonwealth irrespective of race, creed or political opinion.]

INDEX

P